Lala Lajpat Rai

Lala Lajpat Rai

Series Editor
Dr. M.H. Syed

Editor
Anil Kathuria **Bharat Singh**

Himalaya Books Pvt. Ltd.
'Ramdoot', Dr. Bhalerao Marg, Girgaon, Mumbai - 400 004
Tel : (022) 23863863. Fax : (022) 23877178
Email : himpub@vsnl.com

Edition : 2017

Published by : **H.B.P.L.**
"Pooja Apartments", 4-B, Murari Lal Street, Ansari Road,
Darya Ganj, New Delhi-110 002
Phones : 23270392, 23278631
Fax : 011-23256286 Email : hphdel@vsnl.com

Sole Distributers : HIMALAYA PUBLISHING HOUSE PVT. LTD.

Branch Offices

Mumbai : "Ramdoot", Dr. Bhalerao Marg, Girgaon, Mumbai-400 004.
Phones : 23860170/23863863 Fax : 022-23877178
Email : himpub@vsnl.com
Website : www.himpub.com

Nagpur : Kundanlal Chandak Industrial Estate, Ghat Road, **Nagpur - 440 018.**
Phone: 2738731, 3296733 Telefax : 0712-2721215

Bengaluru : No. 16/1 (Old 12/1), 1st Floor, Next to Hotel Highlands, Madhava Nagar, Race Course Road, **Bengaluru - 560 001.**
Phone : 22281541, 22385461, Telefax: 080-22286611

Hyderabad : No. 3-4-184, Lingampally, Besides Raghavendra Swamy Matham, Kachiguda, **Hyderabad - 500 027.** Phone: 040-27560041, 27550139, Mobile:- 09848130433 Telefax: 040-27560041

Chennai : No. 85/50, Bazullah Road, T. Nagar, **Chennai - 600 017.**
Phone: 044-28344020, 32463737, 42124860

Pune : No. 527, "Laksha" Apartment, First Floor, Mehunpura, Shaniwarpeth, (Near Prabhat Theatre), **Pune - 411 030.**
Phone: 020-24496323/24496333/32326733

Lucknow : Jai Baba Bhawan, Near Manas Complex, Church Road, Aliganj, **Lucknow - 226 024.** Phone: 0522-2339329, 9305302158, 9415349385

Ahmedabad : No. 114, "SHAIL", 1st Floor, Opp. Madhu Sudan House, C.G.Road, Navrang Pura, **Ahmedabad – 380 009.**
Phone: 079-26560126, Mobiles: 09327324149, 09314679413

Ernakulam : No. 39/104 A, Lakshmi Apartment, Karikkamuri Cross Rd., Ernakulam, **Cochin – 682011**, Kerala. Phone: 0484-2378012, 2378016, Mob.: 09344199799

Bhubaneswar : 5 Station Square, **Bhubaneswar (Orissa) - 751 001.**
Mobile: 9861046007, E-mail:- orissa@himpub.com

Indore : Kesardeep Avenue Extension, 73, Narayan Bagh.Flat No. 302, IIIrd Floor, Near Humpty Dumpty School, Narayan Bagh, **Indore (M.P.) 452 007**
Mobile: 09301386468

Kolkata : 108/4, Beliaghata, Main Road, Near ID Hospital, Opp. SBI Bank **Kolkata - 700 010.** Mobile: 09910440956, E-mail:- nkmitra@himpub.com

Guwahati : House No. 15, Behind Prajjyotish College, Near Sharma Printing Press, P.O. Bharalumukh, Guwahati - 781009 (Assam
Mobile: 07439040301; 07439040302

Printed by : Infinity Imaging Systems, New Delhi.

Preface

Biography, is now a form of literature, very much in vogue. In fact, biography is a description or account of someone's life and the times, which is usually published in the form of a book. A biography is more than a mention of personal facts (life, education, work, relationships and death), it also portrays the subject's experience of events. Technically speaking, a work is biographical, if it covers, all of a person's life. Biography writing has a long history. A biography is real. Ancient Greeks developed the biographical tradition, which we have inherited, although until the 5th century AD, when the word 'biographia' first appeared, in Damascius' "Life of Isodorus," biographical pieces were called simply "lives". It is quite likely that the Greeks were drawing on a pre-existing eastern tradition. Certainly Herodotus' "Histories" contains more detailed biographical information on Persian kings and subjects. The earliest surviving pieces, which we would identify as biographical are Isocrates' "Life of Evagoras" and Xenophon's "Life of Agesilaos," both from the fifth century BC. "Parallel Lives" by Plutarch, a Greek writing under the Roman empire, is a series of short biographies of eminent men.

The Golden Age of English biography emerged in late eighteenth century, the century in which the terms "biography" and "autobiography" entered English lexicon. The classic works of the period were Samuel Johnson's "Critical Lives of the Poets" and James Boswell's "Massive Life of Johnson". Generally American biography followed English model. By World War I, cheap hardcover reprints had become popular. The decade of the 1920s witnessed a biographical 'boom'. Later, biographical writings developed a lot and today biographies are written and compiled in the finest form of the genre. In India too, biography, as a form of literature has been evolved, cultivated and polished over the years. Here is an effort to promote this tradition further.

This series of biographies of great men, great women and celebrities in all walks of life is an adventurous academic endeavour, in its own right. A team of researchers and compilers has worked for a good period of time to accomplish the project. For this purpose, hundreds of books by eminent authors and editors have been consulted and referred to. We have benefited from various works, liberally, in order to illustrate and enrich this effort of ours. Present book is devoted to the great personality of Lala Lajpat Rai.

Lala Lajpat Rai (1865-1928) was a great author and politician, who is chiefly remembered as a leader in the Indian fight for freedom from the British Raj. He was popularly known as *Punjab Kesari* (The Caesar of Punjab). He was also the founder of Punjab National Bank and Lakshmi Insurance Company. Born in Monga district of Punjab, on 28 January, in 1865, Lajpat Rai created a career of reforming Indian polity through politics and writing. Later, Lala Lajpat Rai's involvement became imperative to the Indian Independence Movement. His actions in anti-imperialist movements led to numerous arrests. He became an important member of the Arya Samaj. Lala Lajpat Rai led political rallies, He, presided over the first session of the All India Trade Union Congress in 1920. In 1923, he became a member of the Imperial Legislative Assembly. Lajpat Rai engaged heavily in direct action and protest against British rule. He was repeatedly arrested. He was not only a good orator but also a prolific and versatile writer. In 1928, Lajpat Rai led a procession to demonstrate against the Simon Commission. During this procession, Rai became the target of a lathi charge by British police. Later, he died of serious injuries.

This is a compact and comprehensive account of the above mentioned great life, which is bound to attract the attention of scholars, researchers, students and the general readers alike. Let's hope this humble effort would receive a warm welcome and due applause.

— ***Editor***

Contents

1

An Illustrious Life

Great leader, Lala Lajpat Rai (1865-1928) was an eminent author and politician, who is chiefly remembered as a leader in the national fight for freedom from the British Raj. He was popularly known as Punjab Kesari (The Caesar of Punjab). He was also the founder of Punjab National Bank and Lakshmi Insurance Company.

Born in Dhudhika in Moga, on 28 January, in 1865 in a Hindu Vysya Family, Lajpat Rai created a career of reforming Indian policy through politics and writing. (When studying law in Lahore, he continued to practice Hinduism. He became a large believer in the idea that Hinduism, above nationality, was the pivotal point upon which an Indian lifestyle must be based). Hinduism, he believed, led to practices of peace to humanity, and the idea that when nationalist ideas were added to this peaceful belief system, a non-secular nation could be formed. His involvement with Hindu Mahasabhaite leaders gathered criticism from the Bharat Sabha as the Mahasabhas were anti-secularism, which did not conform with the system laid out by the Indian National Congress. This focus on Hindu practices in the subcontinent would ultimately lead him to the continuation of peaceful movements to create successful demonstrations for Indian independence.

As the need for partition and independence took an important turn for the possible, Lala Lajpat Rai's involvement became imperative to the Indian Independence Movement. His actions in anti-imperialist movements led to numerous arrests. He became an important member of the Arya Samaj. This political group was full of British-educated Indians who believed that Hinduism had a specific and direct impact on what it meant to be an Indian.

The group also took the ideas of a merged western and eastern world and promoted the view that the subcontinent had benefited from its coagulation. The involvement of the Arya Samaj in constitutional reform supported the freedom movements which took hold of the Indian population. Lala Lajpat Rai led political rallies which taught how the history of the subcontinent had always been heading to the philosophical idea that it would become an independent nation.

(Lajpat Rai presided over the first session of the All India Trade Union Congress in 1920. In 1923, he became a member of the Imperial Legislative Assembly. He also went to Geneva to attend the eighth International Labour Conference in 1926 as a representative of Indian labour. He had an opportunity to watch the labour movement in the USA and England where he was required to prolong his stay for political reasons).

In addition to espousing his philosophical principles, Lajpat Rai engaged heavily in direct action and protest against British rule. [He led the Punjab protests against the Amritsar Massacre (1919), the Non-cooperation Movement (1919-22), and the "Simon go back" demonstrations against the Simon Commission (1928)]. He was repeatedly arrested. He disagreed, however, with Mohandas Gandhi's suspension of the movement due to the Chauri Chaura incident. (He formed the Congress Independence Party, which was particularly pro-Hindu in voice and policy).

He was not only a good orator but also a prolific and versatile writer. His journal Arya Gazette concentrated mainly on subjects related to the Arya Samaj. Bande Mataram and People, contained his inspiring speeches to end oppression by the foreign rulers. He founded the Servants of the People Society, which worked for the freedom movement as well as for social reform in the country. He also wrote an autobiography in English titled The Story of My Life.

In 1928, Lajpat Rai led a procession with Pandit Madan Mohan Malaviya to demonstrate against the Simon Commission. During this procession, Rai became the target of a lathi charge (a form of crowd control in which the police use heavy staves or 'lathis' in Hindi) led by British police. He was severely injured in the charge. Nevertheless, at a meeting held the same evening, he spoke with great vigour. His words at this meeting, "Every blow aimed at me is a nail in the coffin of British imperialism", have become historic. Though he recovered from the fever and pain within three days, his health had received a permanent setback and on November 17, 1928, he died of his injuries. His death led to great disturbances in the country and it inspired national struggle for freedom....he was a great fighter.

Lajpat Rai's journey to the United States during World War I helped him to gather knowledge of how an independent nation formulates a nationalist identity. This is where he gathered information about how foreign nations, specifically Britain's imperialist hold on India, had negative affects on the people, the lifestyles, and the ability to generate bonds with other nations. He wrote articles that persuaded foreign nations to side with the subcontinent's struggle for independence. By accepting that westernised ideals were positive to the creation of nationalities, he gained support for breaking from Britain.

In Europeanisation and the Ancient Culture of India, Lajpat Rai wrote that nationalisation of India was imperative to spread western ideology to the rest of the world. Since the westernisation of India had successfully been adapted while continuing traditions remained a large part of the culture, he believed that India no longer needed an overbearing imperialist government.

He wrote that: "at first sight it seems absurd to give one name to all Indian civilization. But a close examination for facts and data amply proves the unity of Indian civilization, at least for the present geological period." These ideas were passed to foreign countries in order to show that despite cultural differences from the western world, India's society had become a sustainable, functional nation which deserved its own nationality as opposed to being overseen by an alien western country.

(Writings by Lajpat Rai include Josiah Wedgewood — The Man And His Work, The United States of America: A Hindu's impressions and a study, History of the Arya Samaj, Swaraj and social change, England's Debt to India: A historical narrative of Britain's fiscal policy in India, The Problems Of National Education In India and Unhappy India: Being a reply to Katherine Mayo's "Mother India", published in 1928). (Mother India was a polemical account of India's self rule by American historian Katherine Mayo).

The Lala Lajpat Rai Memorial Trust was formed in 1959 on the eve of his Centenary Birth Celebration, to promote education. The trust was founded by a group of Punjabi philanthropists (including R. P. Gupta and B. M. Grover) who have settled and prospered in the Indian State of Maharashtra.

A statue of Lajpat Rai stands at the central square in Shimla, India. Lajpat Nagar and Lajpat Nagar Central Market in New Delhi, Lala Lajpat Rai Hall of Residence at Indian Institutes of Technology (IIT) in Kharagpur and Lala Lajpat Rai Institute of Engineering and Technology, Moga are named in his honour. Also many institutes, Schools and Library in his hometown of Jagraon, district Ludhiana are named after him.

An Intelligent Student

The great patriot Lala Lajpat Rai was born on 28th January 1865 in Dhudika village of Ferozepur District of Punjab Province, His father Lala Radha Kishan was an Urdu teacher in a government school. He belonged to the family of Agarwals, a family noted for its love of freedom and self-respect. Although illiterate, Lajpat Rai's mother Gulab Devi was an ideal Hindu woman. It was from her that Lalaji imbibed patriotic sentiments.

Lalaji was a very intelligent pupil. He won scholarships. Poverty and sickness stood in the way of his higher education. He passed the Entrance Examination of the Calcutta University in the first class in 1880.

The same year he also passed the Entrance Examination of Punjab University. Afterwards he joined the Lahore Government College. At the same time he studied law. Because of the poverty of the family his education was interrupted for two years.

Dawn of Ideals

The two years spent in Lahore were important in Lalaji's life. As he read the history of the past glory of India and the biographies of her great sons, the boy shed tears. The love of freedom and the keen desire to serve the country took root in him at that time. During those days the Arya Samaj founded by Swami Dayananda Saraswati was dynamic in social service. It was a time when enthusiastic Punjabi youths were attracted by the progressive ideals and reformist plans of the Arya Samaj. Lalaji was then hardly sixteen. When he joined the Arya Samaj in 1882 his life of social service began. Patriotism was kindled. The idea took root in his mind that the chains of Indian slavery should be broken.

Brilliant Lawyer

Having passed the first examination in law in 1883 Lala could practice as a *muktiar* (a minor lawyer). He had also to bear the burden of running the family. Eighteen-year-old Lalaji practiced in the revenue court of Jagrav town. After passing the Pleaders' Examination he came to Hissar in South Punjab and commenced practice as a lawyer.

He had no thought of making money in his profession and settling down comfortably. He wanted to devote his life to the service of his country. He wanted to read the biography of Mazzini, the brave revolutionary of Italy. He could not get a copy of the book in India. Lie wrote to a friend in England and got it. Mazzini's bravery, magnanimity and patriotism thrilled him.

Beginning of Public Service

His life of six years in Hissar became the apprenticeship for public service. After the death of Swami Dayananda, Lalaji with his associates toiled to develop the Anglo-Vedic College. The three tenets of Arya Samaj are the reformation of society, the advancement of Hindu Dharma and educational progress. Lalaji earned a thousand rupees a month. He kept aside a part of his earnings to keep his father above want and arranged for the interest on it to be paid to his father. On-tenth of his income was earmarked for work for the nation. The greater part of that sum was being used for Arya Samaj activities.

When the Lieutenant Governor visited Hissar, Lalaji pleaded that the Welcome Address to be presented to him should be in Urdu. To satisfy the British officer a speech had already been prepared in English. Lalaji's suggestion made everyone nervous. But without a trace of fear, he presented the Address in Urdu and there by invited the wrath of the British.

Most of his time was given to Arya Samaj activities. Working ceaselessly he set up branches of the Arya Samaj. He built up educational institutions. But he was not partial towards any community. He was elected unopposed to the Municipal Council from a constituency where there were a number of Muslims.

In Active Politics

In 1888, still a lawyer, he entered politics. The Indian National Congress was fighting for the country's freedom. Realising the dire need for freedom, Lalaji joined the Congress as a freedom fighter. Sir Syed Ahmed who was in the Congress had just then left it. He had begun to argue that Muslims should not join the Congress and that they should support the government. Lala wrote bitter open letters to him in the Urdu weekly Koh-e-noor'. The letters earned high praise in political circles. The same year in the Congress session at Allahabad, when Lalaji arrived with eighty delegates from Punjab, he received a tumultuous welcome, his heroic speech in Urdu there had a great effect on the Congress leaders. Lala was a young man of 23 years. His fame spread quickly in Congress.

Stay at Lahore

The small town of Hissar proved inadequate for his growing social work. After qualifying to practice as an advocate in the Punjab High Court, he settled down in Lahore in 1892. The Congress session of 1893 was held at Lahore. The first Indian to become a member of the British Parliament, Dadabhai Naoroji, was the president of the session. Lalaji served as an enthusiastic volunteer.

Lalaji worked like a bee. There was no time for rest. When he was immersed in Congress work there was a split in the Arya Samaj. Lalaji gave a new shape to the DAV College and stood by it.

Lightning in his Pen

Lalaji was not merely an outstanding politician but also an able writer. The biographies he wrote in Urdu are memorable. He wrote the biographies of the patriots Mazzini and Garibaldi who unified Italy. He also wrote outstanding books about Indian great men Shivaji, Sri Krishna and Dayananda Saraswati. The books on Mazzini and Shivaji contained passages, which encouraged people to fight for freedom. So the government even thought of arresting Lalaji.

Servant of the Suffering

The sense of service shown by Lalaji and his devoted endeavour to help the poor, the downtrodden and those in difficulties bestowed luster on his multifarious exertions. A terrible famine struck the Central Provinces in 1896. The draught shook people. No one can forget the part played by Lalaji at the time. Orphans and the destitute were at the mercy of the Christian missionaries and were being converted to Christianity.

Lalaji began a movement to help the orphans. He saved 250 orphan children from Jabalpur, Bilaspur and other districts, brought them to Punjab and admitted them to the orphanages of the Arya Samaj. He realised that he did not have sufficient time for both social service and legal practice; so in 1898 he reduced his legal practice. In 1899 a worse famine struck Punjab, Rajasthan, Kathiawad and Central Provinces. Again Lalaji led the movement by the Arya Samaj to save helpless children.

It was a trying time for him. He organised an extraordinary movement. Not only were 2,000 helpless persons saved but they were also provided with food, clothing, education and employment. In this movement sometimes there were clashes with Christian missionaries. Government set up a famine relief commission in 1901 and got Lalaji's views. His account of famine conditions and his views led to a change in the government's attitude to the destitute. Hindus and people of other religions were able to establish orphanages for destitute children of their folds.

In 1905 an occasion arose for Lalaji to dive deeper into another matter. There was an earthquake in Kangra district resulting in enormous loss of life and property. The Arya Samaj of Lahore set up a relief committee, as its secretary Lalaji toured Punjab province extensively and collected money for the committee. His service to the people at that time was unforgettable.

Visit to England

The same year general elections were being held in England, the Indian National Congress decided to send two representatives to acquaint the public with conditions in India. Lajpat Rai and Gopal Krishna Gokhale were the two representatives. When they returned from their visit to England, thousands of people welcomed them at the Lahore railway station. Students unhitched the horses and they pulled the carriage.

During his tour of England Lalaji told the people they're about the conditions in India during the British rule. More than this, his reading of the situation was important. It become clear to him that Indians alone could mould their future and for that purpose, the government should be in their hands. He resolved that India should undertake the fight for freedom, the use of articles made in India and boycott of foreign goods. He put forth these views at the 1907 Congress session held in Surat City.

Government's Wrath

1907 witnessed a high-water mark in the adventurous life of Lalaji. That was a time of revolution when the winds of change were blowing across the country; new ideas and a new zest moved the people. There were riots in Lahore and Rawalpindi. In Meerut preparations were being made to observe the fiftieth anniversary of the first fight for freedom (1857). Peasants were upset on account of the proposal of the government to increase the water rates in Punjab. It was a grievous crime in the eyes of the government that Lalaji and certain lawyers addition to this, there were disturbances, supported the ryots.

Sir Densil Ibbotson was the Lieutenant Governor of Punjab. He wrote to Lord Morley, then the minister in the British Cabinet who was in charge of Indian affairs: "It appears that some leaders like Lalaji have sworn to drive the British out of India. An attempt is being made to kindle hatred against Englishmen and break the government administrative machinery."

Those were days when there was a sense of fear in official circles. A poor Indian was murdered. A factual report appeared in newspapers. An attempt was made to foist the guilt on a Punjabi journalist. The people of Punjab protested against the mischief of the government. In addition to this, there were disturbances, because of unjust laws like the Colonial Settlement Act and Land Mortgage Amendment Act and because of increase in the tax on land and water rates. Sir Densil was perturbed. Without any reason he deported Lalaji and with him Ajit Singh (a relative of the great patriot Bhagat Singh) to Mandalay in Burma.

People all over the country opposed the unjust action of the government. Tilak wrote in the newspaper 'Kesari' — "if the British rulers act like the Russian Czars, the people of India will have to react as the people of Russia did." Government had to bow to the vigorous protests of the people and the legal profession; it had no choice. Government realised that the deportation order was improper and illegal; it brought Lalaji to Lahore on November 18 and set him free.

Lalaji was considered one of the famous trinity of the Congress radicals. The three great men were Lala Lajpat Rai of Punjab, Bal Gangadhar Tilak of Maharashtra and Bipin Chandra Pal of Bengal. The country affectionately called them Lal, Bal and Pal. There was a split between the radicals and the moderates in the Congress organisation. Lalaji found that it was not possible to bring about an agreement between the two factions; he therefore kept out of the Congress for a few years.

In 1911, he re-entered the Lahore Municipal Council. When he stood for election to the Municipal Council his popularity was immense. Even the deaf, the dumb and disabled' people turned up to vote for him. A dumb voter brought a photograph of Lalaji to indicate that he would vote for Lalaji.

In other Countries

Lalaji re-entered Congress in 1912. He left for England in April 1914 with the Congress delegation as a representative of Punjab. He had planned to be there for six months. But because of the outbreak of the First World War, he had to change his plans. It did not seem wise to return then. It was likely the British would keep him in detention for a long period. Lalaji went from England to America. His visit to America was a voluntary exile. In America he made a number of speeches about India and conditions of life in this country. He wrote a number of books. As part of the effort to develop the Indian agitation he established the Indian Home Rule League in New York. How could there be dearth of work for the Indian hero in America? He set up the 'India Information Bureau'. He started a journal 'Young India' and gave a fillip to the movement. He himself edited the paper. The paper expounded the Indian culture and explained in detail the necessity for Indian freedom. It attracted the attention of everybody. The circulation increased. Through this paper it became possible for not only Indians but also Americans and people of other countries to understand the aims and objects of Lalaji and to sympathise with India's aims. The movement gained support.

While in America he wrote two books: 'Arya Samaj' and 'England's, Debt to India.' His life in America was not bed of roses. He himself cooked his food. He earned money for his living by writing books and articles. Germany was then at war with England. The German Government attempted to take advantage of the dissatisfaction of the Indians by enticing Lalaji. But he refused to be tempted.

While in America, Lalaji found time to visit Japan. In both the countries he made friendship and won the sympathy of influential people. He conducted himself in such a way that both countries came to trust him. Thus, he made a name for himself. At the end of the great War in 1919 he wanted to return to India. The British Government would not give him a passport. In India in Jalianwala Bagh of Amritsar, British soldiers fired on helpless Indians at a public meeting. Lajpat Rai got news of the dreadful massacre even when he was in New York. He was eager to join his countrymen. He got the passport at the end of the year. In December 1919 Lalaji came from New York to London. There he met the famous author Bernard Shaw and some socialist friends. Then he came to Paris.

Non-cooperation Movement

Lalaji thus brought about a revolution in the attitudes of the people of England and America towards India. He returned in

February 1920. Lokamanya Tilak, Jinnah and Shrimati Annie Besant accorded a heroic welcome to him. Welcome Addresses were presented to him in Bombay, Delhi and Lahore. He was elected as the president of the special session of the Congress held in September 1920.

Next year Mahatma Gandhi started the Non-cooperation Movement. The movement gained momentum in the country. Lalaji jumped into the agitation with his bosom friend, the revolutionary Ajit Singh. In response to Lalaji's stirring call, the whole of Punjab Province joined the movement. The agitation shook the firm foundations of the government. Government schools and colleges were boycotted. Work in courts and offices came to a halt. The people were firmly united against imperialism. Lalaji himself started a national school in Lahore. Tilak opened a political science institution. Thus, enthusiastic youths found guidance. Lalaji undertook a whirlwind tour of Punjab for ten days for that purpose and collected nine lakh rupees. Full of reverence for him, people contributed money enthusiastically.

In Prison

Lajpat Rai's organising ability and heroic speeches were inspiring. Government was finding it difficult to face the intense Non-cooperation Movement growing day by day. All over the country there were agitation and hartals and the rulers were shaken. Lalaji became a dangerous person in the eyes of the government. In December 1921 Lalaji was arrested.

The other leaders of the movement, Motilal Nehru and Chittaranjan Das were also imprisoned. Lalaji was sentenced to 18 months' rigorous imprisonment. Because of the people's protest and the pleadings by lawyers he was released after two months. It was one o' clock in the night when he was released. When he came to the door he was arrested again. He was tried for another offence and was sentenced to rigorous imprisonment for two years.

While in jail he fell ill and his health deteriorated. When the public learnt this vigorous agitation was started throughout the country for his release. Government released him. Lalaji went to Solan to improve his health.

Organising the Community

As soon as his health improved Lalaji become active again. He joined the 'Swaraj Party' of Motilal Nehru. He was elected to the Central Legislative Assembly. By that time the Hindu Muslim unity move shaped by Mahatma Gandhi had failed.

Lalaji had to turn his attention to communal problems. He was himself influenced by the Arya Samaj and was a staunch supporter of the Hindu dharma. But he was aware of the need for Hindu Muslim unity in the fight for Swaraj. The Non-cooperation Movement was crumbling and ill feeling between different communities was reaching dangerous proportions. In the 1924 Hindu-Muslim riots Hindus suffered much in Kohat of North-West Frontier Province. In two days of riots not only were 150 Hindus killed but 400 persons had also to be shifted to Rawalpindi. Mahatma Gandhi undertook a fast.

There was a conference to bring about friendship among the followers of different religions and a national council was set up. But the problem was not solved. The Kohat tragedy pained and disappointed Lalaji. He had to stand by the helpless Hindu community. To counteract associations formed by the Muslims, Lalaji tirelessly fostered movements for 'Purification of Hinduism' and 'Organisation of Hinduism'. As long ago as in 1924 Lalaji expressed the fear that Muslims might want a division of India and demand a separate state for themselves. This shows his far-sightedness.

He presided over the Hindu Mahasabha held at Calcutta in 1925. The speech he made about Hindu dharma and the necessity to uphold it woke up the Hindus. In 1926 Lalaji participated in the International Labour Conference held at Geneva as a representative of workers in India. He also took part in similar conferences held in Britain and France.

"Unhappy India"

Lalaji went to Europe in 1927 to improve his health. Katherine Mayo, a foreign journalist, visited India. She wrote a book called 'Mother India'. It was about Indian civilization, culture and life. She saw only sheer ignorance and filth in India and nothing good or decent. It gave a totally misleading picture of India. In an article Gandhiji protested and called it a 'gutter inspector's report'. The book Mayo wrote was published when Lalaji was in London. The book created uproar in India and Britain. People who were opposed to the freedom of India had given money for the publication of the book. Lalaji read it. He could not keep quiet. Soon after his return to India the first thing he did was to write a book 'Unhappy India.' He gave a fitting reply to the false propaganda of Miss Mayo.

Simon Commission

The Non-cooperation Movement failed. Therefore, there was a lull in political activities. In 1927 the British Government wanted a report on political reforms in India and on amending the Government of India Act. So it appointed a commission. The commission consisted of Sir John Simon and six other members. All of them were members of the British Parliament. There was not a single Indian as member. It was composed solely of White people. The commission was an insult to Indians. These White men were to shape the future of India. The people of India rose as one man against this step. Under Lalaji's leadership, it was resolved to boycott the Simon Commission.

Lajpat Rai moved a resolution in the Central Legislative Assembly in February 1928. "The present Constitution of the Commission and its terms of reference are unworthy of acceptance by this House; therefore, this House advises the Government that it should have nothing to do with the Commission." He made an impassioned speech on that occasion. There were several English men and government officers in the Legislative

Assembly. It was known that they would vote against the resolution. Lalaji appealed to the Indian members thus: "Let the members understand that they are slaves in the eyes of the British Government and of the world. When they vote on the resolution let them remember that in 1919, because of a single epidemic, six crores of people died in our country. Let them remember that in this country ten crores of people do not have even one meal a day."

What right did the British Parliament have to frame a Constitution for India? That was Lalaji's fearless question. Only Indians had the right to decide about their future. They were determined about it. The report of Motilal Nehru and his colleagues was ready. It had protested against the British attitude. Lalaji toured the whole of India to give publicity to the Nehru report. He asserted: "Those who oppose the report are the enemies of Swaraj and enemies of India."

Strike of Imperialism

The 30th of October 1928 was an evil day in India's political history. The Simon Commission was expected to arrive in Lahore on that day. The rulers had taken precautions to prevent a public protest. Prohibitory orders were enforced. Lalaji was ill that day. Still he led the procession to protest against the Commission.

When the Simon Commission arrived, on one side there where traitors to welcome them. On another side the revolutionaries demonstrated against the Commission. In the protest march youths staged a tremendous show. A hartal was observed that day; there was a sea of black flags. Thousands and thousands of hearts and voices shouted "Simon, go back!" The lion of Punjab, Lala Lajpat Rai, led the procession. When the trains reached the station, the cry "Simon, go back!" hit the sky.

Police security arrangements crumbled. The crowd was so thick that movement was impossible. The Police charged with their Lathis (stout sticks). The blood of innocent people began to flow. Lalaji's friends Sukhdev, Yashpal, Bhagavati Charan and others surrounded him, in order to protect him. Police officer Scot saw Lalaji and his bodyguards. He ordered the Police to beat the bodyguards. A Police officer named Sanders came forward to do the job. The Police Lathis rained blows on Lalaji - on the head and all over the body. Lala realised this incident would lead to conflict and a bloodbath. He told the huge crowd of revolutionary youths: "Leave this place." The crowd dispersed.

Last Days and Demise

The same evening there was a mammoth public meeting. The despicable action of the Police was severely condemned and the Simon Commission was boycotted. Police Deputy Superintendent Neal was present at the meeting. Lalaji turned to Neal and said in English so that he could understand him: "The blows, which fell on me today, are the last nails driven into the coffin of British Imperialism."

One word from Lajpat Rai to the youths would have been enough; they would have let loose rivers of blood. But Lalaji practised non-violence strictly. The country had to restrain its anger. In the very week of the incident Lalaji attended the All-India Congress Committee and all-party meetings. He grew weak and returned to Lahore.

Lalaji fell ill and died of a heart attack on 17th November 1928. The whole of India knew that his death was a result of the lathi blows. A deliberate murder by the Police!

More than a lakh of people took up in his funeral procession.

Country did not Forget

The movement did not abate though Lalaji died. In fact it acquired a new vigour. The Congress Party began the no-tax campaign. Punjab could not easily forget Lalaji's death. To avenge the cowardly Whites' attack on their beloved leader, the people of Punjab rose in fierce revolt. The young revolutionary Bhagat Singh murdered the Police officer Sanders, mainly responsible for the attack on Lalaji, in a dreadful manner. This happened on December 17, exactly one month after Lalaji's death. Next year the British sentenced Bhagat Singh to death.

'The Lion of Punjab'

The lesson which the Lion of Punjab Lala Lajpat Rai taught the country was to be brave. To the Indians in the chains of slavery his message was "Begging or prayer cannot bring freedom. You can win it only through struggle and sacrifice." Because throughout his life he fought fearlessly, he was called the Lion of Punjab. The sacrifice of his life was like a warrior's death in battle.

A Multifaced Personality

Lala Lajpat Rai the martyr was a store- house of many good qualities. Efficiency, tireless industry and patriotism gave lustre to his personality. He was friendly. For the sake of his country he won a large number of friends both in India and abroad. From the platform he spoke for hours eloquently. His speeches were fiery and galvanizing. People heard him spellbound and his words opened their eyes. He was indeed a lion among men.

He was a brilliant man and he was devoted, in body and mind, to the cause of education. The DAV College, the National College, the Tilak School of Politics and others are living monuments to his patriotism. His service in the field of journalism was no less valuable. He founded the Urdu weekly Vande Mataram and the English weekly 'The People' - and both maintained high standards. In the field of commerce too, he will be remembered forever. It was Lalaji who established the Punjab National Bank and the Lakshmi Insurance Company. As a member of the Arya Samaj he worked incessantly. He fought against Untouchability. When Gandhiji started the 'Harijan Sevak Sangh' he worked for it. He was like a father to the orphans. He was responsible for starting numerous orphanages in the country. The Gulab Devi Hospital and the Servants of People Society are living monuments to the memory of that great man.

Lalaji was one of those who sowed the seeds of socialism in India. He was well acquainted with Henry Meyers, Beatrice Webb, Lansbury and others who promoted the growth of socialism in Britain. He was in the vanguard of labour organisation. He founded the 'All-India Trade Union Congress' and was himself its president. He started an organised effort to improve the conditions of the working class. He pleaded that a part of the profits of an industry should be given to the workmen.

The people of India were in chains, and they had to be aroused. They had to be organised. Lalaji was the symbol of the power, which did this. As Mahatma Gandhi said: "So long as the sun shines in the Indian sky, persons like Lalaji will not die."

Lajpat Rai once said: "If I had the power to influence Indian journals, I would have the following headlines printed in bold letters on the first page:

Milk for the infants

Food for the adults

Education for all,"

The Legacy

A great national leader who came to be called the 'Lion of Punjab.' Worked tirelessly to improve education, to promote unity among Hindus and to reform society. His clarion call and glorious life inspired the nation. The Lathis of the servants of British imperialism cruelly cut his life short.

It was the evening of October 30, 1928. Standing on the platform at a crowded public meeting in Lahore City, a person known as the 'Lion of Punjab, 'said in an inspiring voice:

> "Every blow on our bodies this afternoon is like a nail driven into the coffin of British imperialism."

Terrible blows had battered the chest and the body of the great man who made that stirring speech. The humiliation inflicted by the high-handedness of the British was more painful than the wounds.

On the morning of the seventeenth day after this, the great revolutionary died. Onward along the path he had trodden his followers marched towards freedom.

The great leader cut down by the high-handedness of the then imperialist Punjab Government was Lala Lajpat Rai.

2

Leader in Making

Beginning and Determination

Barely ten days to the opening event of the season of Christmas festivity, and, of a sudden, Sir Hugh Gough, the British Commander-in-Chief, cancels his grand ball fixed well in advance for the eleventh evening of December.

In the cold season of 1845 things looked pretty grim. The grand ball had to be sacrificed because the British at Ambala got the news that the Sikh army was on the march eastwards and had crossed the Sutlej — the waters that the British had ever insisted must separate Ranjit Singh's domain from theirs. West of Ambala and the Sutlej, Ranjit Singh's successors still ruled, though the British held isolated outposts at Ludhiana and Ferozepore.

Much was at stake for both parties. The Governor-General himself, Henry Hardinge, came down to share the work and worry of the Commander-in-Chief. In the campaign that followed, he would often be seen sitting down to his despatch-boxes under no other canopy than that of a tree, for urgent papers must be dealt with before his camp paraphernalia arrived.

Battle was joined on December 18 at Mudki. Henry Hardinge, himself a tried soldier, directed a part of the British forces, not from a remote and sheltered headquarters, but by galloping into the field the moment heavy cannonade was heard.

On the Sikh side, as a writer of history remarks, "hearts to dare and hands to execute were numerous, but there was no mind to guide and animate the whole". The unlettered but extremely shrewd Ranjit Singh, Lion of the Punjab, had already been dead more than six years. Ranjit Singh had left behind a splendid army, but no worthy successors to put it to good use and to steer the ship of State.

Not more than 48 km from the field of battle, at Jagraon, the same fateful day in December 1845 saw the birth of Radha Kishan, (who later became father of Lajpat Rai), who in turn grew up to revive the old title, Lion of the Punjab.

At Mudki the Sikhs lost. The war had begun well for the British. A few more battles on the neighbouring fields, and all was up. In a month's time at Jagraon itself, the Ferozepore force joined that from Ludhiana. In two months the war had ended. The British denounced the treaty they had so keenly pressed on Ranjit Singh. They had cleared the Upper Sutlej finally. In the next four years the beyond-Sutlej Punjab too was theirs.

When British raj came to the Punjab, the particular branch of Agarwals with which we are here concerned had for generations been living in Malerkotla and the neighbouring territory. Like all Agarwals elsewhere they were a trading and money-lending community, but here they gained additional prestige by filling important administrative offices. In particular they had supplied for generations the khazanchis or custodians of the exchequer to the Muslim rulers of Malerkotla, a small state in the southeastern part of the Punjab.

Malerkotla town is by train some 45 km from Ludhiana, to the south, and has a population of more than 20,000 souls. Originally Maler and Kotla were two distinct townships. The beautiful Moti Bazar connecting the two is a 20th-century addition. The Agarwals of our story were more in evidence at Maler, the bigger of the twins. History tells us of a local disturbance in the turbulent Sikh days which put the clan on the trek, though not for long. In fact, some of them sought shelter next door, not three furlongs away, in Kotla (literally, the "walled" township). The others were scattered in the Ludhiana and Ferozepore districts, but continued to be known as Malerys.

As part of this trek Lajpat Rai's ancestors arrived at Jagraon, a township in the Ludhiana district but not far from Ferozepore. The ancestral house is still there. So also is the school named after their father by Radha Kishan's sons, during his life-time, and since then elevated to college status.

Lajpat Rai's grand Father and Radha Kishan's father had been an employee of the new rulers, a patwari — the time-honoured village official who keeps the land records — in a village not far from Jagraon. He was short of stature and, on his grandson's showing, "very painstaking and courageous... very intelligent and wise and sociable". He had all the virtues and failings of the shopkeeper, that is, of his ancestors through the centuries. In keeping with the code of that class, he was fond of making money in all possible ways. Traditionally a patwari being an ill-paid but indispensable village functionary — one might almost call him a dignitary — suffers from no inconvenient scruples, especially as the law connives at and custom insists on providing many simple ways to extra cash or amenities.

His salary is recognised merely as a retainer or, say, as a supplement to his "extras". To this day when "anti-corruption" campaigns started by those in high authority are advertised so loudly, a patwari without these "extras" is nearly as common as a white crow. Truly speaking, a large part of the petty fees exacted by a patwari is what would properly be called appreciative "tips" rather than outright bribes.

All patwaris collect these tips; the banya patwari may merely have asked for them with greater zest. With this hereditary love of money he combined the adaptability of his stock. A trading community could not be very long-lived when political upheavals were common, unless it displayed exceptional resourcefulness in adapting itself to circumstances. The Muslim rule in Malerkotla, its clashes with the Sikhs, the panicky trek to Jagraon, the petty tyranny in everyday life under the Muslim Rais of Raikot, a spell of Ranjit Singh's Ahluwalia proteges of Kapurthala, the arrival of the British after the Sikh defeat on the battlefield — all these bewildering buffets of history this adaptable clan seems to have thriven on.

The short-statured Malery banya patwari had no schooling worth the name. He was acquainted with the ingenious "short-long hand" of the banya's ledgers, called the "Mahajani", but had no acquaintance with Persian and Urdu in which the land records were maintained. His was the advantage, however, of having come from a stock which accepted any situation in which it was placed, and adapted itself quickly to the altered circumstances. Possibly those who had the advantage of knowing Persian and Urdu were yet trying to get their own bearings in the quick and cataclysmic changes that history had staged.

These practical people, however, wasted little time in idle gazing and futile introspection. They were adepts in trimming their economic sails to any political wind that blew. So they would supply a patwari, and one who would well manage his business in spite of his handicaps. They furnished a patwari, because in the tossing about by history they had found their feet earlier than those with the necessary training and qualifications. Their patwari ran true to type and like his jat bhais he was orthodox and strict in his religious observances. He performed his devotional rites twice a day regularly, and hospitably cultivated the company of the ascetic gurus — Shvetambara (white-robed) Jain sadhus.

His wife was a bit "different". Not in being illiterate, or in her incapacity to count beyond twenty — handicaps common to most women of her generation — but in not being money-minded. "I have not seen another woman" says Lajpat Rai of his grandmother, "as righteous, as pure-hearted, as hospitable, as generous and as simple. She was incapable of keeping money and her husband never gave her much. All her life she never used a lock and never kept a key in her custody. She was not fond of jewellery or of dressing well. She was so generous that practically all she got from her husband was given away to her neighbours."

Could the invisible fingers that join chromosomes and prepare the packet of heredity combine this woman's generous indifference towards money with the money-shrewdness and practical sense of her husband?

This "different" woman, we are told, was also a study in abnormal psychology — a subject, if you like, for parapsychology, or for psychical research. Occasionally the spirit of her husband's deceased sister seemed to possess her. The family would gather round her and consult her as an oracle, whenever she was in this state of trance. She would foretell the future or make revelations about matters not known to anybody. Later events corroborated her prophecies: the family anyway had great faith in her. Her grandson had often seen her, as a boy, in such a trance, and wrote what we have just quoted, without offering any explanation of the phenomenon, adding only that "tricks or fraud or humbugging my grandmother knew not, and that "she kept excellent health and seldom fell ill".

Her husband showed indications of a wanderlust, though we are not aware if he ever undertook really long tramps in those pre-railway days. His last illness lasted but a day, and he died practically in harness.

Born of these parents, Radha Kishan exhibited an unusual interest in religion. Macaulay had already written his famous note on educational policy in India, when Radha Kishan went to school. The madrasah set up by Macaulay's countrymen in Radha Kishan's village was conducted by a Maulvi and imparted what was known as Persian education. Radha Kishan was a bright pupil, ever securing the top position in the class, and in the final Normal School examination he came out first in the Punjab, securing the full quota of marks in "exact learning", i.e., in mathematics and physical science.

He was more than merely intelligent, much more than a mere winner of prizes and positions in examinations. He had an intellectual sturdiness about him that gave to things of the mind a definite precedence over the mere running after cash. He had not his mother's complete apathy towards money, nor was he like his father prone to "making money by all possible means". He evinced great interest in religion; but to him this did not signify the routine ritual that had been accepted by his ancestors for centuries. He wanted to study, to ponder, to scrutinise and only then to accept. The one religion that he could study at his school was that of his teacher, a pious Sunni Mussalman, "very firm in his religion and honest and righteous". His lofty character, we learn, made his Islam contagious, for several of his non-Muslim pupils embraced Islam later in life. Some of those who fought shy of apostasy, in their heart of hearts renounced their own faith in favour of the pious teachers. So did Radha Kishan. He said his namaz, fasted during the Ramzan, and he sought friends amongst the ulema. For years he was on the verge of formal conversion but fought shy of it fearing the tremendous domestic difficulties it would for certain bring in its trail. He studied Islam with a sincere devotion to truth. Ever responsive to new stimuli, he combined the receptive quality with the critical.

When Sir Syed Ahmad Khan started his liberal interpretation of Islam, which came to be dubbed popularly as "natural theology", Radha Kishan avidly drank in the new tenets. He read with zest all that Sir Syed wrote, and for years was in correspondence with him. Once in a letter he asked Sir Syed if to become a Mussalman it would be necessary for him to cease to be Radha Kishan, and to be known by an Islamic name. Sir Syed's reply suited Radha Kishan admirably, for it said that change in name was not in the least fundamental, the essentials being a firm monotheistic faith in Allah, and in Muhammad as his prophet. This reply must have gone a long way in appeasing Radha Kishan's conscience.

Duni Chand, the lawyer, shared with his intimate friend, Radha Kishan, his peculiar faith, and his peculiar difficulties about apostasy. One day, however, it appears, the two friends resolved to embrace Islam openly. With this intention they set out for the masjid. Radha Kishan's wife somehow came to know of their plans and successfully thwarted them! She had felt bitterly, as any Hindu woman would, the heresy of her husband, but she had tolerated it with the tact and adaptability peculiar to Hindu wives. Her parents believed in the Sikh gurus.

She had been taught their bant in her childhood, and in Radha Kishan's house she kept up her regular recital of Japji, the Sikh mattins. Radha Kishan would bring his Muslim friends to his house to dine with him. In those days of orthodoxy (though not of political 'communalism') this was regarded as outrageous in a Hindu home. But Radha Kishan's wife created no scenes. She satisfied her husband by serving his friends in her own plates and afterwards satisfied orthodoxy by cleansing the plates (of metal, as usual in Hindu homes) in fire. A non-vegetarian Aggarwal in those days was regarded by his people as little short of a monster. But Radha Kishan who in his thinking had ceased to be Jain or Hindu and Aggarwal would at times carry home a meat dish cooked in the house of a Muslim friend.

All these outrageous doings his wife put up with; but he knew she would draw a line somewhere - he knew exactly where. The day he became an avowed Muslim, he strongly suspected, she would leave his roof taking away the children and would seek either his father's roof or that of her own. "That my father did not become a convert to Islam... is nothing short of a miracle, and the credit of having wrought this miracle goes to my mother," so wrote Radha Kishan's son.

But a friend of the family gave the credit for this shuddhi (or conversion back to Hinduism) miracle to the baby Lajpat in Gulab Devi's lap when she overtook her husband on the steps of the masjid and appealed to him in the name of their little one. While the father in Radha Kishan listened and hesitated, the babe bewildered by this unfamiliar scene started crying, and this coming at a tense moment supported the mother's beseeching so successfully that overcome by domestic emotion, the near-Muslim halted just as he was about to cross the barrier, and returned home unconverted.

Radha Kishan's wife must have been a wonderful woman in her own way. The handling of such an erratic husband made extraordinary demands on her tact and again as a housewife she needed to be no less skilful in managing a house on his meagre income. As a teacher he was getting just twenty-five rupees a month. He was much too absorbed in his theological studies and in the pursuit of learning to bother about currying favour with the officials of his department, and so was never thought of-in connection with any preferment, though superb as a teacher and so adored by his pupils.

After years of keen interest in education Lajpat Rai wrote of Munshiji as a teacher: "In India I have never come across a better teacher." In his whole career he is said to have been granted an increment twice — each time a five-rupee one so that when he retired he had been getting the munificent salary of thirty-five rupees a month! His wife had to bring up a large family on this slender income. In all she bore him ten children; at the time of her death six of these, four sons and two daughters, were alive. How she managed to feed and clothe this large family and to observe in addition all the religious feasts and festivals and samskaras — for we are told she missed none of these — within this income seems little short of a miracle. Yet her bigger miracle was that of fortitude which her husband was for ever straining to a breaking-point by his sacrilegious enormities.

She suffered deeply, but all in silence — a living monument of fortitude. No rows, no ugly scenes, and that made her suffering the more intense. Sorrow she kept strictly to herself. Lajpat, as a two-year-old, often watched her for hours shedding tears of grief at her husband's incorrigible ways. "For days together," wrote her son afterwards, "she would not taste her food, and would be sighing in grief with her children in her lap. But she would never think of deserting her husband. In fact she always lived with him and was never away from him for any appreciably long period of time" — we suppose to suffer, to serve, and thus to avert if possible the calamity of apostasy.

Good and remarkable in many ways, she was altogether unlettered. Her husband tried time and again to teach her, and later on her son tried too. But her frail health, the perpetual worry about her husband, the heavy household routine of a housewife on a meagre allowance for a large family, and the fact that most Hindu women of her generation even in families better favoured by fortune were uneducated, made her remain content with her unlettered lot.

Radha Kishan remained an "unofficial" Muslim till about his fortieth year. He not merely admired Islam zealously and sincerely, but cultivated in himself all the aggressiveness of a new convert in denouncing the religion and ritual of his forefathers. To have done so secretly or even privately would have been entirely unlike him. He wrote out his denunciations in newspaper articles which found ready publication in the Brahmo Press of those days. His attitude towards Hindu religion, philosophy and culture changed only when his son had become an ardent follower of the principles of a new Hinduism which the Arya Samaj had laid bare. He was able to show his father that beneath an exterior that had become ugly and even putrid, Hinduism at its core was pervaded by a beautiful aroma all its own. Radha Kishan was never wilfully blind but he knew no Sanskrit; and a keen seeker after truth as he was, the milieu of his school days had not favoured his seeing Hinduism in the true perspective.

When he became aware of this lack he readily tried to correct himself. He studied all about Hinduism that was accessible to him. But he never joined the church for which his son so devotedly worked. His studies led him not to the Arya Samaj, but to Vedanta. The subtleties of the Vedantic philosophy held out a strong intellectual appeal and in his old age he found solace in the teaching of the Upanishads.

All his life Radha Kishan remained a keen student of religion. He could not go to the Hindu source books as he had done in studying Islam. But whatever was available to him in Urdu (or even Hindi or Gurmukhi), he read with avidity and studied with industry and conscientious scrupulousness.

Besides newspaper articles he occasionally wrote small books and had some title to authorship. His religious studies resulted in a book in Urdu called *Tehqiq-e-Mazahib* (Enquiry into Religions), a brief comparative study of the fundamental tenets of the principal religions, advertised as "the fruit of the author's study of different religions extending over a period of 22 years". We do riot know whether Munshiji ever composed verse, but he is known to have sported the penname of Azad as appropriately betokening his spirit and his outlook.

His published tracts included one on metempsychosis called *Risalah-e-Tanasukh* in which he particularly compared the teachings of his erstwhile guru, Sir Syed Ahmad, with those of the Hindu philosophers, generally to the advantage of the latter. But he himself did not subscribe to the views of any one particular school. He joined issue with Swami Dayananda in his doctrine according to which even souls that had attained *moksha* (salvation) enjoyed such beatitude not eternally but for an essentially limited, though a very long period. This doctrine he found to be contrary both to the teachings of ancient Indian philosophers and to the dictates of his own reason. Radha Kishan throughout tried to be logical and terse and confined his attention only to the point at issue. He had his chapter and verse ready in support of his contentions and generally let the different philosophers he was discussing speak for themselves. His writing is dispassionate in the extreme, completely devoid of all attempts at decoration. In fact, it is ascetically bald, and definitely wanting in grace of presentation.

His studies in history resulted in an Urdu booklet of about 150 pages called Bir Charitra which was mainly a selection from Todd's Annals and Antiquities of Rajasthan. In a preface Munshi Radha Kishan speaks of the value of historical study and shows his peculiar fondness for it. The book enjoyed a vogue for some time, and even a second edition was called for.

Lala Lajpat Rai had given away the house of 2 Court Street, Lahore to the Society and had built himself a smaller two-storeyed one in the same compound. His father did not shift to the new house, but continued to occupy in the old one a small low-ceilinged room in the south corner of the verandah. A cot and an office chair were about all the furniture one could notice in this room, besides the very conspicuously-unvarnished, crudely-planed thick strong plank of wood running continuously along three walls, at a convenient height.

This shelving came handy for stowing away books, papers and odds and ends and underlined the ascetic aspect of the bed-cum-living room of Munshi Radha Kishan. This was perhaps the only room in the house the ascetic aspect of which never accepted a glass-pane in door, window or ventilator. In summer, of course, he slept in the verandah or in the open. In the morning he would get up and would be seen reading one of his favourite books, or last evening's paper — for, Lahore in those days boasted of no morning paper — till it was time for breakfast.

After breakfast he would walk to the shop of his second son, Ranpat Rai (a paper merchant on Ganpat Road, Anarkali) and spend his day there, most of the time reading. His supper he used to have at Ranpat Rai's, after which he would return to his own small room at 2 Court Street, with the afternoon's Bandemataram in his hand. He never went to sleep without having first done his reading.

Among the books that he was particularly fond of was an Urdu translation of Draper's classic Conflict between Religion and Science. Often he would dip into this early in the morning or else pick it out in the evening for a read when going to bed. His other favourites were mostly books on religion or history.

When he died he was eighty-two. His father's death was keenly felt by Lajpat Rai — the more so because being in prison at the time he could not be by his deathbed for a filial fulfilment. He sent special instructions that all expenses for the obsequies must be met out of his (Lajpat Rai's) royalties as a writer which he regarded as a particularly pure portion of his fortune.

The Upbringing

Munshi Radha Kishan taught for some eight years at the Government Middle School, Rupar, in Ambala district. During the Rupar days, early in 1865 — January 28 — he became a father. The first child, a son whom he named Lajpat Rai, arrived in a small mud house in his father-in-law's village, Dhudike. As is the custom largely even now, the expectant mother had moved to her father's home for her first childbirth. Dhudike is a small village in the Moga tehsil of the Ferozepore district, and about 8 km from Radha Kishan's own Jagraon, which is in the Ludhiana district.

The father happened to be away at Delhi for a short professional course. News reached him there that the new arrival was a puny thing. Tall and vigorous himself and devoted to physical exercise, this was not exactly what he had looked forward to.

Early childhood in malaria-infested Rupar did not go to make of Lajpat a model of health and vigour. When he grew up into a schoolboy he was more fond of books than of play. He became a constant victim to malaria, and early acquired an enlarged spleen.

The boy's schooling at first was largely carried on by Radha Kishan at home, where the lessons of the classroom were abundantly supplemented. The boy was intelligent and hardworking and as prize-winning as his father had been in his own day. The father taught him not merely the three R's, but soon began to interest him in that most interesting of all R's - Religion. The boy read parts of the Quran with his father and like him used to say his namaz and occasionally even observed the Ramzan fast.

Young Lajpat must have been puzzled about feelings about religion as he saw it practised in his home. His father's father was an orthodox Jain; his own father a firm, though an unofficial, Muslim; his mother in perpetual agony about her husbands Islam but scrupulously regular in her Sikh recitals. If ever he went to her parents' house he must have seen plenty of Sikhism in evidence. How could he help feeling perplexed whenever he took stock of his situation even in a boyish way? Anyhow Munshi Radha Kishan succeeded in imparting to his son the contagion of religious enquiry and curiosity which continued unblended through mature years, even though the boy before very long gave up Islamic observances.

From his father he also inherited his fondness for the study of history which in fact meant a fondness for the 'epic' in the widest possible sense. Radha Kishan started the boy early on Firdausi's immortal Shahnama, which is regarded as the Persian counterpart of Homer's epic or of Vyasa's Mahabharata. Again and again he read parts of Firdausi with his father, and when he had grown up, he continued to read them all by himself. The studies at once satisfied a craving, and created an appetite for more. It is to the early schooling in Shahnama that Lajpat in later years traced his passion for books of history, and it might be it was the dramatic declamations of Firdausi's heroes that first kindled in the child's mind an interest in oratory.

Perhaps to this schooling might even be traced his life-long fondness for the dynamic, the heroic and the epic in any work. Like Vyasa and Homer, Firdausi is not content with a mere chronicle of what happens on the battlefield. In that sense he was very unlike the official historians of yore. He is all-embracing and presents an exhaustive picture of the life and culture of the times his verse celebrates. The boy nurtured on this intellectual diet naturally sought ever after in books of history the same large sweep, the same encyclopaedic range.

Preoccupation with Holy Quran and the Shahnama and rather frequent interludes of malaria notwithstanding, he did not neglect his school-books. Almost always he occupied the top position. Being also the youngest boy in the school he was looked upon as a prodigy. He completed the Rupar school course consisting of six forms. Soon after the closing of that school, Munshi Radha

Kishan was transferred to Shimla. He could not take his wife and children there because his meagre salary would not suffice to meet the expenses of that place. Lajpat had been sent to Lahore for further schooling. The education department granted him a stipend of seven rupees a month and from Lahore he went to Delhi. He was there for about three months, but the climate of Delhi did not suit the sickly boy. By then the father had gone away to Shimla, and Lajpat went with his mother to their home in Jagraon.

Before he was thirteen and while yet at the middle school, the boy had been married. Of course it was an arranged match, in the orthodox way, linking one Aggarwal family with another. Radha Devi, the bride, came from a Hissar family and had seen there more affluence than was visible at the house of the ill-paid teacher. We shall have occasion to speak of her and of the married life of the couple later. For the moment we are concerned with the education of the bridegroom.

After having left Delhi, and having spent a few months at home at Jagraon, he joined the Mission High School at Ludhiana, where also he was granted a stipend as a promising boy, and where again he fell ill and left the school after a few months. About this time Munshi Radha Kishan again received orders of transfer, this time to Ambala. There his wife and children joined him. At Rupar two more children were born to him — Mela Ram, who died young, and a daughter. In his Ambala days, three more sons were born — Ranpat Rai, Dhanpat Rai and Nand Rai, later named Dalpat Rai in better consonance with the names of his brothers. Also, incidentally, a Dalpat Rai at Lahore was a very successful lawyer in those days.

Sickly Lajpat had not been at Ambala quite two months when he fell dangerously ill, and for nearly four months had to be nursed in bed. This time it was an abscess which had to be operated on twice or thrice. Thinking of those days he later wrote:

> "I have been a source of trouble and anxiety! to my parents all my life, but that year I put them to so much trouble that I can never possibly forget it."

All the same he matriculated that year. In fact, he did a double matriculation. The University of the Punjab was yet in its infancy, and Dr. Leitner was trying various experiments to pattern it differently from the other universities. The infant university did not enjoy much prestige even in its home province, whereas the diplomas and degrees granted by the Calcutta University were at a premium. Lajpat solved the problem by taking both the examinations, the Calcutta and the Punjab ones.

He was successful in both, and got a first class in his Calcutta examination, in spite of his long illness. For his Calcutta matric he took up Persian as second language, but in the Punjab he was examined in Arabic and Urdu and physical science, besides all the Calcutta subjects. His father had been keen that he should learn Arabic, and in early boyhood he devoted a good deal of time to Arabic accedence and syntax; but in reality he was not much interested in the study, and his success in the examination was a tour de force. Dr. Leitner's university turned out barely 106 matriculates that year; the educational factories were working slow and Lajpat Rai stood somewhere in the middle of the turnout.

Impressions and Attachments

Lajpat Rai's further education became a serious problem. The boy was no doubt gifted and keen on his studies. To his father so genuinely interested in education, it would have been painful indeed to wean such an eager and promising lad away from his books so soon, and yet where was the money to send him up to college? The difficulties were formidable, but eventually Radha Kishan made up his mind to give his son the benefit of a college education, whatever hardship that might entail on the family at home. A man of Munshiji's independent character could not go about begging support from friends.

The only friend whose help he is said to have ever sought was a much respected Mussalman of Jagraon, one Sajawal Biloch, who had been his schoolmate, probably his classmate, and with whom Radha Kishan's relations were cordial and intimate. Sajawal would have willingly financed the high-school education of the boy at Lahore. But it does not seem he was ever called upon to make good his word for, as we have seen, Lajpat's stay at Lahore for school education was extremely brief. For his college education he depended on the stipends he could secure and a meagre allowance of eight to ten rupees a month from home, which sum, of course, was a considerable part of his father's earnings.

In February 1881, a little after he had turned sixteen, Lajpat joined the only college that Lahore (or the Punjab) had, known as Government College.

The struggle with poverty at college must have been grim indeed. He had not seen prosperity at home, but a frugal standard within their slender means was maintained there, and whenever he fell ill, his parents could look after him. At Lahore, with the utmost that could be squeezed out of the family budget, supplemented by sundry stipends, he was constantly being reminded of his penury.

To the first two or three months, he himself says, "I had to face great embarrassment. My eyes gave me great trouble. Besides, I had at times to go without food. After a good deal of struggle I succeeded in getting a stipend of three rupees a month from the university. I had come to Lahore merely with the idea of studying for an arts degree, but on the advice of certain fellow-students in the hostel I joined the law school also.

Out of my monthly stipends I was paying two rupees as tuition fee in the Government College, three rupees in the law school and perhaps one rupee as hostel fee. My father could, with difficulty, manage only eight to ten rupees a month, and I had to live within that amount. Law books were pretty expensive, but I got the more essential among them rather cheap, by buying them second-hand, or I depended on friends for their loan. I used the same economy in securing the arts books and got along by borrowing these. My parents were undergoing great hardship for my sake, and were even prepared to run into debt. But I did not want to put them to this trouble, and so lived very frugally."

The grim struggle soon persuaded him that the first thing was to complete the law course and get the diploma that would enable him to earn a living. Liberal education soon came to occupy a subsidiary place in his plans. For his law examination he worked hard enough to qualify at the end of the year for *mukhtarship* — and also for jaundice. He continued on the college rolls for two years more, but without passing any more university examinations.

Frequent illness, the law-school priority, preoccupation with certain live issues in public life, and absorption in education of a type very different from the university curriculum, all combined in 1883 to keep his name out of the list of successful candidates in the intermediate arts examination.

But his Government College days were otherwise very important in his life. Here his classmates included names that later became famous — Mahatma Hans Raj, Pandit Guru Dutt Vidyarthi, Raja Narendranath and Professor Ruchi Ram Sahni. A college class in those days was a smaller affair. Although the number of students taking the corresponding examinations of the successor universities at Chandigarh and Lahore, nowadays, runs well beyond 50,000 yearly, it is doubtful if any other year in the Punjab's academic annals has seen a batch that will outshine this 1882-83 galaxy.

Five men who have had half as much to do with the shaping of the modern Punjab, as Lajpat Rai, Hans Raj, Narendranath, Guru Dutt and Ruchi Ram, all of whom took their intermediate examination in 1883, could not easily be named out of students in any class. Some of his comrades were for Lajpat Rai much more than mere fellow-students; in fact, Guru Dutt, Hans Raj, Lajpat Rai, Chetan Anand and Rai Shiv Nath, who formed a coterie at college, had a great deal to do with one another's lives even after their college days. A puritanic way of living was a common bond. Rai Shiv Nath, later an engineer in the UP, was perhaps the most ascetic of them all. He went about barefoot and was a zealous collector of ancient Indian, curios and books: his Dehra Dun house was indeed a private museum with a unique feature displayed in its geometrical reproductions of the old Aryan yajnashalas worked out from ancient texts with devotion and industry!

Issue of Urdu and Hindi

Many of among Lajpat's teachers at the Government College could by later judgement be regarded as nearly so important as the brilliant galaxy of his classmates. The only memorable names from amongst the teachers seem those of Dr. Leitner and Muhammad Hussain Azad. Dr. Leitner's ambition was to be a shaper of educational policy, but his plan of creating a sort of oriental seminary under the aegis of the University of the Punjab met with little success. But he has a claim to be remembered as the scrupulous and painstaking author of an important report on Indigenous Education in the Punjab which brought to light facts showing that literacy, far from being such a scarce commodity in the pre-British days, was perhaps commoner then than after a century of British rule.

As a teacher he was brilliant and versatile, and covered a wide and variegated range extending over the Arts, Oriental and Law Schools. He also had a number of linguistic, mainly Oriental, studies to his credit. But administration was a different affair, and the official history of the university seems to suggest that the brilliant Dr. Leitner had to go because under him there was too much laxity regarding the funds and accounts of the university.

Muhammad Hussain Azad was shaping history at the Government College in a different way. Steeped in Persian and Arabic erudition, he was keenly aware also that literature and learning must change with the times, and he had addressed himself to the task of enriching Urdu and of making of it a better vehicle for the new literary requirements arising mainly out of the western impact His verse is of little significance, but indubitably he ranks among the makers of Urdu prose.

He produced the first comprehensive and systematic history of Urdu literature and so powerful and vivid was his style of writing that even where his facts have been shown by later research to be utterly baseless, his obiter dicta cannot be obliterated from the popular mind; for he is a clever literary portraitist, and his minutiae, and the anecdotes ingratiate themselves into the readers' imagination and abide there tenaciously. Historians may repudiate Macaulay when he says that a convict was offered the choice of reading Guiccardiani's History or working at the galleys, and after a trial of both chose the galleys as the lesser torture, but the story has stuck to Guiccardiani. Muhammad Hussain Azad had the same dangerous gift.

When he made up his mind to give a particular character to an Urdu poet, always the stories came pat to support him. Most of the anecdotes he circulated about the ill-temper of the pathetic genius, Meer, have been found by later scholarship to be fables, but for generations Meer seems doomed to go down much as Azad portrayed him.

Lajpat Rai attended Azad's Arabic classes for only a few days, but those few days remained indelibly impressed on his memory. Azad could indulge in a broad joke even in the class room, as Lajpat Rai learnt to his cost, the very first day. However, it was not because of banter that he left the Arabic class. He left it for more ponderable reasons. The language controversy was just then starting. In the United Provinces (now named Uttar Pradesh) a movement was afoot that resulted a few years later in the recognition of Hindi as the language of the law courts. In the Punjab the Arya Samaj was laying great emphasis on the importance of Hindi and Sanskrit for Hindus. Lajpat Rai's Samajist friends at college, having definitely espoused the cause of Hindi and Sanskrit, beseeched him to discard Arabic in favour of Sanskrit — of which he knew not a word — as a sacrifice for the cause.

Professor Azad's own attitude helped Lajpat Rai in yielding to the importunity. Azad used to boast that as a Shia and as a Persian scholar he considered Iran and not India as his home. This offended the patriotic awareness already fast developing in young Lajpat's bosom and made him suspect that there was a denationalising influence lurking in the study of Arabic and Persian. The enemy lay in ambush, and he must beware. He made up his mind to leave his Arabic class and to give a trial to Sanskrit. But if he had made poor progress in Arabic, he was not destined to fare any better in Sanskrit. Even during his staunch Arya Samajist days, he had access to Sanskrit wisdom only through translations.

Let no one run away with the impression that Azad was a sort of anti-Hindi bigot He was, in fact, neither anti-Hindi nor a hater of India. He loved India in his own way. Perhaps in a different set of circumstances no one would have accused him of hostility to Hindi, even though his own contribution went only to Urdu. Azad found that Urdu literature was not only poor but was definitely suffering from stagnation. Prose had attracted little talent, and verse was wasting lavish amounts of it in outmoded channels. If it continued in the rut into which it had then fallen, there was no hope of its ever coming out to serve the many uses to which modern minds might put it. The modernising of Urdu literature had its birth in the Punjab. The initiative was taken by Muhammad Hussain Azad. The great and almost unbelievable miracle of Urdu literature is that the modernising which is supposed to have come out of the impact of the West (made mostly through English) was achieved mainly by those who had little or no knowledge of English — by Azad and Hali, and next to them by Sir Syed Ahmad and Shibli.

Amongst these four, the first place in the new movement must be given to Muhammad Hussain Azad. He set the movement going and under his influence it gathered momentum in the province. At his instance it was that Hali came down to Lahore and the combined efforts of the two resulted in something of a literary revolution. It was while Urdu was undergoing this invigorating metamorphosis that the Hindi Movement made its appearance in the Punjab and the Hindi-Urdu question became one of the major controversies of the day.

Lajpat Rai threw in his lot with the Hindi enthusiasts. But he was not to shake off so easily the influence of Muhammad Hussain Azad. He left his class, because he thought there was a danger of his falling under the spell of Azad's Iranian leanings. Yet his national pride was destined to derive nourishment from the writings of this very Muhammad Hussain Azad and, in his autobiography, he paid a handsome tribute to this influence on his life. His father had been his first great teacher, and he had formed the boy's mind mainly by teaching him Firdausi's Shahnama. Muhammad Hussain Azad was to be his second great teacher, for it was from his very well-written slender Urdu book, Qasis-e-Hind, that Lajpat first became aware of India's glorious past. These chapters of Indian history in the form of legend and story presented her past in language that made their author's pride in the Indian heritage highly infectious.

Incidentally it proved to him that his father had not been altogether right in concluding that pre-Muslim India had nothing to boast of. Both the Shahnama and the Qasis he continued to read off and on long after his school and college days. Later on he became acquainted with Col. Todd's Annals and Antiquities of Rajasthan; these annals and Arya Samaj's revealing to him the manifold glories of India's ancient past changed for him the image of his motherland; but the beginning had surely been made by Azad's narratives in the Qasis-e-Hind.

His admiration for Muhammad Hussain Azad's dignified prose must also have started at this period of his life. At any rate it continued to the end of his days. Azad, Sir Syed, Shibli — these three were his perennial favourites.

Between Brahmos and Aryas

The Hindi Movement soon found in him an active missionary. This was in fact the beginning of Lajpat Rai's public life — a precocious beginning rather, for he was barely out of school. He and Guru Dutt and Hans Raj started their public careers with this movement, while (all three) still "freshers" at college. Guru Dutt and Lajpat Rai had a busy time collecting thousands of signatures to a pro-Hindi memorial.

The first public speech that young Lajpat Rai made was in the cause of Hindi, at Ambala in 1882, when he was only eighteen. He had gone there especially for this propaganda. A subordinate magistrate happened to be among the audience and sent up a report to the Principal of the Government College who duly administered a warning to the young enthusiast pointing out that students were expected to keep at a safe distance from all such agitation.

Lajpat Rai's active participation in Hindi propaganda did not necessarily imply acceptance of the Arya Samaj. In fact for a time he wavered between the Brahmo and the Arya Samajas. The Punjab Brahmo Samaj was much under the influence of Navin Chandra Roy, and unlike some other Bengali leaders of his day, Navin Babu attached the utmost importance to the Hindi Movement. He regarded Hindi as the foundation on which the entire edifice of Indian nationalism would one day rest.

Agnihotri who later founded the Dev Samaj, the church without God, was in those days a pillar of the Punjab Brahmo Samaj. Lajpat had brought to Lahore an introduction to him from his father. Agnihotri was still a drawing master or Art teacher at the Government school, and was also editing an Urdu paper, called the *Biradar-e-Hind* (literally "Brother of India"). Munshi

Radha Kishan used to attack the Arya Samaj and orthodox Hinduism in the hospitable columns of this paper. At Lahore Lajpat Rai was very much under the influence of Agnihotri. Probably he went out occasionally with Agnihotri on lecturing tours. He read a paper on the life of Rammohan Roy at one of the Brahmo Samaj meetings. In 1882, he was formally initiated into the Brahmo Samaj by his father's friend. Agnihotri was a most eloquent public speaker and it is possible that the first realisation of what a mighty force a moving speech can be came to Lajpat through contact with him.

But Lajpat did not stay a Brahmo very long. At college, as we have already seen, his chief friends were Guru Dutt and Hans Raj and they frequently talked of the Arya Samaj to him. Guru Dutt was a prodigy; his towering intellect, his vast fund of knowledge in all branches of learning, his all-round dazzling brilliance made a profound impression on Lajpat Rai's mind. Yet it was not Guru Dutt who enlisted Lajpat Rai for the Arya Samaj but another who, though he had few intellectual pretensions, undoubtedly possessed a magnetic personality and a sound judgement regarding men. This was Sain Das, then President of the Lahore Arya Samaj. He often used to go to the college hostel, in search of converts for his church, and he knew how to attract a promising young man when he saw one.

Sain Das happened to be present at the Brahmo Samaj meeting at which Lajpat Rai received initiation at the hands of Agnihotri. As he came out of the meeting Sain Das accosted him, and in a pitying tone remarked that a worthwhile young man had been misguided and entrapped.

Inside the Punjab Brahmo Samaj, things seemed moving towards a crisis, with three factions striving for ascendancy. The bickerings bewildered the young lad from Rupar and Jagraon.

Towards the end of the year the Arya Samaj at Lahore was celebrating its anniversary. Lajpat Rai had heard a lot about this other Samaj from his friends, Guru Dutt and Hans Raj. At the time of the anniversary curiosity led his footsteps towards the Arya Samaj. He had never before witnessed an Arya Samajist gathering. Having watched the anniversary meeting the first day, he went there the next day too. The principal speaker that day was one who knew him well and had great affection for him. He took him aside to the top of the building to show him a draft of the speech he was about to deliver, and it must have flattered the young student thus to be invited to give his opinion.

Lala Sain Das urged him to join the Arya Samaj. Lajpat Rai agreed. "Indescribable joy illuminated Lala Sain Das's face."

Early Venerability of Aryas

Ones in the Arya Samaj, he was soon in its inner counsels, and before long among its front rank leaders. Sain Das, President of the Arya Samaj at Lahore, soon after selected Lajpat for a deputation to Rajputana and the United Provinces. He visited Meerut, Ajmer, Farrukhabad and other places, addressed public meetings, raised funds and everywhere met the Arya fraternity and exchanged notes with them. Growing intimacy with its working revealed the Samaj as a body extraordinarily fervent and dynamic, a well-knit determined lot that might work as the leaven for a vast quantity of inert dough. It provided just the environment that he had long yearned for: he had at last arrived where he felt at his ease.

It was not the theological or doctrinal superiority of the Arya Samajic teaching that had attracted him. It had rather been the patriotic zeal of its members, their ambition of restoring Aryavarta to its ancient glory, that inspired and permeated all activities sponsored by the Samaj and promoted by its members.

He had no doubt been influenced by the company of Guru Dutt and Hans Raj, his closest friends at college. How had these been drawn to the Samaj? Guru Dutt was precocious, and a much-talked-of prodigy of his day. As a very young lad he had displayed an interest in science and philosophy altogether beyond his years. He became a keen student of metaphysics. He had a facility for learning languages too.

He studied Sanskrit while a schoolboy with the earnestness of an accomplished scholar of mature years. His studies in Western philosophy led him to the agnosticism so much in vogue among the European thinkers of the eighties and nineties. But his agnosticism was not without streaks of faith. Spiritualism with its promise of mystical experience fascinated him as much as agnosticism did with its intellectual challenge to belief. He became interested in yoga, and the subtleties of Sanskrit grammar and philosophy attracted him even more than Bentham and Mill and Herbert Spencer had done.

Yet he was not merely a man of books. He took his books too seriously to be content merely with reading and academically pondering over them. He wanted life to tally rigidly with thought. He kept a journal which showed a perpetual struggle to secure this concord. Flesh was weak and would often fail. With this earnest man, however, every such failure called forth immediately an entry of self-reproach in his journal - and fresh endeavour. He had met a yogi in his early youth when he still vacillated between faith and agnosticism.

This yogi made a profound impression on him and Guru Dutt wanted to accompany him as a disciple; but friends intervened, and the ties of home and friendship proved stronger than the love of yoga. It is said that the last shreds of his agnosticism vanished when he saw Dayananda on his deathbed.

The dying founder of the Samaj won a convert who came to be regarded as the greatest intellectual among his followers. Guru Dutt was an eccentric. He would often put on winter clothes in summer and summer clothes in winter. By these austerities he sought to make his mind and body perfect and obedient tools.

With some slight alteration somewhere in his methods he might perhaps have become a Gandhi long before Gandhi had been discovered even by himself. And perhaps out of this revised Guru Dutt you could have made not only a Gandhi but a couple of intellectuals too from what was left over.

From out of the products of the University of the Punjab, for sheer intellect nobody attracted as much attention as Guru Dutt, with the possible exception of Har Dayal, another intellectual that Lajpat Rai was to have a good deal to do with in later years at Lahore and in Europe, and above all (through Har Dayal's followers and lieutenants) in the States.

These two, in fact, resembled each other much. Both were eccentric in personal habits as well as in their thinking. Both were too much weighed down by a heavy earnestness. Both possessed great gifts of mind and memory — curiosity, receptiveness, a strong will and a flail for languages and for expression, for logical thinking, for a contagious persuasiveness. Both pushed their thinking to the extreme, and could hop from one extreme to another — from the westernmost to the easternmost, or from a cosmopolitanism that left internationalism lagging far behind to the narrowest and most parochial nationalism, from agnosticism to perfect faith and spiritualism. Both had a remarkable knack of collecting around them friends and admirers who never tired of offering incense to them.

Both had a strong streak of asceticism, Har Dayal's remained unaffected alike in the midst of American materialism and the gaiety of Paris. If like Guru Dutt Har Dayal kept a journal and if it were unearthed one day it will be interesting to see if this too is full of self-reproach and of renewed resolutions for mortifying the flesh.

Those interested in yogic philosophy and exercises aim generally at personal salvation. But Guru Dutt did not lose his sense of social and collective values in this endeavour at individualistic perfection. Though he would not be reckoned amongst the 'politically-minded' he was by no means wanting in patriotism. As a student he had been as little examination-minded as his friend Lajpat Rai, but because of his greater precocity he could not help outshining all competitors in an examination. He was an equally keen student of Sanskrit and the Vedas, and of Western thought and modern science. He passed his M.A. in physical science in 1886 and because of his brilliant university career was offered an assistant professorship in physics at the Government College, Lahore. As his journal shows, he kept on wavering between continuing in this career and giving it up in favour of a yogic pursuit of perfection.

All the time, however, he continued to work hard for the Arya Samaj, by lecturing, by writing, by organising, by guiding and by exercising his personal magnetism on a large circle of friends and admirers. His intellectual gifts and attainments, and even more than these, his earnestness and sincerity and his readily sacrificing personal interest, profoundly impressed the youngest of the trio, Lajpat Rai. In shaping his own career Lajpat Rai at every step consulted him. Even apart from the service rules Guru Dutt's bias and temperament seemed removed from the sphere of politics. A directly political movement had not yet arrived — at least not in the Punjab. Even if it had, it is possible that "plunged in thought" Guru Dutt would have "let the thundering legions pass". But he was certainly patriotic in a broader sense, and the contagion that affected those coming within his orbit was not without an ingredient of patriotism. Lajpat was attracted by that part of Guru Dutt's idealism which demanded sacrifices in a cause, rather than by his high intellectual attainment or even yogic pursuit of personal perfection. This pursuit too he may have admired — somewhat from a distance, and with little inclination to emulate.

In his pamphleteering fervour for the Samaj Guru Dutt was then editing a magazine in English, appropriately styled the Regenerator of Aryavarta, which rather suggested a patriotic mission. The patriotic side of Guru Dutt was to no small extent responsible for Lajpat Rai's being won over by the Arya Samaj. In choosing his own vocation he consulted Guru Dutt. At one stage he had to consider whether he should give up law and dedicate himself to the educational movement being set afoot by the Samaj. It was proposed that Hans Raj should" work as headmaster (they had then started only the high school; the college was to come later) and Lajpat Rai should be his second in command. He himself felt diffident. Hans Raj had taken his B.A. degree — a rather rare bit of parchment then — while Lajpat Rai had no academic credentials. The trio pondered over the matter, and eventually it was decided that Lajpat Rai could be more useful to the college by continuing at the bar.

Guru Dutt himself had a choice of careers before him — apart from the extreme alternative of discarding all worldly careers. He could have become an "extra assistant commissioner", a provincial civil service man, in other words. He had been offered this: he could go up the rungs of the ladder of administrative jobs, and with his rare gifts he might go as high as any Indian was in those days permitted. After some anxious thinking he decided that work at the Government College could suit him best. He continued there, though he was a member — and a very prominent one — of the DAV College Society too.

Guru Dutt lived a life of voluntary poverty. His personal wants were very few and easily met. A large part of his salary always went to help others, and to buy books for which Guru Dutt had a passion. Hoarding money he regarded as a sin, and at his death it was found that he had saved nothing for his wife and children.

Before Guru Dutt died, two schools of thought had arisen in the Arya Samaj. One was dominated by men supposed to have a modern outlook, those who would think and talk in terms of what is practicable and expedient, rather than in terms of scriptural sanction of text and canon and of dogma. The other school denounced this worship of expediency and wanted to go by rigid principle and the letter of the text.

It was generally believed that the first school was more political and patriotic in its outlook, while the horizon of the second school was dominated by dogma and theology. Guru Dutt was much respected by both. It was during his last illness that the cleavage became definitely pronounced. After his death the best tribute that was paid to him was that each party quoted him in its own support Lajpat Rai's personal tribute to his dearly loved friend was paid in the form of a biographical sketch, published both in English and Urdu in the early-90s — Lajpat Rai's first claim to authorship, if we leave aside a few small tracts and pamphlets written for the Arya Samaj, and perhaps a minor professional production, dealing with criminal courts and litigation said to have been written during his Hissar days.

This was by no means one of his important books; the author's craft had not yet been acquired by him, and the book bore marks throughout of an amateur hand and of haste. But one can perceive that even in the crudest of its pages breathes the feeling of tenderness that actuated the attempt. It is significant that Lajpat Rai began his career as an author with an essay on biography. Till the end he retained a fondness for biographies. As an author he was to attempt a number of biographies later on, some of which enjoyed considerable vogue; and, as we shall see, of all his books the one which helped most in bringing about a national awakening, especially in the Punjab, was his biography of Mazzini in Urdu.

Hans Raj, Lajpat Rai's other great friend at college, was temperamentally a contrast to Guru Dutt. Without the dazzling brilliance of Guru Dutt, Hans Raj was endowed with gifts that made for greater stability. He too had joined the Arya Samaj before he came to college but he had not been directed thither by any Sanskrit erudition. He never acquired proficiency in Sanskrit, and could never have been much interested in yogic culture. He was actuated by a sincere passion to serve others, but he wanted to do so in the manner of a hard-headed practical man, and not that of an idealist pushing ideas to their logical extreme or seeking after perfection here and now.. He could not draw round him a coterie of young enthusiasts, but he had a wonderful knack of managing things. He decided on a life of simplicity, even poverty and service. When the DAV College was conceived, he identified himself with the institution, with almost a Jesuitical single-mindedness. His critics have averred that the institution had been intended to be just a means, not an end in itself, and that Hans Raj treated the means as an end. That, alas, is the common failing of those dedicated to institutions. Hans Raj's special talent was for organisation; he would build up an institution entrusted to his care, inch by inch with meticulous devotion to detail, a devotion bordering on an idolatry which in jealously guarding the idol at times checked rudely the onslaught of a great and dynamic movement embodying a national aspiration.

Hans Raj was not interested in the subtleties of metaphysics and of theology, Vedic grammar and exegesis. For him it was enough that the Arya Samaj as a progressive movement was destined to play a vital part in the reorganisation of Hindu society. In other words, he had been drawn to the Samaj more by its patriotic than its philosophical or dogmatic side.

Lajpat Rai stood midway between the extremes of perfectionist idealism and of expediency; but his approach to problems interesting the Arya Samaj was much nearer that of Hans Raj than that of Guru Dutt. For him as for Hans Raj the supreme merit of the Samaj lay in its social, educational and welfare work, and in its stimulating a patriotic awareness in Hindu society.

It was good for the friendship of this trio and, incidentally for the DAV College, that their spheres of activity remained distinct Lajpat Rai had intended to dedicate his life to the DAV College, like Hans Raj, and not having a university degree, to be for ever his subordinate. It was likewise suggested that Guru Dutt should take over the DAV College as Principal.

The results in either eventuality could have been disastrous. Temperamentally the three friends differed too widely from one another to make a good team. They were bound to differ at some stage, and then the consequences might have been ruinous as much for their friendship as for the institution equally dear to them all.

3

Influence of Arya Samaj

Youthful and highly receptive, Lajpat Rai was drinking in through every pore of his being the ideas of the Arya Samaj - ideas that made up its real core rather than those that constituted its corpus of dogma. To understand the shaping of his outlook it is necessary to grasp the Samajic ideas of the eighties and the 'nineties, and we need to know a little more here of the elderly men then guiding the destinies of the Samaj.

First of all there was Sain Das, at that time President of the Lahore Arya Samaj who, as we have seen, had been immediately responsible for winning over Lajpat Rai for the Arya Samaj. What was his conception of the mission of the Samaj? Was he interested keenly in theological and metaphysical subtleties, or in the yogic pursuit, or in the practice of austerities for the attainment of individual perfection and salvation of the soul? Or did all these things combined interest him less than serving his people through the Samaj in a more secular way, by promoting social, educational or relief and welfare work, and inculcating a spirit of patriotism and self-reliance among them? He himself held a clerical job in a Government office.

He could not directly be connected with any political movement. We do not hear of any yogis. Whom he pursued for the deliverance of his soul. He carried no heavy load of Sanskrit grammar or theological erudition in his head. But he was one of the shrewdest men going in the Arya Samaj, with an uncanny judgement about men and affairs. A harder-headed man with greater abundance of common sense would be difficult to find. He had no pretensions to being an intellectual, but it is remark able that he too had a claim to authorship. The only book that he wrote dealt not with Vedic exegesis or with Aryan philosophy, but curiously enough it was a translation of the essays of Francis Bacon. This may be some indication of the philosophy of life that guided this leader of the Arya Samaj.

Much controversy arose in later years as to whether the Samaj was a political or a religious movement. The truth is that the founder of the Samaj was a religious personage and not a politician; all the same his work had a conspicuous streak of patriotism running through it. And he attracted round him not a few who were drawn as much by his patriotism as by his learning and spiritual accomplishments, and to whom patriotism was a sort of religion and a religion void of patriotism meant nothing at all. Some of these men were bound by their inherent bias to play an active and important role later on in political movements, when these made their appearance.

But it was absurd to look upon the Arya Samaj as a camouflaged school of political thought or as a semi-secret political movement which had put on a religious mask to deceive the authorities. We shall remember that though Dayananda is rightly regarded as the founder of the Arya Samaj, the Samaj as a movement and as an organisation was really the result of the joint deliberations of the Swami and several of his disciples and friends some of whom in their thinking attached the highest importance to social reform and to a patriotic renascence. The fundamental principles — the ten basic tenets — and the Constitution of the Samaj were very largely drawn up by the Swamiji's Punjabi admirers and advisers, prominent among them being Rai Bahadur Mul Raj.

We may usefully indulge in a digression about Mul Raj, whose ideas seemed to be better defined than those of most other leaders of the Samaj, and who, even though, keeping largely behind the scenes, made an intellectual contribution of special importance. He took care not to be loud, but he was certainly articulate, and he had a knack of making himself effective through influencing the key men of the movement.

Without the ambition of political leadership, he played an effective role behind the scenes in various movements. He thought much about the political emancipation of his country. In later years Lajpat Rai used to say that Mul Raj had conceived the principles and programme of Gandhian non-cooperation when Gandhi must have been a mere schoolboy. But he was never known for bold action. He was himself in Government service, though he preached to young men who met him that they must never hanker after a career of that kind. He was an evangel of swadeshi — long before the Swadeshi Movement of the anti-partition days was born. He conceived industrial and financial reconstruction in the interests of swadeshi, combined with a political non-cooperation with the Government Lajpat Rai in his autobiography had something to say about Mul Raj:

> "Rai Mul Raj — he was the Rai Sahib — had with him a history of the secret societies of Europe in two volumes which he had borrowed from some library. He read the whole book. I read a few pages then and there but Rai Mul Raj did not permit me to carry the book home with me...."

Later Lajpat Rai got the book from England and satisfied his curiosity.

This early convert to swadeshism, though he wanted India to get rid of foreign rule, had no faith in Hindu-Muslim unity. His influence on Lajpat Rai's early outlook is revealed in a passage in the autobiography, without naming Mul Raj:

"The cause of my indifference towards the Congress after 1889 was the opinion of my Arya Samajist friends. After 1889 I had the privilege of being in the company of a respectable friend who was a staunch opponent of the Congress. The grounds for his opposition briefly were:

- The Congress has been founded by a few Englishmen; as Englishmen love their own country it is not possible that the Congress should win political freedom for India. The English derive great benefits from their rule in India; it is impossible that they should willingly restore India to freedom. Being afraid lest the intelligentsia should organise a deep political movement aimed at England's supremacy, they had provided this Innocuous occupation for the intelligentsia so that they might gratify themselves by two or three days of 'speechifying! and by seeing themselves eulogised in the papers. In those days this gentleman looked upon every Englishman as an enemy of India.... He regarded the Congress not merely as useless, but even detrimental to the interests of India. What he then thought necessary was that Indians should make themselves stronger by education, by the spread of swadeshi and by the smuggling of arms, and then bide their time till they were strong enough to turn out the English.

- This gentleman had no faith in Hindu-Muslim unity. He believed that attempts at unity would harm the Hindus. The Hindus were void of internal solidarity, religious fervour and communal self-respect; the Muslims excelled in these virtues and would therefore always be the gainers in the attempts at unity. Also, the Islamic supremacy continued in Afghanistan, Turkey and elsewhere. So the attempts at unity would make the Muslims politically very strong. To him it appeared that the primary need was that the Hindus be strengthened and be shown the way to ultimate solidarity and that national fervour be instilled into them. The Congress Movement, he argued, would divert energy from the work for Hindu solidarity and Hindu reform and set the Hindus a futile task.
- A further argument was that the political movement would make the Britishers suspicious of the Hindus, and they would therefore not only obstruct the progress of the Hindus, but harm them in all possible ways."

The Arya Samajist leaders generally shared these views which constituted the common credo of Mul Raj, Sain Das and Lal Chand (who later became a judge of the Chief Court in the Punjab). All three of them were in Government service. Sain Das, we are told, clad himself in nothing but swadeshi, and preached swadeshi even in 1881. Mul Raj too believed in swadeshi, even though he did not practise it as rigidly as Sain Das. Of their younger colleagues Hans Raj took to swadeshi very early in life. Many of the leading men in the Arya Samaj were preaching swadeshi long before the Swadeshi Movement had been born in Bengal and Maharashtra. Not all of them had been converted to swadeshi by the Samaj; possibly some of them had become swadeshi and patriotic before they joined the Samaj; but there can be little doubt these people found an affinity between the teachings, activities and the whole atmosphere of the Samaj, and their own swadeshi outlook. Some of them had conceived the idea of non-cooperation with the foreign government nearly half a century before the Congress thought of it. We read in Lajpat Rai's autobiography:

> "Lala Sain Das and Lala Mul Raj often regretted that the best Indian brains were being used to strengthen the rule by a foreign nation. They used to dissuade the most brilliant Indian students from entering Government service....Lala Sain Das felt it keenly that the pandits of Kashi should have brought Hinduism into disrepute by drawing the cart of Lord Ripon. The acme of public morality for Hindus, according to him, was that in their religious and social reform and educational affairs they should have nothing to do with the Government or with the Britishers, and should seek no help from them in the form of money, consultation, or guidance. Whatever the Hindus wanted, they must try to get by their own effort, and they must generate in themselves a spirit of self-reliance."

The nationalism of these worthies was primarily a 'Hindu nationalism'. The memory of the days when the Muslims were the rulers and the Hindus the ruled was as yet too fresh. The flame of patriotism in the heart of these Arya Samaj leaders was fed by a feeling for the degenerate condition of the Hindus.

Sain Das had more to do with the shaping of the Arya Samaj in the eighties than any other single person. You could say his religion was three-fourths 'political' and yet you could say his politics were three-fourths love of the Hindu nation, and if that be religion, his politics were three-fourths religion.

These were some of the men in the Samaj with whom youthful Lajpat came into intimate contact. Whatever their shortcomings, they were a dynamic group, determined to have a hand in shaping the events. They were just the company that Lajpat Rai's soul yearned for. And youthful, firm, earnest, dynamic Lajpat Rai was just the worker that the Samaj wanted. So he casts his lot with them to work with them and for them for long years to come; and even when he outgrows the Samaj and they part company, he will not altogether discard the Samajic impression on his outlook and on his methods of work. Whatever departments of public activity he chose in the later years of his career, he could never forget that he had received his early training in the Arya Samaj.

It was there he first schooled himself into a public speaker, and as a journalist, as a pamphleteer and a compiler of biographies, as a writer in Urdu and in English, as a leader of movements, and an organiser of big institutions, as a zealous social worker leading relief campaigns wherever famines or earthquakes wrought havoc, or when orphans, those 'waifs of the storm' of life, needed the establishment of a permanent home to turn them into capable citizens. It was in the Arya Samaj that he acquired the art of appealing to the hearts of his audience and making them empty their pockets for great causes and institutions.

A Mofussil Lawyer

Valuable as this training was, it hardly helped solve the question of a living. His father had made great sacrifice and put the whole family to severe hardship to provide for him the benefits of "education. He had qualified as mukhtar in 1881. He had passed no university examination in his arts course, having been too busy with other things.

Meanwhile he had become a married man. He must earn his own living and must also afford some relief to his father who had to maintain a large family on a slender income. The father impatiently looked forward to the day when this badly needed relief would come. The son was haunted by a desire to serve the people, the miserable millions; yet he could not ignore the hardships of his own family, and he could not begin by being an ingrate to his own father. He lived in an agony, torn between these two opposing calls.

His heart turned away from his books. "My spirit wanted to soar higher, but poverty and the hardships of my parents made me despair. Again and again the Penal Code or some other law book might lie open before me while I finished in my mind the periods of a speech addressing people of a by-gone age." He thought of dedicating himself to the service of his people. He tried to train himself for this task and preferred self-devised tests to those imposed by the University. But, ah, the bitts that chain poor mortals down to sordid earth when their spirits yearn to soar higher and higher! For the moment it was with sordid circumstances that the last word lay. He had to set up as a mukhtar and to begin earning.

He went to his small native town, Jagraon, to practise in the law courts as a mukhtar. He found both the profession and the town uncongenial. The place was too small for him. He was fast growing beyond it. He felt choked in that little town where nobody thought of the big problems, where he could get no contacts which would yield nourishment to his spirit. His soul felt frustrated. The mukhtarship too was uncongenial — much more so than Jagraon, for it was humiliating. He had fed his spirit on heroic stories about the Rajputs. Could a Rajput do all the kowtowing before all the arrogant petty officials clad in brief authority? Yet if he wanted to succeed with them, he had to get all the fool Rajput things out of his head.

He was fed up with Jagraon, and to improve things at least a little he shifted to Rohtak, where his father was now posted. Rohtak was a bigger place than Jagraon and perhaps his dislike of kowtowing would not he such a handicap at the headquarters of a district as it had been at Jagraon.

He felt keenly the humiliation of being a mukhtar, and if he must practise law this must be as a member of the higher hierarchy of vakils. He had made an attempt at getting through this examination in 1883, but because of his preoccupation with so many other things he had failed. His father goaded him to a second attempt as also did the humiliation felt deeply by a sensitive soul. But again he had been dividing his time between work as a mukhtar, and work for the Rohtak Arya Samaj and preparation for the examination — with the result that once again he was among the 55 unsuccessful candidates and not among the successful ten. Three more marks would have done the trick! The failure was disheartening but his father insisted that he should make yet another attempt.

He would not neglect his Samaj work. He had found the Samaj at Rohtak in a sorry plight and was working hard to infuse some life into it. Besides, the social work was taking him to Lahore very frequently, for committee meetings, and consultations at headquarters. The DAV College had been conceived in 1883, and he was taking an active interest in the preliminary work and in the planning out of things. At Rohtak he kept busy finding support for the proposed college chiefly in the shape of funds. The college work interested him much more than did law.

Though he could not follow the example of Hans Raj he might have envied his friend's B.A. degree, and his having an elder brother who had undertaken to maintain him. Lajpat Rai could look for no such support; on the other hand he had a family to maintain. Already as a mukhtar he was earning Rs. 200 a month. Not a princely income, but certainly a substantial one as compared with what he had ever seen in his father's house. His sensitive soul had for the moment to reconcile itself to the humiliation of a mukhtar's job.

During one of his visits to Lahore he made up his mind not to go back to the mukhtar's job, whatever the consequences. Yet he did not know what he should turn to next. His friend, philosopher and guide, Guru Dutt, discovering him in a state of spiritual agony, asked for the cause. Lajpat Rai laid bare before him his inmost heart. Guru Dutt, before he could advise him definitely, wanted to know whether he was having better luck in his third attempt at the law examination. The two of them, as was customary in such situations in those days, tipped a clerk to know Lajpat Rai's fate before the result was announced, and they were happy to learn that his third shot at vakilship had not gone amiss. When the result was published, Lajpat Rai stood second amongst the candidates. Guru Dutt sent him back to Rohtak to work as a vakil, telling him plainly that he could be more useful to the movement from there than by working as a second-master under Hans Raj.

At Rohtak he did some work in the local Arya Samaj and participated extensively in the Samaj and DAV College deliberations at headquarters. He also wrote occasionally for the press. Sometimes he wrote in English but more generally he wrote for the Urdu *Rafiq-e-Hind* conducted by his young friend, Maulvi Muharram Ali Chishti.

He had patriotic impulses and an earnest desire to serve his people, but the raw youth had little to offer by way of serious study of political problems of his country. He was by no means a fire-brand — opposing Government for opposition's sake. Indeed in accordance with the fashion of the day he used to be laud the Government in his speeches at the Arya Samaj.

He had completely rid himself of the pro-Islamic bias that his father had fostered in him and had even moved away to the extent of feeling somewhat grateful to the British for having ended the oppression of Muslim rule. His political ideas were yet being formed. But he had started writing for public print. He and his friends felt that the Arya Samaj needed its own press.

They decided on an Urdu journal to be named Bharat Desha Sudharak and an English journal, entrusted to Guru Dutt and Hans Raj and christened (at Lajpat Rai's suggestion) Regenerator of Aryavarta. The Urdu journal was to be Lajpat Rai's care but his absence from the headquarters prevented his carrying out this task. For the moment he had to be content with occasional articles in *Rafiq-e-Hind* and any other journal that cared to publish his stuff.

He had no reason to be dissatisfied with the progress he was making at the bar, but he doss not appear to have struck root at Rohtak. On the whole the Rohtak days were unimportant as a formative period. He himself writes that his spirit was famished in the 1883-85 period. He had arrived at Rohtak in 1884. In 1885 he had qualified as a vakil.

In 1886 he accepted a somewhat important brief in the adjoining district of Hissar and finding that place more congenial settled down there. For the first time he felt he was striking root. He remained at Hissar for about six years, and those years made considerable contribution to the maturity of his mind, and to his work for the Samaj, and above all to his initiation in politics.

At Rohtak the Arya Samaj had arrived before him but had shown no strong growth. At Hissar he had to enlist the help of his friends to prepare the ground, and sow the seed; but the soil was more congenial and the new growth was soon flourishing vigorously. In fact Hissar was soon reckoned among the most active of Arya Samaj centres in the province.

In his autobiography Lajpat Rai ascribes this achievement to the fact that the Hissar Arya Samaj was favoured with a set of leaders of calibre, and with tender delineation he has given us sketches of these leaders. Amongst them he contracted some of the most enduring friendships of his life. There was, for instance, Lala Chandu Lal, the "Sardar of Haryana". He was not associated with extremist politics. But a man more loyal to his friends could not easily be found. Even when Lajpat Rai was deported as an inconvenient extremist, Chandu Lal was one of the few friends who stood by him.

His closest friends who had shared his political ideas and ideals disowned him but Chandu Lal stood by him openly as if nothing at all had happened. He had occasion to associate himself with officials, but he never tried to please them by disowning Lajpat Rai or even by trying to conceal the friendship. He openly said he was a friend of Lajpat Rai and firmly believed in his innocence. He wrote letters to Lajpat Rai and received the deportee's instructions about the conduct of his personal and family affairs. Of all the Hissar portraits done by Lajpat Rai in his autobiography, that of this loyal friend is drawn with the tenderest touch.

The Hissar leaders made the Arya Samaj a movement of the masses, instead of the vociferous intelligentsia. Here it was in genuine touch with the soil. Elsewhere the Samaj consisted of Babus; here it consisted of peasants. At Hissar, Chandu Lal and Lajpat Rai and Lakhpat Rai made the Samaj deeply vital. The experiment must be regarded as something unique in the history of the Arya Samaj.

At Hissar he was before long not merely a successful lawyer, but in many ways a leading figure, particularly known for his hospitality and for his being a voracious reader over a wide range. The self-schooling of the young man who had to leave the Government College without a degree had started in right earnest.

His was soon a notable private collection of books, something distinctive enough in such a place to attract occasional visits from the European district head. He was a highly respected citizen in the new locality which elected him to its municipal body - from a constituency with a preponderance of Muslim voters. This municipality he served for some time as its secretary in an honorary capacity. The Hissar days were important for him not merely because of the Arya Samaj work but also as the formative period in his civic and political training.

Writing Pursuit

In Hissar period, coincided with the earliest days of the Indian National Congress which held its first session in Bombay in December 1885 under the presidentship of W. C. Benerjee. Mul Raj, the shrewd and keen-eyed Samajist, as we have seen, had declared the new movement suspect However, Lajpat Rai was not guided very long by such mistrust in advance. In 1888, Ali Muhammad Bhimji was deputed to tour the Punjab on behalf of the Congress. The young lawyer at Hissar invited him to his town and arranged a public meeting for him. This was his first contact with the Congress, then hardly three years old.

When Hume started the Congress, Sir Syed Ahmad Khan opposed it in the name of the Muslim community. The Aligarh leader advised his co-religionists to keep aloof from the new movement. He wanted the Muslims to further their interests by standing behind the rulers of the land.

Lajpat Rai had already travelled far from the Syed-inspired teachings of his father. When he saw Sir Syed in this new and unpatriotic role, his respect for the Aligarh leader dwindled further. He wrote a series of "Open Letters" to Sir Syed in the press in Which he showed how Sir Syed was going back upon all that he had preached in former days. These letters gave a copious amount of English translations of the earlier writings (in Urdu) of Sir Syed which went to show that therein he had been preaching just the reverse of his new gospel. The "Open Letters" by "An Admirer" bore a Hissar date-line; and Hissar could not boast of many men in those days who could aspire to such polemical effort. Those who, knew Lajpat Rai had no difficulty in guessing who the real author of the "Open Letters" was. He had no particular reason to conceal his identity; but he had not yet become much of a leader, and modesty impelled him to remain anonymous.

In an Urdu version the letters appeared in the weekly *Koh-e-Noor* over the name of Munshi Radha Kishan. In English the first of these letters dated Hissar, October 27, 1888 is subscribed "The Son of an Old Follower of Yours". When Sir Syed started his campaign against the Indian National Congress little could he have thought that his old writings would be flung in his face by one who had read with such care and thoroughness every word that he ever published in his books and magazines. Besides the proverbial short memory of his public, Sir Syed had the advantage that his writings had mostly been published in Urdu, and, therefore, Wedderburn and Yule and Hume and the Bengal, Bombay and Madras leaders of the Congress who dominated its counsels could not have been aware of their existence. The writer of the "Open Letters" — at the very outset warned Sir Syed that he had been "a constant reader and admirer" of his writings.

"From childhood I was taught to respect the opinions of the white-bearded Syed of Aligarh. Your Social Reformer was constantly read to me by my fond father, who looked upon you as no less than a prophet of the nineteenth century. Your writings in the Aligarh Institute Gazette and your speeches in Council and other public meetings were constantly studied by me and preserved as a sacred trust by my revered parent."

The writer then reminded Sir Syed of the days when he had admired Jolin Stuart Mill's On Liberty, and when Bentham's Utility was translated for his Reformer at his behest. Most telling of the quotations were those from Sir Syed's Causes of the Indian Revolt which had been written within a year of the "mutiny" and for the enlightenment of British MPs had in 1873 been circulated in an English version. In this book Sir Syed had advocated the principles of representative government "Most men, I believe Sir Syed had said, "agree in thinking that it is highly conducive to the welfare and prosperity of Government; indeed, that it is essential to its stability that the people should have a voice in its counsels. It is from the voice of the people that Government can learn whether its projects are likely to be well received. The voice of the people can alone nip errors in the bud and warn us of dangers before they burst upon and destroy us. This voice, however, can never be heard, and this security never acquired, unless the people are allowed a share in the consultations of the Government. Sir Syed had explained in his brochure how the conceding of the principles of representation would have averted a catastrophe like the fifty-seven "mutiny".

"If Hindustanis had been in the legislative councils, they would have explained everything to their countrymen, and these evils which have happened to us would have been averted."

This book of Sir Syed's had been rendered into English by Sir Auckland Colvin (at the time of the "Open Letters" Lieutenant Governor of the North-Western Province) and Lt.-Col. Graham, Sir Syed's official biographer. These worthies obviously had seen nothing 'seditious' in Sir Syed's insistence on some form of representative government — an offence for which Sir Syed was now denouncing the Indian National Congress as a body of sedition mongers. Home rule, self-government, swaraj had not yet been declared the goal of the Congress which spoke in much humbler accents — at the worst it made a demand that the principle of representation should be conceded and an elected element be introduced into the legislative councils of the Provincial Governors.

True, some "natives" had, in a patronising way, been nominated councillors. But, pertinently asked one of the "Open Letters":

> "Can men like Raja Shiv Prasad and yourself be properly considered as representatives of the people, and the method of selection by which you are sent to the Council Chamber be accepted as of any value? I think no reasonable man would contend that it would have been possible, if Raja Shiv Prasad had been an elected representative of the people of India, for him to have libelled the whole Indian nation, as he did, in his notorious speech on the Ilbert bill. Could Raja Pearey Mohan Mukherjee and other native members have consented to the raising of the salt tax if they had thought that their seats depended on the voices of the people, whose throats were, so to speak, to be cut by that obnoxious and inhuman measure?"

Nor was the young critic of Sir Syed Ahmad content with quotations from his writings thirty years old. He produced excerpts from his much more recent articles to show that till about seven years previously Sir Syed had been writing in the same strain.

In 1881 when the question of raising the University College at Lahore to the status of a university was under consideration Sir Syed had written:

> "Whatever may be stated by way of flattery, the fact is that in reality the relations of Hindustanis to their rulers are no better than those of slaves to masters."

A most pertinent excerpt on the question of representative government was dug out from an address Sir Syed Ahmad had delivered when laying the foundation-stone of the New Ghazipore College (later the Victoria College) which read:

> "The appointment of natives to the Supreme Council was a memorable incident in the history of India. The day is not far distant, I trust, and when it does come you will remember my words, when that Council will be composed of representatives from every division or district, and that thus the laws which it will pass will be laws enacted by the feeling of the entire country."

Quoting this, the "Open Letter" commented: "Sir Syed, have the happiness to know that the day which you in 1864 said was not far distant is coming nearer and nearer and that you need no longer feel so much ashamed of your countrymen for not conforming to the age.

Your prophecy is not fulfilled yet, but we are certain that some time or other it is sure to be fulfilled, and then you will, have the satisfaction of feeling that you did not prophesy in vain. Sir Syed, do you wish to withdraw this prophecy of yours?"

Sir Syed had criticised the Lucknow speech of the Hon'ble Pandit Ayodhya Nath of Allahabad and asked Congressmen if any of their agitations had existed when the Government "granted all the boons which we enjoy".

But came the reply: "I have quoted largely from your own writings to show that such an agitation did exist, and that you yourself were one of the most prominent agitators." Then Sir Syed had written":

> "I am afraid that a feeling of fear — fear that the Government or the district authorities would esteem you factious and discontented, were you to inaugurate a measure like this — deters you from coming forward for your country's good. Believe me that this moral cowardice is wrong, the apprehension unfounded, that there is not an Englishman of a liberal turn of mind in India who would regard with feelings other than those of pleasure and hope, such a healthy sign of increased civilization on the part of its inhabitants.... Far better would it be...for India were her people openly and honestly to express their opinions as to the justice or otherwise of the acts of Government. Now as a critic of the Congress Sir Syed seemed to forswear all that he had stood for before."

Not so very long before, the Aligarh-veteran had been known as an evangel of broad-mindedness and unity, and now he was raising a hue and cry that 'the interests of Hindus, and Muslims clashed and that therefore the Mussalmans must keep away from the Congress. It was Sir Syed who had contributed the beautiful classic image of national unity by visualising the Hindu and the Muslim as the two eyes of Mother India. Could the right eye clash with the left? His youthful critic, who had once been his admirer, had no difficulty in confronting him with passages From his speeches which had preached the oneness of Hindu and Muslim interests and which strangely contrasted with the new gospel that Sir Syed had started preaching. All these earlier speeches had by no means become ancient history. During his Punjab visit, justly regarded as a notable event for the Punjab in the eighties, Sir Syed had laid the greatest stress on a single Indian nationhood claiming Hindus and Muslims and Christians alike. At Gurdaspur he had said:

> "From the oldest times the word 'nation' is applied to the inhabitants of one country, though they differ in

> some peculiarities which are characteristic of their own.... Remember that the words Hindu and Muslim are only meant for religious distinction — otherwise all persons whether Hindu or Muslim, even the Christians who reside in this country, are all in this respect belonging to one and the same nation... They must, each and all unite for the good of the country which is common to all."

And yet when soon after a common national platform was actually being created, he had gone over to the other extreme and started preaching a gospel of clash of interests. The Gurdaspur speech had been made in January 1884. Only a year later Sir Syed seemed to have undergone an ugly transformation.

His speech at Lahore, on February 3, 1884, had been perhaps even more emphatic than the Gurdaspur utterance. In reply to an address by the Indian Association of Lahore, Sir Syed had said:

> "Even granting that the majority of those composing this Association are Hindus, still I say that this light has been diffused by the same whom I call by the epithet of 'Bengalees' — I assure you that the Bengalees are the suffer equally. These are the different grounds upon which I call both these races which inhabit India by one word, i.e., 'Hindu', meaning...... to say that they are the inhabitants of Hindustan. While in the legislative council, I was always anxious for the prosperity of this nation."

There was not a demand put forward by the then Congress nor a principle or policy advocated by it that Sir Syed had not himself advocated at one time or another. But when the National Congress came into being he seemed to have altogether changed in principles and policies.

The Congress was being condemned as "seditious" by narrow-minded critics, for daring to suggest the creation of Indian volunteers. When in March 1883 (i.e., a short while before the Congress formally came into being) Hume had advocated the cause of "native volunteers" in India, and Lt.-Col. Graham (Sir Syed's biographer) had tried to rebut his arguments in the columns of The Pioneer, Sir Syed had taken up the cudgels not on behalf of Lt.-Col. Graham, but of A. O. Hume. He wrote to Lt.-Col. Graham:

> "I have perused your reply to Mr. Hume's letter advocating the volunteering of the natives of India. In not allowing the natives to become volunteers, the Government mean to say that they do not trust the natives of India. Its consequence should be judged from the saying: 'If you want us to trust you, you should also trust us.' There yet exists a wide gulf between Europeans and the natives of India and unless it be filled up, nothing can secure and improve the prosperity of the country"

The last ten words were Italicised by the admirer turned critic, who did not fail to remind Sir Syed that the letter he was quoting had been written only about four years earlier. Lt.-Col. Graham, now "would be the selection, by the local authorities in 11 large stations in India, of a certain number of picked native volunteers — men of good family and well known to their loyalty — to be placed under the command of the officer commanding the European volunteers. I would let them only people in our country whom we can properly be proud of, and it is only due to them that knowledge, liberty and patriotism have progressed in our country. I can thereby say that they are the head and crown of all the different communities of Hindustan.... I myself.. heartily wished to serve my country and my nation faithfully. In the word 'nation' I included both Hindus and Muslims because that is the only meaning which I can attach to it (Le., 'nation' or '*qaum*') — We inhabit the same land, are subject to the rule of the same governors, the fountains of benefit for all are the same and the pangs of famine also we select their own company officers; and once started, I would also permit them to select their own recruits as vacancies occurred. Give us this much, and we will be satisfied for a long time to come."

The strange contrast in the Syed of days before the Congress and the Syed of the days subsequent to the founding of the Congress reminded his critic of the classic opening of the Tale of Two Cities, and the third of his letters opened thus:

> "Well, may we say, that it is 'the best of times' as well as 'the worst of times'. Best, as the country is on the point of taking as nation, worst as a particular section of the community wants to check the progress of the country and unfortunately is headed or at least is said to be headed by a man who has been a frequent advocate of representative government in India.'"

Quite forcefully the parallel continued through references to the 'age of wisdom' and 'foolishness', the 'epoch of belief and incredulity', the 'spring of hope' and the 'winter of despair' since 'we see her own sons deserting the cause of awakened India'.

The critic exhorted Sir Syed to feel happy that his country — men were awakening, that his dreams and prophecies were about to come true, that the people had made up their minds not to be deterred by opposition — even if that came from Sir Syed himself!

The "Open Letters" were by no means a mere collection of excerpts from Sir Syed's writings and speeches strung together. The comments accompanying them were quite a castigation - combining taunt, irony, satire, sarcasm and downright tomahawking — though the craftsmanship was at times crude and the youthful hand struck rather relentlessly. Here and there, in view of the veteran's white beard — particularly in a country: where respect for white beards is traditionally strong — the reader might even have been offended by what would seem the impertinence of a jackanapes.

Why there was this inconsistency in the attitude of the veteran was the problem. At the end of the first letter the author referred to insinuations by 'some people' that "these writings which I have quoted came from an honest, uncorrupted mind, at a time when the author had no prospect of being raised to the Legislative Council by mere favour". He dismissed the insinuations, pausing for another solution of the riddle. The second letter once again dismissed as "childish" a possible claim to consistency "in the face of the above quotations" and Sir Syed's fall was likened to that of Adam:

> "Just as Satan is said to be the cause of the fall of that progenitor of our race, this seeking after worldly honours seems to be the real explanation of your decline."

The jackanapes strain continues:

> "It is nothing to you, because your term in this world must at no very distant, date expire; but to us who are yet, we hope, to live long and to fight out the bloodless battles of liberty, it is destined to remain a permanent disgrace."

A footnote to the last of these letters carried an insinuation of a different kind: "Can it be that your once massive, manly intellect, succumbed to the feeble, school-girl-like sophistries of your shallow-pated employee; that, Merlin-like, the great heart that once beat true for India is now pulseless, and that you lie bound inextricably, by the treacherous spells of a modern Vivien?"

Here and there, the letters bore marks of callowness, but on the whole they were a creditable performance for a mofussil lawyer yet in his early-20s.

This was the first big polemic of his career. He made a promising beginning. He who would succeed in the rough and tumble called politics must needs know how to deal with his adversary in controversy. He must have an eye for the enemy's weak spot, and sharp tooth and claw to swoop down on it.

Even in his early-20s Lajpat Rai seemed possessed of sensitive political antennae for later developments have fully borne out his apprehensions of the dangers lurking in Sir Syed's preachment of Hindus and Muslims being two separate nations. The seed sown then bore fruit in Jinnah's day. But his hard hitting on this occasion never blinded Lajpat Rai to Syed's great qualities. He even considered him pre-eminent amongst those who developed Urdu prose, and till the end he continued to command the Aligarh leader's advice to his co-religionists against the lure of Pan-Islamism and against looking for saviours in other Islamic countries.

But weaning Muslims away from the national awakening and seeking salvation as a separate nation through the grace of the British rulers was bound to spell disaster, though no doubt even in such ill-advised or ill-considered doings Sir Syed had no personal axe to grind, for, as Lajpat Rai always fully acknowledged, he was a man of high character and dedicated to ideals and sought to serve his people in an unselfish spirit.

His First Ideal

The "Open Letters" created a great stir. Hume who had been feeling nervous found them very helpful. It was suggested to the author that the letters should be put together and reprinted as a pamphlet. He readily agreed. Hume himself revised or edited the letters. Here and there the phrasing must have been improved.

The pamphlet, debunking the great Muslim leader with such deadly effect and confronting him with his own utterances, was Issued on the eve of a Congress session, and almost overnight it made Lajpat Rai a man of India-wide fame in political discussion.

The last of the letters to Sir Syed was published just a few days before the Congress met for its annual session at Allahabad. The ink of the letters had hardly dried when Junius emerged out of anonymity (unlike the original Junius whose identity continues to puzzle scholars to this day) and rushed to Allahabad to be received at the railway station with an ovation by Malaviya and Ayodhya Nath and to find that he had become a famous name in India's national politics. He was known as the controversialist who had so effectively exposed no less an adversary that the great Sir Syed Ahmad Khan of Aligarh. He made two Speeches at the Congress session, one of them being a sort of continuation of the Open Letters. This he delivered as the founder of the principal resolution of the day, the one relating to the expansion of Legislative Councils by the introduction of an elective element. In this speech he showed that Sir Syed; who was now seen as a leading opponent of the Congress, and in particular of its demand for elections to legislatures, had formerly spoken in different accents, and thirty years earlier in his book on the "mutiny" had himself made the same demand.

The official historian of the Congress, Dr. Pattabhi Sitaramayya, commenting on the 1888 session, says:

> "Lajpat Rai was doubtless a man of true vision, for he spoke in Urdu at the Congress of 1888 and proposed that half a day be set apart for educational and industrial matters. The resolution was accepted and the industrial exhibitions since organised are a direct result of the recommendations of the committee appointed in that behalf."

Of his two speeches the first may have won more applause as-topical controversy, but the second led to solid work. Even at that time when the Congress conducted its business entirely in English, Lajpat Rai addressed it in Hindustani. He gave a clear indication that if he played a role of consequence in the affairs of the Congress, he would strive to make it the real mouthpiece of the masses. His emphasis on industrial exhibitions showed that he was no mere politician, but attached great importance to constructive work.

The 1888 session of the Congress definitely threw Lajpat Rai into a movement directly political. With brief spells of comparative indifference he was to work for the Congress for the rest of his life, that is, for the next four decades. He had to attended any of the first three sessions of the Congress, but he had not been indifferent, although (mainly because of the influence of Mul Raj) he had entertained honest misgivings, about the Congress, He had read the writings of A.O. Hume and been moved by them profoundly, but Mul Raj had declared the new organisation a trap set by wily. Englishmen who appeared in the dangerous guise of friends. By the time of the third session of the Congress (held at Madras under the presidentship of Badruddin Tyyabji), Lajpat Rai had been converted into Congressman. He has recorded in his autobiography that this session "impressed me greatly".

About this issue he says, "There were published two by Mr. Hume — The Star of the East and An Old Man's Hope., I have yet to come across in Congress literature another brace of pamphlets as good as these. A wave of liberty surged through their pages and they impressed me profoundly."

With his "Open Letters" and his speeches at the following, session at Allahabad he had of course definitely cast his lot with the Congress though, as we have said, there were in his career brief intervals of comparative indifference both towards its organisation and its immediate policies. At Allahabad, the Punjab delegates deputed him to invite the Congress to hold its next session at Lahore, but Bombay was chosen. Though he attended the Bombay session his enthusiasm began to wane. He felt that the Congress leaders cared more for name and pomp than for the interests of the country.

Till 1893 Lajpat Rai kept away from the Congress sessions and this was his first spell of indifference towards the Congress. Even more than the Congress, his admiration for Mazzini urged him on towards the freedom movement. Perhaps if he had not adopted Mazzini as his guru the Congress might not have interested him so much. He had been led to the writings of the great Italian by. Surendranath Banerjee's Speeches of Joseph Mazzini included in a collection of the Bengal orator's utterances which Lajpat Rai happened to come across at the beginning of the eighties.

"One Speech" he records in the autobiography, "moved me to tears several times as I read it. It made a great impression on my tender heart and I determined that all my life I would follow the teaching of Mazzini, and serve my nation. I made Mazzini my guru, and so he continues to be to this day."

This was before he joined the Arya Samaj. His first 'guru' according to his own testimony, was Mazzini and not Dayananda. He had been soaked in patriotism before he joined the Arya Samaj. He felt drawn towards the Samaj because in it he saw a patriotic mission. No direct political movement had started as yet to which he might dedicate himself at the altar of his country, For a time he had to wait and hold his soul in patience.

He looked for the life and teachings of Mazzini at bookstalls and eventually got a volume from England through a Punjabi friend of his. He read it avidly from cover to cover, "and I was moved by it far more intensely than I had been several years before by Babu Surendranath Banerjee's speech about Mazzini. The profound nationalism of the great Italian, his troubles and tribulations, his moral superiority, his broad humanitarian sympathies, enthralled me." He translated the Duties of Man into Urdu and when the manuscript was ready he sent it to a journalist friend in Lahore who, after giving it some touches, published it in his own name.

Later on, he was to produce in Urdu the life of Mazzini, and that of Garibaldi. These books, particularly that on Mazzini, were to be among the major influences that at this period affected the mind of the Punjab. We shall have occasion to speak of this later. Meanwhile, it is important to remember that Mazzini was the first guru that satisfied the longings of his restless heart. Before he joined the Arya Samaj and the Congress, his mind had already been formed. Both the Samaj and the Congress were to be the channels through which he was to work for the fulfilment of his mission, which had been formulated for him at its clearest in the writings of the great Italian teacher.

In 1883 Swami Dayananda Sarasvati died. The Arya Samaj was thrown into gloom on the Dipavali Day. The Samajists gathered to mourn the loss of their great master. Guru Dutt had attended upon the Swami during his last illness at Ajmer and had been profoundly moved by the deathbed and serenity that his eyes saw. He got up to address the Lahore gathering but his words utterly failed. Speaker after speaker failed; and the meeting was finally addressed by the young convert, Lajpat Rai,' who spoke with fine feeling. For two hours he held the audience spellbound. It was this speech that made his reputation is a public speaker. He came to be regarded as the most effective orator of the Samaj. It is noteworthy that he made his reputation in public speaking first not as a stump orator, as is the usual thing with politicians or even such of them as later became dignified statesmen, but in the classic way of Greek orators, with what was practically a funeral oration.

After the death of Swami Dayananda, his followers and admirers gave much thought to the question of raising a befitting memorial. The Dayananda Anglo-Vedic College scheme was the final upshot of these deliberations and when they were to take practical shape, Lajpat Rai did more than his share. By the close of the eighties we find him still at Hissar, as an active leader in the much wider field of the Arya Samaj with the established reputation of being its greatest public speaker, a fairly important figure in politics after the flutter caused by the "Open Letters" episode. He was giving a good deal of his time to public works now, and at the same time making quite a fine success of his job as a lawyer.

He seldom made less than a thousand a month, and often doubled that figure. This was by no means a rare achievement in the profession but was sufficiently remarkable for a young man whose ambitions already lay largely in other nobler fields of activity. He commanded fees deemed handsome by any mofussil lawyer, and if he had given more time to his work at the bar lie could certainly have made a good deal more, for by his able handling of briefs and his skilful advocacy he inspired' confidence among his clients to the same extent, as he did by his sincerity and force of expression among the people at large. He now persuaded his father to give up his ill-paid teaching job. He set apart enough money for his father to retire and to provide for educating, bringing up and marrying off the young children.

This was a mere precaution against emergency, for Lajpat Rai was himself meeting all the expenses, of the father and the household, and neither for the education of his children nor for their weddings was Munshiji called upon to touch his reserve. Lajpat Rat saw all three of his brothers properly settled in life. The money set apart for the father simply accumulated with interest. In his Hissar days offers came of property that would be sure to appreciate and yield him sizable unearned increment at a later date. Those who availed themselves of such offers made goodly fortunes, but as his ambitions lay in other directions he shunned all such offers. Possibly he was all along thinking of leaving Hissar one day to settle down in the metropolitan Lahore, and did not want to be tied down to the provincial town by the shackles of real estate. He made no investments of that kind.

New Agitation

Lajpat Rai returned to settle in life early in the nineties was vastly different from the Lahore of his student days. When he had got down at the railway station, the first time, for his matriculation examination, the most conspicuous sight had been the police constables bawling out warnings against pickpockets and swindlers, and the boy Lajpat as he trudged along followed by a porter carrying his baggage, had wondered all the time whether he would be led into a trap, done out of his small belongings and left stranded. Now Lahore was no longer so savagely insecure for the newcomer - no policeman could be heard shouting anyway; and he, of course, was neither a lad at school, nor a stranger in Lahore. He did not have to trudge along either. He could pay for a comfortable conveyance, and a horse and *gharry* would soon 'be his own as necessary paraphernalia for his professional and public activity.

The British Raj was already half a century old. The administration had time to consolidate and it seemed to be expanding by its own momentum. Its offices were multiplying and this meant a continuous influx of a 'babu' population into Lahore. And of course the mills turning out these babus were working more and more vigorously. Soon they would have got into their full stride.

Though Lahore was growing rapidly no factories could yet be seen sprouting up. Banking and insurance had witnessed no enterprise from Indians; but European commercial offices were a good deal in evidence, most of these being the remote ends of tentacles reaching out from Calcutta or. Bombay or even the Imperial octopus in London. These also absorbed some of the babus, but the majority were employed in State and railway offices. And with the growth of educational institutions, the student population too was swelling — babus and potential babus.

Lawyers also were increasing in number — not as yet very quickly, but steadily. Thanks to all those newcomers, Anarkali was developing into a prosperous bazaar. The sahibs and memsahibs did their shopping on the Mall at stores housed mostly in bungalows — all built essentially after the model devised by some unknown genius of the Public Works Department, beautifully innocent of all architectural sense and bold enough to think out a pattern that looked a complete exotic in the East, and had never been known in the West.

These hordes — babus, lawyers, students — had to be housed. And physically Lahore seemed to be expanding like a tapeworm — cell added on to cell of brick and mortar. Wilderness could be built upon and made to yield substantial rents. Hoarded fortunes come as 'unearned increment' or as 'the reward of abstinence?' Let learned economists wrangle over that.

Even more than the face of Lahore, its mind seemed to be undergoing a change. Whatever the causes, no one could help noticing that a ferment was at work. Vaguely, you could name education and religion, to some extent politics, as the ingredients of this ferment. The babus and the lawyers were the people it affected most of all.

A non-official purely Indian venture in education had not yet been thought of in Lajpat Rai's student days, but the Christian missionaries with Dr. Forman at the head had been active in this field before Lajpat Rai had become a vakil; and in 1889 the Forman Chiristian College had been founded. The missionaries, of course, had vast resources behind their endeavour and they wielded unbounded influence with the rulers. Broad acres were theirs as a gift, from Government for the manifold institutions they had planned or might plan. These missionaries certainly had a lot to do with the ferment in Lahore.

They indirectly provided the impetus for indigenous endeavour to raise institutions that would impart the new education. So, besides the haphazard houses for babus, the bungalows and Government buildings like the Dayananda School were sprouting up too. The site where the DAV School had since sprung up, the Lajpat Rai's student days had been an unsafe — frightfully unsafe — wilderness. The ferment was manifesting itself in brick and mortar and in the conversion of what had been wilderness.

In his student days he had watched the University of the Punjab more or less in the process of being born. Dr. Leitner who acted in a capacity had his own notions about the baby. By now these had been definitely discarded and his experiments more or less liquidated. The university had set into a routine shaped after the accepted pattern of the universities at Calcutta and Madras. What used to be styled the University College had grown into the university, the college had dome to be known as the Government College.

To this university were attached law and medical and oriental colleges (the last in a way a creation of Dr. Leitner's).. The missionaries too had raised their college under the auspices of this university, and Indian leaders might follow suit now - leaders of the ferment.

In the eighties in Lahore, the two rival channels for the ferment had been the Brahmo Samaj and the Arya Samaj. Things had somewhat changed since the eighties.

Pandit Shiv Narayan Agnihotri, who as his father's friend had been a sort of guardian to the boy Lajpat, had now given up his job as a schoolmaster. He had also left the Brahmo Samaj, and founded a church of his own called the Dev Samaj. From Pandit Agnihotri he had thereby come to be known to his followers as "Dev Guru Bhagwan". He also weaned away many of the active spirits away from the Brahmo Samaj, thereby enfeebling it in the Punjab" and making it easier for its rival, the Arya Samaj, to elbow it almost out of the field- To the new progressive element that was turned out by the new educational machine, the more dynamic and quite, aggressive Arya Samaj could make a bolder appeal." And since education was a main activity of the day, the Arya Samaj had also set up a school and named it after its founder.

This practically decided the issue against the Brahmos and in favour of the Aryas. Already their school had added on a college department. The head of this was a young man who after graduating had not sought a job and a career like other graduates, but had dedicated himself to the institution. He was the Honorary Principal a title that would not have been easily understood in Lajpat Rai's school days.

The Arya Samaj had definitely struck root among the intelligentsia. Its activity was expanding every year both at Lahore and throughout the Punjab. It professed to revive the Vedic religion. It harked back — like all revivalist movements. It compared the ancient glories of India with her present degenerate condition. It thus fostered sentiments of patriotism. That was one of its several facets. Another represented its activity in modernising Hindu society, of refitting it so that it might be able to tackle the modern problems with efficiency.

It may be that all the evils in Hindu society had been unvedic; but the paradox remained that many of the Arya Samaj enthusiasts, paying homage to the Vedas, had more first-hand acquaintance with the modern writers, thinkers, historians and statesmen of Europe than with the Vedas and rishis. They wanted to equip the Hindu society for the struggle in the modern world. They wanted to eradicate child marriage, to abolish hereditary priesthood and to simplify all ritual, to lift the ban on the marriage of widows, and on crossing the seas, to introduce (or reintroduce) an Aryan monotheism as rigid as the Semitic one. Most of these things they shared with the Brahmo Samaj, but they were more aggressive and had more of rough and tumble in them. They had not much use for an eclecticism that stressed the good points of all religions. They wished to give tit for tat when the missionaries of other religions assailed Hinduism, and they wanted Hinduism to become aggressive and proselytising like its rivals — They laid great stress on the removal of untouchability and started a 'Reclamation' Movement. They underlined the importance of Devanagari and Hindi, and here too their zeal perhaps outstripped that of the Brahmos. Their leadership may have lacked some refinement and culture, but it could put a more enthusiastic shoulder to the wheel.

In the nineties the Arya Samaj seemed to promise a ubiquity that would pervade all walks in the public life of the Punjab. The dynamic and progressive element among the Hindus rallied more and more round its banner. The more the educated element concentrated in Lahore, the more grist there was for the very efficient mills of the Arya Samaj, The mind of Lahore was changing fast indeed. Revivalism and modernism alike were attacking the massive but lethargic forces of sacrosanct superstition.

Politics also was being talked about increasingly. A branch of the Congress had yet to be established, but that of the Indian Association existed. Politics was becoming the hobby of the lawyers. Law was a very lucrative profession. It meant money as well as respect. In it a man with brains could rise without an investment and once he had arrived in the upper hierarchy he could command big fees. True, the Punjab did not abound in big landlords and rajas who could conveniently be fleeced to the tune of lakhs, but successful lawyers could get decent fees from prosperous middle class people. A princely income at the bar was not possible but one ensuring comfort and respect certainly was to be had without too much drudgery. The lawyers dominated in politics as a matter of right, as they were the "independent" half of the intelligentsia (those who had received education and enlightenment), the other half being bound by the "rules of conduct" for Government services — The more "Babus" there were in Lahore, the greater the number of potential Arya Samajists; the more lawyers there were, the greater the number of potential politicians.

Whilst the Brahmo and Arya Samaj activity among the Hindus made this stir, the Muslims too were hearing new voices — that of Sir Syed Ahmad Khan who had toured in the Punjab in 1883-84 and of a new sect called the Ahmadiyyas. In many ways the Syed school with its modernistic liberal tendencies resembled the Brahmo Movement among the Hindus (or rather the resemblance was very striking till he started his narrow-minded campaign against the Congress); while the aggressive Ahmadiyyas resembled the Arya Samajists in their zeal and pugnacity. It was about this time that the Sikhs happened to become aware that they were distinct from Hindus.

Hitherto most people had supposed them to be one of the several semi-autonomous units in the loose federation of Hinduism. It was in Lajpat's college days (as sometimes, reminiscing about those days, he once recalled) that the students noted in the admission forms of the examination that they had to enter whether they were Sikh, Hindu, Christian or Muslim. Before that, Sikh and Hindu had not been thus differentiated. Macauliff was persuaded in 1893 to give up his judicial career to translate the Sikh scriptures into English — the version then undertaken resulting in his six volumes on the Sikh Religion... Dr. Trump who had translated the Adi Granth for the Secretary of State had died eight years earlier. John Bull had begun to take an interest in the Sikhs. They had proved so useful in the 'mutiny of 1857' that imperialism wisely decided they must receive especial treatment.

The ferment seemed to pervade all communities alike and from Lahore it radiated to remote corners of the Punjab, Thanks to the ferment, Lahore was becoming more and more the metropolis of the Punjab more and more the nerve-centre of its body-politic.

Ferment, public life, politics — in other terms, the nerve-centre of the Punjab, Lahore was giving an increased importance to the press. The 'intelligentsia' ruled the roost The "dumb millions" were as yet very very dumb. Naturally, prestige and power were with the press conducted in English. The Civil and Military Gazette had come into being soon after the annexation of the Punjab by the English. Indians wanted a paper too. The munificence of Dyal Singh Majithia resulted in the founding of the weekly Tribune in 1881.

In the mid-eighties the Tribune had begun to appear twice a week. This was the principal Indian paper in English that Lahore then had. In the 'nineties it began to come out thrice a week with an editor Nagendranath Gupta who hailed from Bengal.

The mind and face of Lahore were thus changing swiftly when Lajpat Rai arrived there in the early-90s to settle down, to practise at the bar and to be at the nerve-centre of the public life of the Punjab. The ferment that was working the change gave just the opportunity that his talent sought, and just the sort of adventure that his spirit craved for an adventure far bigger than was to be found in a purely bread-winning career.

Arya Samaj in Crisis

The Arya Samaj was now his principal field of activity. The Samaj was growing, undoubtedly, but at the same time it was passing through a grave crisis. Things seemed to be heading towards a split between the Little Indians and the Big Indians — with this interesting variation on the Lilliput theme that here one of the factions in its strict adhcrence to vegetarianism held as taboo the little end as well as the big. Sain Das and Guru Dutt, who had represented the two different trends of thought among the Arya Samajists, were now both dead. But the two schools of thought that they represented were ill at ease in each other's company. The DAV managing committee had passed a resolution authorising the opening of the college department while Guru Dutt was still alive. Trouble started over it not long after his death. The causes that underlay these squabbles were thus described by Lajpat Rai, who in his autobiography has left a critical if not very detailed account of this split in the Arya Samaj:

> "Firstly, Lala Hans Raj's personal unpopularity. People got the impression that he was haughty and conceited and grasping. His reserve, his aloofness, his sternness in administration, all went to make him unpopular. Secondly, the question of vegetarianism. Underlying this was the question of tile authority of Swami Dayananda Saraswati. Pandit Guru Dutt had in his last days become such a devotee of the Swami that he would not tolerate the smallest deviation from the doctrines laid down by the Swami. In his overzealous moments he often maintained that the Satyartha

> Prakasha of Dayananda was true in every syllable. The same spirit worked among the Pandit's disciples and followers. When they raised he controversy about vegetarianism, naturally the opposite group maintained that it was not binding on any Arya Samajist to accept Swami Dayananda's teachings in their entirety, and that the Swami was not infallible."

In the administration of the college differences became acute (soon after Guru Dutt's death in 1890) over the place of Sanskrit in its scheme of studies, and still more over the details of the Sanskrit syllabus itself. Dayananda's Satyartha Prakasha carried a chapter on education in which was set forth a detailed syllabus covering the entire range of elementary as well as higher teaching. In this puritanic scheme there was no room for Kalidasa or Bhavabhuti. In fact the Sanskrit drama was completely unrepresented, and in poetry only the epics of Valmiki and Vyasa tolerated, not as poetry but as history.

The corner-stone of Sanskrit studies was to be Panini (with Patanjali's great commentary), for the Swami vehemently condemned the later grammarians. It was a fundamental belief with Rishi Dayananda that between books composed by the rishis and those perpetrated by ordinary mortals lay an unbridgeable gulf, and the scholars to be prepared for realising the highest truths in the Vedas were to be nurtured only on the sacred fare provided by the rishis. The literalists regarded the Satyartha Prakasha as infallible and as essential a part of the Master's teaching as any other doctrine or dictum found in his voluminous works. At least so their professions ran, for when they had to work out a scheme they too made concession and compromise.

The more practical-minded people held that the Satyartha Prakasha curriculum was not meant for present-day conditions and that underlying it was the presumption of a Sanskrit-speaking Aryavarta. The Anglo-Vedic College raised by Dayananda's followers in his memory was from the beginning intended to be different from the master's ideal scheme. Its very name proclaimed its spirit of compromise. Guru Dutt had been a party to that name and to the original manifesto setting forth the promoters' aim and object which certainly were inspired by this spirit of compromise.

Two years after the issuing of this manifesto nothing seemed to have materialised excepting a modest sum (considerably less than a lakh) but as soon as his friend Hans Raj offered his honorary services to the proposed institution he pressed for the starting of the school classes forthwith.

Again when about three years later the Managing Committee decided (by a majority of one) to start college classes he (like Lajpat Rai) was amongst the six who voted for this step. He had served on the subcommittee of five appointed to implement that decision. As secretary to this subcommittee he had himself drawn up its report outlining the scheme of studies — still another compromise affair. Guru Dutt worked in a spirit of give and take; but there can be no denying that the trend of his own thought was different from that of Sain Das.

The two trends produced a violent clash amongst the friends of Sain Das and the disciples of Guru Dutt, when both of them were no more. The doctrinaire group became more and more fanatical and began to condemn openly and vehemently the way the college was being run. Eventually this group broke loose from the college, and to translate the master's ideas into practice founded the Gurukula University. The other group worked to make the college a success by acquiring funds for it and tangible assets of brick and mortar, and by attracting a large number of scholars.

Their Samajic conscience was quite satisfied if they felt that besides helping in the spread of education in a general way, they had created a most important agency for making Hindi popular in the Punjab and for inculcating a love of Sanskrit among some of the students that came to them even though they could not adhere to the ideal of compulsory Sanskrit and Sanskrit taught in strict accord with Dayananda's curriculum for all of them; that even if their scholars did not go through the strict brahmacharya enjoined by the Swami, their school and college served as useful recruiting-grounds for the Samaj; and that their institutions were helping the broad patriotic purposes dear to their hearts. If these things their college could achieve, they would not make it compulsory for all their students to study the intricacies of Panin's grammar, though Panini and Patanjali had been so much extolled by Dayananda. They were not willing to scare away all their students for the pleasure of a literal adherence to an impracticable scheme of studies.

When Lajpat Rai arrived on the Scene, the cleavage was becoming increasingly marked. For a while he tried to remain non-partisan. He could not see the feasibility of converting the college into an institution that would adhere literally to what Dayananda had prescribed in Sanskrit curriculum or idolatry. He was rationalistic and valued intellectual independence too much to accept the 'infallibility' of the Swami or of anyone else. He was not able to see the sinfulness of his flesh diet. He had adopted Mazzini as his guru and he found that his ambition of patriotic service to his people was shared more by the 'cultured' section than by the 'vegetarian' faddists. The latter seemed to him too dogma-ridden, too unpractical, too other, worldly. Also he felt that his friend Hans Raj was being misunderstood and misrepresented, and was the aggrieved party. He cast his lot with the group led by Hans Raj. Once he had declared his partiality, he was called upon to do a lot of propaganda for the party. When the controversy raged over the Sanskrit curriculum, he produced a brochure in Urdu to show that the DAV College had not neglected Sanskrit, as its 'Mahatma' vegetarian critics made out. He had to write to the press frequently to defend his party or to attack its opponents. He had to take his share of consultations and committee meetings. Like others he too violated at times the code decorous. He did not like all he had to do as a partisan but he did it.

How deeply he had been affected by these unseemly squabbles of his co-religionists may be gathered from his reflections on the 1891 election of the Samaj, though they relate to the Hissar period.

"These scenes I saw with my own eyes. They moved me immensely and I used to keep awake at night pondering over them and wondering whether God himself could cure us of our national malady of disunity. To end dissensions and to unify the people we had put ourselves under God's own care, but even there we could not rid ourselves of our sins and the result of our dark deeds was that instead of being united we had begun to quarrel with each other, and that too in a manner the indecency of which knew no bounds. When I went back to Hissar after the

'91 anniversary I was sick at heart and the condition of the Samaj and my own uneasiness over it compelled me to leave Hissar permanently for Lahore."

Discussing "the blackest episode" in this warfare, he comes to the conclusion that both the parties were equally to blame, "In my opinion," says he, "Lala Hans Raj's responsibility was as great as that of Lala Munshi Ram".

The actual split came about towards the end of 1892, at the time of the annual election of the Lahore Arya Samaj. On the evening previous to the election, the party with which Lajpat Rai had cast his lot met at the house of one of their prominent leaders, Lala (afterwards Mr. Justice) Lal Chand. Their object was to decide what course of action, they should adopt the next day, in view of all the irregularities and malpractices that the other section was supposed to have perpetrated to ensure a packed house.

Some chronicles Lajpat Rai, "wanted to take possession of the Samaj mandir with the aid of the police. Others wanted a decision by a court of law fixing different timings for the meetings of the two parties. Still others would dispense with the police, capture the mandir by force of lathis at night, and give battle if there was resistance. A fourth group, in which I was included, was of the opinion that since it was impossible to cooperate with the mahatmas it was better to part company with them and for the time being to rent a house for our separate weekly meetings."

In a characteristic speech Lajpat Rai said at this meeting, memorable in the history of the Arya Samaj:

> "Principles and not brick and stone constitute the Samaj. We joined the Samaj to reform our lives and to serve the people, not to take possession of houses or to quarrel over them.... I am entirely opposed to quarrelling or fighting or inviting the police or a court of law to our aid.
>
> This sane and large-hearted appeal succeeded. The party passed a formal resolution of separation and founded the next day what came to be known as the Anarkali Arya Samaj. The idea of abandoning the

original Samaj mandir in Vachhowali was very painful to Lala Hans Raj; even so he agreed."

Of this Samaj Lajpat Rai was chosen the first President.

Later he had to review his own conduct with severity as he realised that in the heat of his partisanship he had formed an uncharitable opinion of Mahatma Munshi Ram (Swami Shraddhananda), the leader of the other section.

"I must say," wrote Lajpat Rai in his autobiography, "that I have largely revised the opinion I had of him in 1892-93 and for several years after, that he was a mischief monger, and a hankerer after fame, and ambitious to become a leader. Now I believe it was unjust to pronounce upon Lala Munshi Ram's-character on the basis of what he did in party spirit for party ends. Like all great men Lala Munshi Ram had his own failings and those who hung round him often exploited them; Those by whom he was always surrounded largely influenced his opinion and his actions....

But I am certainly far from saying that he was a mischief-making or a vindictive person. In moments of heat I formed an opinion which I had to change afterwards and I am extremely sorry I should ever have done him such injustice. Lala Munshi Ram was by nature ' impulsive; lofty and noble impulses-dominated him, and not the petty or ignoble ones. He was generous and hospitable and was actuated by a high sense of public service. He knew what it was to suffer and sacrifice. As a friend he was very loyal. As a man he was very frank and open and pious."

This was written in 1915. There is little doubt that Shraddhananda rose still higher, very much higher indeed, in Lajpat Rai's estimation in the period beginning with 1919 — days of Martial Law in the Punjab — and ending in 1926 with the Swami's martyrdom. How often did he envy the glorious death that crowned Shraddhananda's career!

Energetic and industrious as he always Was, the work he had to put in those days must have been pretty strenuous even for Lajpat Rai. He had to work hard in his career at the bar and to work harder in his dearer career in public life. Almost all his off days at the court he had to spend in touring about to raise funds for the college, for he was becoming not only its chief public speaker, but also its chief beggar. The split in the Samaj and the mutual hostility of the two groups made the burden peculiarly heavy. As a small instance, Lajpat Rai mentions that once he had to rush straight from Shimla to Peshawar, for "had I arrived at Peshawar even a few hours later I would have got nothing. In two days I collected Rs. 3,000 in cash. Then the Mahatma deputation arrived and the college collection stopped."

Though the two groups in the Samaj had separated in 1892, the separation was not complete. The Samaj mandirs were separate; but the "Mahatmas" who were on the College Managing Committee started wrecking tactics there, and from 1897 it was a period of severe struggle.

One day the fight took the form of an exchange of lathi blows. Sunder Das, eldest son of the late Sain Das, had his skull fractured and laid down his life for the sake of his party; somebody from the other side also paid the same heavy price."

There was hard work aid there was this nerve-racking strife. No wonder that his health suffered badly, and at one time during this period he was at death's door from pneumonia. Both lungs were seriously affected and he went through more than one crisis, being confined to bed for about two months. "Doctor Beli Ram tended me with great affection and took great pains to save me. To him I remain indebted as long as I live, he wrote gratefully afterwards.

4

In Political Arena

Lahore Congress Session

We have seen that after attending its Bombay session in Lajpat Rai's enthusiasm for the National Congress abated a good deal. He did not trouble to attend any more of its yearly Christmas gatherings, till at last the 'mountain came to Muhammad' in 1893. The Punjab had invited the Congress at the suggestion of one of the DAV College leaders, Bakhshi Jaishi Ram (father of Mr. Justice Bakhshi Tek Chand). Lajpat Rai too joined the Reception Committee, but he was not among its most active participants. Although the Congress had been invited at the suggestion of one of their important leaders, the Arya Samajists were rather lukewarm.

There were others more willing, particularly Dyal Singh Majithia the philanthropist, and young Harkishan Lal, the latter by no means favourably inclined towards Bakhshi Jaishi Ram and his Arya Samajists. So the Congress session was the care not so much of the Aryas as of the Brahmos and so Navin Chandra Roy, an outstanding Brahmo in Lahore, was Chairman of the Reception Committee. Lajpat Rai made two or three speeches at the Congress-session. "What was most worthy of note is," he records, "that Rai Mul Raj took a large part" This gentleman, as we have seen, was a Government servant, and, what is more, he was-part of the judiciary. He was thus supposed to be doubly dead to politics. But as a matter of fact he was busy pulling the wires from behind the scenes and at informal meetings. He had drafted the Arya Samaj Constitution for Swami Dayananda and he wanted the Congress to adopt one somewhat on the same lines. His suspicions about Hume still continued and the demand for a Constitution was probably his way of putting these to the test, anticipating that Hume would not find it convenient to accept the suggestion. The anticipation was not falsified by events. Hume saw no necessity for any Constitution and did not let the proposal materialise.

Today it may sound unbelievable that the Congress remained practically without a Constitution all these years. Till the 1899 session in Lucknow it was without any Constitution whatsoever and the one adopted that year hardly met the essential points of the proposals inspired by Mul Raj, i.e. a representative character for the delegates and some sort of machinery for their election, and a standing organisation with regional branches for carrying on the work all through the year. Provincial Committees for such work were not thought of by the Congress leaders till 1908. The Punjab delegates insisted at several sessions on the Congress giving itself a Constitution before it got the country one and the idea of course had originated with Mul Raj, that inscrutable man who always revelled in putting his ideas forward from behind a smoke-screen.

Even in 1904 the Punjab contingent headed by Lajpat Rai and his friend Dwarka Das urged in vain that the Congress should define its Constitution. Now the high priest of the Congress was the grand and imperious Sir Pherozeshah Mehta. As Duni Chand (of Ambala) who was present at this Bombay Congress session says:

> "Both Lala Lajpat Rai and Lala Dwarka Das pleaded in vain for a Constitution for the Congress; the Parsee Knight coerced them into silence without much difficulty. Lala Lajpat Rai had not by that time developed that personality which he did only two years later."

This "two years later" is a reference to the memorable Banaras session, to the happenings of which we shall devote a chapter later. Here let it suffice that already in 1893 Lajpat Rai and his friends had realised the necessity of a proper Constitution for the Congress, and the resistance they thus evoked must have impressed on them how hard they would have to struggle before a Constitution could be wrung for India from the unwilling hands of her alien rulers, seeing that even the patriotic autocrats of the Congress were so unwilling to become constitutional rulers of their own organisation. It was at this second session of the Congress at Lahore that Lajpat Rai for the first time met the two leaders from Poona, G. K. Gokhale and Bal Gangadhar Tilak, acquaintance with whom in later years developed into the most valued friendships of his life.

Discarding a Blooming Exercise

How did a busy lawyer find time for so much of extraneous activity? As lawyers are fond, of putting it, law is a jealous mistress. Lajpat Rai's literary output was that of a whole time writer and editor. His touring, lecturing, raising of funds, attending to office routine of the several institutions he was connected with, committee meetings and organising work in the Samaj, the college, the famine relief campaigns, the orphanages easily equalled the burden carried by two or three competent whole-timers. A host in himself one would say. Even so no one in his profession could have engaged himself in "half that enormous amount of public activity without its affecting the number of clients who came to him, and without having to turn down some of the briefs. He was proving a great success at the Chief Court and was noticeably rising to the top. This seemed to happen in spite of himself, for Lajpat Rai's heart was not in these briefs. "My practice," he writes, "hampered my public activity, and my public activity hampered my practice." He was faced with the difficult situation of having to manage two jealous mistresses at once.

At times he felt impelled to make a choice. He could not think of deserting the mistress of his ruling passion, with the other, it had been an affair of convenience or of sheer necessity for making a living to begin with, and that pressing necessity being no longer felt, he wondered if time had not come for ending the cumbersome bigamous arrangement. But of course this would have important consequences for his family, and he was told he could not take a decision all by himself. He was now the father of three children — two sons and a daughter all born in the nineties. (The youngest of his children was to come early in the next decade). They were too young to have a voice in the family counsels, but a father's obligations were inescapable. His brothers had by now completed their education and were settled in life. His wife perhaps did not have very much of a say. It is not without significance that in his autobiography there are passages full of deep affection for his parents; there are tender sentiments occasionally expressed for some of his brothers or children. But there is very little said about his wife. The way Gandhi discussed, we might say dissected, Kasturba in his Experiments with Truth had not been to Lajpat Rai's taste. His autobiography refers but little to his wife, though that little is utterly frank writing.

His parents had married him off while he was still at school, but domestic life began some years later. It certainly remained free from rows and squabbles, but it does not seem to have been blessed with much of felicity of a higher type.

It may be a problem for psychologists whether his passionate zeal for reform, for creative work, and his wanderlust would not have been much less in evidence, if he had been more passionately attached to his wife and home. As it was, he had a sort of grievance that his partner in life could not take much interest in what life meant to him. His wife seems to have realised this fully, and was on the whole content with looking after her husband's comfort — which indeed she did devotedly. Perhaps she felt very justifiably that the husband was not always fair to his home and children and seldom did by them all that he could or should, judged by accepted standards.

But she must have realised early that there was no mending his ways and kept her feelings to herself and must be given credit for thus adjusting herself to a way of life so little of her own choosing. If she did not make much of a contribution by an active participation in what he considered a richer life, she put no obstacles in his way, scrupulously avoided doing anything that might make for unhappiness or domestic tension. No jarring note, and taking the peculiar context fully into consideration, this was a considerable, even if not a positive, contribution. And thus by mutual consent (or her acquiescence) she had no effective say in the big decisions in Lajpat Rai's life, and the only members of the family to be consulted when the question of his retiring so early from the profession arose were his parents.

Munshi Radha Kishan was glad of the prosperity that his lawyer son's fees had ushered in. At the son's suggestion he had himself, long ago, somewhat prematurely, thrown away his teaching job. He strongly disapproved of Lajpat Rai's ideas of retiring from practice while still full of youth. Father and son disagreed "Work at the Bar" so the son wrote afterwards, was not after my liking. I wanted to give it up and to devote myself entirely to the service of my country. But my father stood in my way. He wanted that I should make my pile and provide adequately for my brothers and my children. I used to reply that I had already discharged the obligation of educating my brothers and that I had with me enough to support my children.... In this noble resolve of mine my mother offered no resistance. Her sympathy was with me."

A tug of war went on for some time till on the occasion of the Lahore Arya Samaj anniversary in 1898 he announced his resolve to curtail his work at the bar and devote his time more and more "to the service of the college, the Samaj and my country". He now set up an office for himself in a room in the school building where, when not out touring, he would go every day to work for the college and the Samaj. His visits to the mofussil Samajas became much more frequent, for after the announcement every Arya Samaj in the province (owning allegiance to the College section) thought it had a right and a duty to invite him to its annual celebrations.

He started lecturing on Indian history at the college though he could not keep this up beyond a couple of months. He wrote a small book in Urdu, mainly for the use of school boys, (but actually it was appreciated by grown up people as we!) giving an account of the ancient Aryan civilization. This was in a way a forerunner to something more ambitious dealing with ancient India which he may have conceived then, but which was actually written much later during his non-cooperation prison term. He compiled also an English reader for schools. For a while it looked as if he were setting up as a full-time teacher and educationist.

He was systematically reducing his work for his clients. To make his new resolve more effective he took a further step about two years later, by deciding to give away whatever he earned at the bar. This he announced in a letter to his friend Principal Hans Raj, and for several years he continued to offer his earnings, thus dedicated in advance, to the DAV College (and the Samaj). He was generally understood to have earmarked his entire income exclusively for the college and the Samaj. As a matter of fact his resolve related only to his professional fees as a lawyer, his main object being to take the edge off the temptation to be wasting time and energy in swelling his earnings.

Adding to the pile must no longer come between him and his dedicated work. Although for a number of years Tie gave away this income mostly to the college and the Samaj, his pledge left him free to divert it to any other good cause at his own discretion. This kind of sacrifice was novel, perhaps unique, and it created a profound impression. It was this sacrifice, this utter disregard for money as a personal possession, as much as the eloquence and vigour of his speech that made him such a dangerous beggar. His appeal for funds became a regular feature of the Arya Samaj anniversaries and, instead of scaring away people, it ever proved a great draw. His moving eloquence made the stingiest loosen their purse strings and helped in the collection on the spot of large amounts that were only too welcome to the yet scantily lined coffers of the Samaj and the college.

'The Punjabee' Newspaper

Lajpat Rai entered on the new century with horizons very much widened, and still widening every day. The Arya Samaj and the Punjab were beginning to look too small to utilise fully the new energy that he felt surging within him and seeking appropriate outlets. The Punjab was coming to know him more as the author of those booklets on Mazzini and Garibaldi that were stimulating a new national awakening and a passion for freedom than as a leader in a socio-religious movement. The smaller things were all right in their own place but his spirit yearned for a big epic theme.

The Congress seemed too tame as yet to serve this purpose, but it had potentialities. There seemed to be no hot blood coursing in its veins. But given such a galvanising force, it could certainly serve.

After the 1900 session of Lahore the Punjab, as we have seen, was experiencing one of its periodic lapses into apathy. Even Harkishan Lal who was supposed to be running the Congress seemed to have had enough of it All this was not much to the liking of Lajpat Rai, He began to devote his time and attention more and more to work directly political, and ere long he realised that the first and supreme need for making such work effective was a newspaper. He and those of his way of thinking did not believe that the existing press was willing to do its share in laying those sound foundations of popular education without which no political superstructure worth the name could be built up.

One day a situation arose which was simply unbearable. The editor of the leading Indian paper of Lahore has shown himself unworthy of any confidence and ignorant of the fundamentals of journalistic ethics by handing over to the Principal of the Government College the original manuscript of an anonymously published communication from some of his students. The students were victimised. Following this, Lajpat Rai and his friends could no longer resist the conclusion that a paper of their own must be started at once. Ten of them met and agreed to put in if need be and to lose a thousand rupees apiece in the venture.

They lost nothing in fact for they chose for manager a man with a sound business instinct, Jaswant Rai a lecturer at the DAV College. The Punjabee — so the paper was named — was launched in October 1904. Front its very first issue it confirmed the public expectation that it would take a bold stand. The policy of the paper, it was well known, would be generally guided and controlled by Lajpat Rai. He appointed K. K. Athavale as editor, at the suggestion of Tilak, and himself wrote signed articles quite frequently, besides almost regularly writing unsigned editorials. The Punjabee was not meant to be just one more newspaper.

It was definitely intended to work week after week, and in a variety of ways, for the creation of a new political consciousness in the Punjab. Whatever it may have appeared to be to other people, to Lajpat Rai it was no doubt a weekly continuation of the work started years ago by his Mazzini booklet. The task in both cases was the same: journalism was just one more medium of preaching the same gospel. And an effective one too, for it dealt in concrete terms with the day-to-day application of that gospel. He started The Punjabee because it was necessary to whip up a lazy public opinion, that had steadily grown more indolent during the past three years. He felt too that the time was at hand when it would be proved how salutary and timely this castigation had been.

Judged by the standards of today, The Punjabee was not a great newspaper. Judged by the standards of tomorrow, it will appear to be a poorer thing still. It was an eight-page weekly, turned out by an insignificant press. It had no resources for news 'stories' — in those days such journalistic signification of 'story' did not seem familiar in Indian newspaper offices — nor an elaborate staff to prepare a varied banquet. What are called 'features' were then unknown. A half-tone block was a rarity, for to get one made you had to go to Bombay or Poona or Calcutta. Typography and make-up tricks had not yet been mastered by many news editors, and the readers were none too fastidious in these matters. The Punjabee might appear crude in its ways; but it was alert and effective.

It knew what to say and how to say it with its real purpose ever in view — preparing the Punjab for the big battle inevitably coming and already instinctively being anticipated, if not so much by the older Congress leaders, certainly by some of the younger ones, and by Lajpat Rai who always seemed to sense in a mysterious instinctive manner the coming on of big events. For this object The Punjabee worked most effectively; week after week, the local grievances, police high-handedness and race arrogance were dealt with in its columns. Then there were India-wide issues like the Universities Bill of Lord Curzon, and foreign and international events which could be used to further the same end. From the very beginning The Punjabee devoted great attention to the lessons of the Japanese victories against Czarist Russia. These victories were going to affect the awareness of the entire East and The Punjabee saw to it that its readers did not escape the invigorating influence.

The big battle that Lajpat Rai and The Punjabee were preparing for soon came — perhaps sooner than they expected. In Bengal it arrived with proconsul Curzon's bureaucratic act ill cutting up the Presidency into two; in the Punjab it came with the Lieutenant-Governor Ibbetson's Land and Canal Colony laws. The Punjabee played an important role both in creating public opinion on these issues and in giving a true and bold expression to it when the agitation had become a swelling, onward rushing tide.

Congress Session in Bombay

The Punjabee Group decided to renew contacts with the Congress and accordingly they sent a contingent of delegates to the 1904 session in Bombay. Lajpat Rai and his friend Dwarka Das (after whom Lajpat Rai named the library he presented to the Servants of the People Society) were amongst the prominent leaders of this group in the Congress session. The Congress did not yet have much fight in it and it did little 'constructive work'. It held a sort of an annual festival at which its orators gave excellent account of themselves. Its chief purpose till then seems to have been to give a public expression to the year's grievances (in addition to the stock or standing grievances).

It remained a somewhat amorphous body. The Arya Samajists, used to well-nit organisations and well-planned public work, did not much admire the ways of the Congress. They urged again, with Lajpat Rai and Dwarka Das as their spokesmen, the need for a Constitution that would set up machinery for sustained work throughout the year. But in this second attempt they were easily snuffed out by Sir Pherozeshah Mehta, who at that time was the grand potentate of the Congress.

However, this session proved of some consequence to Lajpat Rai in another way, as we shall presently see. Immediately after it he took a boat to Sri Lanka, looked at and admired the landscape and the seascape of the Malabar Coast and on his way back made a pilgrimage to Rameshwaram and visited the famous temple of Madurai. This was his first visit to the south. For three days he stayed at Madras as the guest of G. Subramania Iyyer and then proceeded to Calcutta.

It was in the course of these wanderings after the 1904 Congress session that he had his first significant meeting with? Gokhale, who happened to be in Calcutta for the Supreme Council. Gokhale took him as a visitor to the Council which was that day discussing a validating bill in regard to the irregularities of Curzon's University Act. He heard Gokhale speak from the non-official side. He heard other speeches too and recorded that "the mockery of the whole thing made a great impression on my mind"!

Feeling sore at the policies initiated by Curzon, the Congress; leaders decided on sending a deputation to the Viceroy. Curzon refused to see the Congress President and thus "slapped the Congress in the face". The leaders "felt offended, they fretted and fumed... resolved to appeal to the British public". To place the grievances of India before the British public, therefore, the Bombay session decided to send out a deputation at the time of the impending general elections in England... Gokhale suggested that Lajpat Rai should be one of the proposed deputation to England, and Lajpat Rai readily agreed, feeling that he could be of use to the deputation, and that the experience abroad would certainly be worth his while. The contact with Gokhale he valued highly, and soon a friendship based on mutual esteem grew up between the two for the sake of which Lajpat Rai later made sacrifices without ever regretting them. The political outlook of the two was not identical, and in days that soon followed the difference became accentuated, but that never meant a clash.

Through Gokhale he made certain other notable contacts in Calcutta, and he esteemed that with Sister Nivedita as a rare experience. Possibly he was already acquainted with her writings on "aggressive Hinduism" and kindred subjects. The Arya Samaj was nothing if not "aggressive Hinduism" and by now his Arya Samaj had become a good deal liberalised. In interpreting Hinduism the emphasis in his outlook too was on the underlying genius of Hinduism rather than on this or that sectarian dogma. In action, the emphasis was on an all-round liberation of the people, particularly political liberation.

He had not accepted Vedantism as his father had done, but he had now culture and understanding enough to be able to appreciate the beauty of that philosophy. Nivedita was working in the cultural and spiritual fields; he more and more in the political and active sphere. But they could understand each other well. The contact developed into one of two kindred souls. They talked politics also and talked without reservation. On their way to the office of Mr. S. K. Radcliffe (who was then editing The Statesman) they had a frank exchange of views.

"I can never forget," he wrote afterwards, "the things I heard on the way from her lips. She was a great hater of British raj, and a great lover of Indians. In politics she stood for the first principles that Mazzini had expounded. In short, this interview further confirmed me in my own convictions and gave me profound joy."

It left behind sweet memories. When in later years he sometimes recalled them, he did so in a joyous mood and they came forth fresh and fragrant like treasured things perennially laid up in lavender.

In the Company of Gokhale

The general elections in Britain were delayed. The British voter, supposed to be the ultimate master of the British Parliament, could not thus have the pleasure of conveniently receiving in audience the delegation from India for the next few months. Gokhale changed his plans. The day (May 10, 1905) Lajpat Rai was starting from Lahore, he received a telegram saying that Gokhale had been advised by Sir William Wedderburn, head of the British Committee of the Indian National Congress, to put off his visit till July and had done so accordingly. Lajpat Rai found this extremely awkward; he had completed his preparations for his first visit to Europe and his friends at Lahore had already given him a grand fare-well. All that might now appear to have been much ado about nothing. General elections or no, he was not going to alter his plans.

As Lajpat Rai found out subsequently, Wedderburn had merely intimated the election schedule — which was misunderstood in Bombay as suggesting a like change in Indian delegate's schedule!

He kept his schedule. On his way to Bombay he halted at Poona where during his brief stoppage he was the guest partly of Gokhale and partly of Tilak and the next day he set sail.

He could not continue the unsigned editorials for The Punjabee, but he took the earliest opportunity of sending it letters about his travels and activities abroad. His travelogue-detailed his impressions of Port Said and of Naples and Rome and Milan places that he visited *en route*. On June 10, 1905 he arrived in London.

Some propaganda on behalf of the Indian National Congress, which was already a 20-year-old organisation, was being conducted in London by an India Committee of which Sir William Wedderburn was the chairman. This committee issued a small monthly about Indian affairs called India. The Congress was annually voting substantial sums for this journal. Dadabhai Naoroji too was in England most of the time. He lived in South Kensington and devoted much of his time to canvassing support for the Indian cause. He had already presided over a Congress session in 1886 and again in 1893. Dadabhai had a pathetic faith in the Englishman's "instinctive love of justice and fair-play" and most of his time was spent in appealing in vain to this "instinctive love" on behalf of India. Dadabhai and Wedderburn were the chief spokesmen of the Indian National Congress in England.

Younger and keener men were very much dissatisfied with the tame and staid politics of Congress leaders and of their India Committee in (London, Shyamji Krishna Verma was the moving spirit and leader of this younger group; Shyamji had started as a disciple of Swami Dayananda, at whose recommendation Professor Monier Williams, the renowned Sanskritist, had taken him to England for help in his researches.

After qualifying there for the bar, Shyamji had returned to India, tried his hand at a few odd jobs in the course of a few years and then finally left India, finding conditions in this country too uncongenial for a lover of freedom. He seemed to have settled down in London. He had been deeply influenced by the writings of Herbert Spencer and when he started a journal in England he called it the Indian Sociologist.

Sociology owed is vogue largely to Herbert Spencer and the name of the journal was intended to proclaim the Spencerian leanings of its editor in social thought. This journal made vigorous attacks on the Congress leaders, on Gokhale and Dadabhai and on the British friends of the Congress. It was a sort of counterblast to India. Shyamji was a difficult man to get on with, and though he was initially considered the brain and the chief inspirer of the Indian Revolutionary Movement abroad, he made no lasting friendship and attracted no loyal disciple. For one thing, his stinginess was a serious limitation. He could make money always, but was ever loath to part with it. All the same he acted as a very potent influence in creating discontent against the sober and staid politics of the Congress leaders.

"To say that Har Dayal and Savarkar were his 'disciples' would be to belittle these two great men, but there can be no doubt that Shyamji's ideas did influence them," writes Lajpat Rai, and the implication clearly is that since Har Dayal and Savarkar are known to have influenced the entire Revolutionary Movement, Shyamji's role may not be dismissed lightly merely because of this lack of devoted disciples.

In 1905 Shyamji was very active with his Indian Sociologist and with his India House, a hostel intended to attract Indian students. He called on Lajpat Rai at his hotel and exchanged notes with him and invited him to stay at India House — an invitation availed of somewhat later.

The India House in Highgate was formally opened about this time, and Lajpat Rai was present on that occasion.

For about a month Lajpat Rai toured about visiting the English counties and Scotland, addressing meetings for the cause he represented, and when he got back to London in August responding to Shyamji's invitation he put up at the India House.

However, his stay at the India House could not have found favour in the eyes of some of the members of the India Committee of the Congress in London. When one day Shyamji and Lajpat Rai addressed a Labour or Socialist meeting in Holborn Hall in favour of Home Rule, a flutter could be seen in the India Committee dovecots. (Lajpat Rai had not yet moved in to Shyamji's India House. The meeting had been called by a labour organisation and Lajpat Rai invited by Dadabhai Naoroji, its vice-president

Lajpat Rai Writes:

> "When Sir Henry Cotton learnt that Shyamji and myself had made speeches from the same platform in favour of Home Rule, he felt greatly annoyed and brought a motion before the British Committee to the effect that as I was in England as a delegate such conduct on my part was objectionable."

Sir William Wedderburn, however, did not support Sir Henry and Lajpat Rai himself "made it plain that by becoming a Congress delegate I had not bartered away my liberty, that though my speech contained nothing to which a Congressman could take exception, if it was suggested that (being a 'delegate') I had no liberty to express my views in that country, I was quite prepared to resign from the delegation, but would in no case sacrifice my freedom."

Sir Henry Cotton at last put the blame on the inaccurate reporting of the speech and the incident was closed.

Lajpat Rai would not lightly let his freedom be taken away, and he exercised it fully. He addressed meetings in Manchester, Edinburgh, Liverpool and elsewhere. Gokhale had also arrived. Often they spoke from the same platform. Sometimes they toured about and spoke separately. They delivered their message to the British voter leaving, of course, the decision to his good sense.

In an article on India and British party politics, contributed to The Punjabee, Lajpat Rai wrote that there was nothing to choose between Liberals and Tories and the only people from whom some friendship might be expected were Labourites. (Till then the Labour group was only a part of the Liberal party). Through Shyamji and Lajpat Rai made some friendships in radical circles. He particularly mentions the British socialist writer, H. M. Hyndman and some of the Irish leaders.

The Gaekwad of Baroda who also happened to be in London, gave a reception at the Cecil where he was staying. The guests included Lajpat Rai and Shyamji, these constituting two-thirds of the entire number of Indian guests. They were introduced to Her Highness the Maharanee. The Gaekwad whispered to them asking them not to hurry away when the reception broke up. They stayed on after the English guests had departed and had a talk "in which the Maharaja laid bare his heart before us", to render Lajpat Rai's Urdu literally, "the blisters of a scorched heart".

Before returning to India Lajpat Rai made a brief trip to the United States, in the company of Dewan Badri Nath, the scion of a well-known family of Punjab chiefs, at that time a young, man with progressive views.

In October he was back again in London and Sir William Wedderburn had drawn up the programme of another lecture to for him. Both he and Gokhale addressed a large number of meetings, several of these, particularly Lajpat Rai's, arranged under Labour auspices.

Gokhale's choice of Lajpat Rai as a fellow-delegate to England had been readily endorsed by the Punjab branch of the Indian Association and it had sent round an appeal for money for the delegate's expenses. On his return to Lahore Lajpat Rai announced that the three thousand or so thus collected had remained intact to be used for other public causes. It may be that his earnings at the bar for this year went to political work abroad instead of the DAV College.

Motivation at Young Age

Early in November 1905 Lajpat Rai left the shores of England, at Marseilles taking tie very steamer S. S. Peninsular, by which Lord Minto was coming to India to take over as Viceroy, landing in Bombay on November 17.

At Lahore an unprecedented welcome awaited him. A huge crowd had collected on the platform and outside the railway station and just as he stepped out of his compartment, a very distinguished citizen, the Brahmo leader, Babu Jogendra Chandra Bose lifting him up put him on his shoulders. He could thus be seen by the eager crowd and at the same time be spared the jostling. As he got into his carriage, the students unharnessed the horses, themselves drawing the carriage for the three km and more right into his Court Street house. The students simply adored-Lajpat Rai and when the round of parties and addresses of welcome started, they by no means lagged behind - even those of the Government Colleges came forward with their address of welcome.

As he looked round, he could immediately read the portents foreshadowing big events. For the Arya Samaj anniversary he had of course been announced, and that had drawn such an unexpectedly big crowd that the meeting had to be adjourned to improvise adequate arrangements. He addressed the crowd later in the DAV College hostel. It was at this meeting that he said that the credit for whatever was good in him belonged to the Samaj.

However, the speech became more memorable for certain other passages in it. For, it was nice speech that later on the official apologists sought justification for his deportation. In concluding the speech he foresaw "blood raining down from the Indian sky. At the moment it was a seemingly clear sky but tiny red specks were already visible.

The Lajpat Rai menace in CLD records was obviously swelling. The "blood raining" speech was followed, soon after by this one threatening "unpleasant consequences" and, besides, perpetrating the dangerous heresy of "conditioned loyalty". Lahore, where a short while before the officials had thought all was so quiet, had galvanised of a sudden and become so dangerous. That the very first meeting of protest against a lathi charge in far-off Barisal would be held at Lahore must have seemed incredible to the official mind. Shocked and bewildered, officialdom had to wake up to an intolerable state of affairs, and to the new phenomenon of Lajpat Rai's Lahore, Lajpat Rai's Punjab.

And it was not all imported or vicarious resentment. The Punjab had its own grievances in the new land measures.

A measure restricting the alienation of land had been enacted. This evoked much hostility, but it was supported by the classes which it sheltered in its ample schedules as "agriculturist". Lajpat Rai and The Punjabee opposed the bill. At the next Congress session a resolution was passed against this measure. Later on when the Congress saw that a large "body of Muslim landholders supported the measure as affording just protection to their rights, it dropped its opposition.

Far more intense was the opposition to Ibbetson's Land Colonisation Bills. Here Hindu, Sikh and Muslim, urban and rural, agriculturist and non-agriculturist joined hands, and soon the Punjab was in the grip of a whirlwind agrarian agitation.

A few days after the Barisal conference, the Congress met for its annual session at Banaras. For the first time "left" and "right", then styled "extremists" and "moderates", openly clashed.

In Bengali the new spirit had been visible in the columns of Aurobindo's Bandemataram. In Maharashtra Tilak's party decried the moderate methods of Gokhale and his followers. In the Punjab,

Lajpat Rai was already the idol of the people, especially of the younger generation, and he had left little 'doubt in anybody's mind that he was with Tilak and Aurobindo and Bipin Chandra Pal, rather than with Gokhale and Dadabhai Naoroji, and Pherozeshah Mehta.

At Banaras the new spirit loomed large; all round there was far more of fervour than had been witnessed at previous Congress sessions. The presidential procession with its enthusiastic scenes was a flattering homage to tie moderate leader, Gokhale; but the fervour was engendered not by moderatism but entirely by the new spirit In the presidential carriage with Gokhale was his colleague in England, Lajpat Rai, and he recorded afterwards:

> "The citizens of Banaras gave a splendid reception to Gokhale. I was sitting in the same carriage with him. On the footboard stood a volunteer whose shouts deafened the ears. Looking at this reception one thought that the nation's evil days were coming to an end. Gokhale was joyous. If only we had worked, there would be enough appreciation and fervour amongst the people observed he, and tears were seen in his eyes. It was a wonderful sight indeed."

Lal-Bal-Pal

The year nineteen hundred and six but underlined the changed temper as seen at Banaras. The more virile element had definitely made its presence felt at the Congress session in the holy city. An annual iteration of neatly drafted resolutions,, supported by superb oratory with rounded periods that wan applause and yet left the people cold and the alien ruler unperturbed, could no longer do. Not words but dynamic action, mass agitation that would know no rest till it had won something worthwhile. A basic law of dynamics about action and reaction being opposite and equal could be seen very well illustrated.

The bureaucracy under Curzon had been in a correspondingly high mood, feeding the resentment against his' Universities Act and against his bisection of Bengal, and against numerous other unpopular doings the cumulative effect of which was enormous.

Curzon went away in 1905, but the imperious mood continued as part of the legacy left behind by him. The New Party - as the very assertive school of thought! represented "by the advanced nationalists in Bengal by Pal and Aurobindo and the Bande matararn, in Maharashtra by Tilak and his Kesari, and by Lajpat Rai and The Punjabee in the Punjab came to be characterised - were intensifying their campaign of swadeshi and boycott. The vows and pledges in Bengal, originally binding "till the annulment of the partition", were now made absolute.

The boycott of British goods, particularly of British cloth, was becoming stiffen The indents to Manchester, made not by political enthusiasts but by hard-headed Marwaris when they ushered in their new year, in the winter of 1906 shrank very nearly to the vanishing point. The boycott was far from becoming as ridiculous as its critics had prophesied. On the contrary, it was being effectively preached from a thousand house-tops and being enforced by a thousand volunteer pickets. The national education movement was affecting the mind of the students. They picketed White-way Laidlaw's in Calcutta, and fashionable ladies had to accept with good grace their brotherly supplication, unless they were prepared literally to trample over the pickets' bodies.

Curzon's fiat had created a new province in East Bengal. But when the Lieutenant-Governor of this province wanted to buy a piece of Manchester mull in Barisal, his men were told at the stores that they would have first to obtain the writ of Ashwini Kumar Dutta, the New Party leader of East Bengal! Bipin Chandra Pal, as the chief orator of the New Party, was widening the scope of "boycott" so as to include all avoidable association with the alien ruler or his governmental machine — to signify in fact an attitude that a decade later was adopted under the colourless negative label of "non-cooperation" with Pal's customary vehemence attacking the NCO programmes.

Things were taking a serious turn, and the bureaucracy seemed definitely jittery. In a fluster they were led to so many things that revealed symptoms of psychosis. There was an infamous circular regarding students and the Swadeshi Movement in Calcutta about which the leading Anglo-Indian paper, The Statesman, wrote:

> "We should really like to know the name of the imbecile official at whose instance the Lieutenant-Governor sanctioned this order. Government has blundered apparently into a childish and futile policy which can only have the effect of manufacturing an army of martyrs."

Most infamous of the many circulars, perhaps, was the one in East Bengal that forbade the shouting of Bande mataram in public. A direct result of this circular was the crisis precipitated when the Bengalis assembled all their heavy artillery in a provincial conference at Barisal in April. Surendranath was arrested and the meeting broken up by regulation lathis. There was intense resentment against the brutalities at Barisal. In Lajpat Rai's Lahore, as we have seen, a public meeting-voiced this resentment promptly and vigorously, and Lahore's lead was followed in principal towns in different parts of India. Bengal, Maharashtra and the Punjab were regarded as the strongholds of "extremism". Undoubtedly the Punjab was in the thick of the fight.

The movement acquired fresh strength from the lathis used at Barisal. The year was to close with the Congress session at Calcutta. The moderate leaders of the Congress had reason to be nervous. To prevent things passing completely into the hands of the "extremists" they got Dadabhai Naoroji to come from England and guide the deliberations from the presidential chair, even though that meant for him the adventure of a long voyage in his 82nd year. Dadabhai was respected by the extremist wing as much as by the moderates. His presence prevented the cleavage from becoming patent though the differences in outlook between the two groups could escape no discerning eye.

On the whole, the Calcutta Congress was a further triumph for the more virile elements. Its resolutions endorsed swadeshi and boycott (though not in the all-out Pal style) and national education, the three-fold programme of the Bengal school. What is more, Dadabhai Naoroji himself in his presidential address, hit upon a potent word which was to serve as an even greater rallying cry than swadeshi- It was he who first uttered the word "Swaraj" from the Congress rostrum. "Swaraj, Swadeshi, Boycott" now became the thrice-sacred mantram of nationalism.

Writes Lajpat Rai: "This session, satisfied the nationalists-very much, whilst some of the moderates were grumbling at the impropriety of the ideas so boldly expounded by the leader whom they had brought over from England in the expectancy of having a moderate address. But that was the only possible thing to do in Bengal at that juncture. Any other course would have jeopardised the very existence of the Congress.

A tonsorial casualty deserves to be noted here. Like many of the Arya Samaj leaders of his day Lajpat Rai had worn a long beard for many years. Bengali crowds had of course given a most enthusiastic welcome to Dadabhai Naoroji, the President-elect. But the Lal-Bal-Pal phase in Indian politics had already set in, and Bengal of course was overwhelmingly aligned with this school, and emphatic evidence of this was afforded by the extraordinary fervour with which teeming, crowds paid their homage to their two idols from Maharashtra and the Punjab. As he alighted from the train at the Howrah railway station the beard served a distinctive emblem for the crowds to spot the Lala from a distance.

Yet, at the start of the Congress session when the chairman called upon Lajpat Rai to second Dadabhai's name for the presidentship it was someone without a beard that walked up to the rostrum — The audience felt puzzled — but as soon as the would-be seconder opened his lips, his voice dispelled all doubts. The voice that could hold such sway was the real Lala, not the beard.

He had arrived at the house of his host, Rai Bahadur Rallia Ram (a Punjabi and Arya Samajist, serving as Superintending Engineer in the Bengal Eastern Railway), with a flowing beard, and from there arrived at the Congress session with a clean chin. In fact many of his admirers who had assembled in the evening to meet him at his host's residence had to keep enquiring — but where is Lalaji himself, till in puzzlement they heard the Lala's voice come out of a beardless source! He never again grew a beard, though his moustache remained intact till the last.

The closing months of 1906, as also the early ones of 1907, were quite a stormy period. In the Punjab and resounding as were the echoes of the boycott started in Bengal, more important than these and far more important than the resentment amongst the educated classes against the Curzonian ways was the crop of grievances raised by the Lieutenant-Governor. Sir Denzil Ibbetson, through his Canal Colonies legislation and his measures increasing water rates and land revenue. In Bengal the movement was mostly a bhadralok affair; in the Punjab an agrarian situation was fast developing.

Bengal had its Bande mataram edited by Aurobindo and Maharashtra Tilak's Kesari, the Punjab had The Punjabee, with Athavale as its editor, but guided and controlled, as everyone knew, by Lajpat Rai. He was himself virtually the editor. His morning routine usually included a visit to the press to pars the final proofs. The Punjabee, started as a weekly, had now three issues instead of one every week. Its circulation and influence were increasing. The Government's annoyance with it was naturally increasing too. Every now and then there were rumours that The Punjabee was getting into trouble; but though it took a bold line, its proofs were scrutinised by Lajpat Rai as a careful lawyer.

At last, however, the Government initiated a prosecution against its editor, K. K. Athavale, and its printer, Jaswant Rai Objection was taken to an article calling attention to the mystery surrounding the death of a police constable. This appeared in an issue not seen by Lajpat Rai in proof, otherwise the article might not have been permitted to stand as it was, though it may be doubted whether that could have averted a prosecution against The Punjabee on one ground or another.

The proceedings, as could be expected, make The Punjabee more popular and more influential than ever, particularly as the facts contained in the article were widely believed to be true. The paper enlisted Muslim sympathy too, for the can-stable in whose death it had interested itself was a Mussalman. Jaswant Rai and Athavale were arrested, bailed out, tried, convicted and awarded hard labour.

The Punjabee trial added a good deal to the excitement and the tension in the Punjab. The day its editor and printer were sentenced marked one of the peaks of excitement in Lahore in that period.

Later, the Sessions Court reduced Jaswant Rai's sentence to six months. An appeal was taken to the Chief Court.

About this time Gokhale was touring in northern India. Lajpat Rai and Gokhale now were generally supposed to belong to different schools of political thought, but the mutual personal esteem had no whit been affected. Lajpat Rai invited Gokhale to Lahore on behalf of the Indian Association (of which he was the President then) and Gokhale readily accepted the invitation. He arrived in Lahore the day of the exciting happenings just described — when Jaswant Rai was jailed for two years and bailed out. The crowd that in the morning cheered The Punjabee heroes and jeered at the Anglo-Indian reporter arrived in the afternoon at the railway station to receive Gokhale.

He was given a grand reception. A wave of enthusiasm surged in the crowd. The Punjabee sentences and the continual friction between the crowd and the police had surcharged the atmosphere to a high voltage. But the pleasure of such an enthusiastic reception and of sky-rending shouts was somewhat marred for Gokhale when the procession arrived in Anarkali, and heroes of the day, Jaswant Rai and Athavale (already enlarged on bail) joined in, and the crowd without consulting either their wishes or Gokhale's convenience, simply lifted them and put them in the same carriage in which Gokhale, and, at his insistence, Lajpat Rai were.

During The Punjabee trial came a great bereavement. Dr. Jai Chand of Dehra Dun married to Lajpat Rai's only daughter, Parvati Devi, died, leaving behind a young widow and an only son just a few days old. Getting the news in the court room while in the middle of arguments for The Punjabee friends, Lajpat Rai felt the heavy blow; but with characteristic stoicism he refused to interrupt his work. He gave his son appropriate instructions, sent him off to Dehra Dun, and himself went on with the day's work.

Most of his domestic affection was ever after reserved for the widowed Parvati. He interested her in his own work; she was quite a success at public meetings, and went to prison in the Non-cooperation Movement. Eight years after his "death, when the Congress fought elections to the reformed provincial assemblies, she was elected an MLA from the Lahore women's constituency; but soon after she developed a serious illness and died in January 1938.

Punjab in Revolt

The year nineteen hundred and seven sent the wave of agitation sweeping virtually through the entire land. In the Punjab it took on the form decidedly of an agrarian revolt and was generally described as the zamindar agitation. The 'zamindar' in the Punjab context mostly connotes a peasant proprietorship. The new land measures had created serious discontent and day by day this was becoming more and more vocal.

The Canal Colonies bill created a stir among the peasantry of the canal-irrigated area; of this ferment Lyallpur, the principal Canal Colony town was the natural focus. In the western Punjab, Rawalpindi was as bad as Lyallpur, for there the Government had, most unreasonably, enhanced the land revenue as assessed by their own settlement officer. Lajpat Rai voiced the grievances but did not quite plunge into this agrarian agitation. He did not keep aloof either — the zamindars would not permit him to.

Ajit Singh, the 'Bharat Mata' firebrand, like his brother Kishan Singh (father of Bhagat Singh), had been a student at the Anglo-Sanskrit School, Jalandhar, where Sunder Das, eldest son of the Arya Samaj leader Sain Das, was the headmaster. Ajit Singh was a favourite pupil of his, and in Lajpat Rai's opinion "there can be no doubt it was Lala Sunder Das who first inoculated the two brothers with the germs of patriotism". Lajpat Rai had known Kishan Singh as a relief worker under him in the 1897 famine in the Central Provinces. He did excellent work there. When he returned with a batch of orphans, he was made superintendent of the newly started orphanage at Lahore. Lajpat Rai was the secretary of the orphanage for several years and had often occasion to see the superintendent, but does not seem to have been much impressed by his brother.

Ajit Singh, writes, "he was at that time a student of the DAV College and had rather spendthrift habits... To me Kishan Singh appeared to be superior to his brother. At the 1906 Congress Ajit Singh was noticed at the meetings of the extremist group. He had besides started taking part in public debates and was writing for the press. With Sufi Amba Parshad he founded, in 1907, a society, called the 'Bharat Mata', and young men under its auspices openly promulgated the doctrines of the extreme wing and made vigorous speeches against the British Government."

Lajpat Rai had no connection with 'Bharat Mata', and the young men conducting it did various things that he could not possibly have approved of. All the same, the young men looked up to him for help and were convinced that Lajpat Rai knew them to be patriotic, a claim they well understood to be irresistible for him.

"About this time," writes Lajpat Rai, "Ajit Singh approached me repeatedly for financial aid, though he did not care to fulfil the conditions I laid down."

Ajit Singh and his 'Bharat Mata' took a prominent part in the zamindars' agitation. A Jat by birth, he had every right to speak in the name of the peasantry, but unlike many other Jats taking part in this agitation he and his brother were not merely interested in the repeal of the Colonies Act — they were using this agitation for creating discontent against Firangi Raj.

Ajit Singh was developing into an effective agitator. He toured about and addressed meetings all over the province, and everywhere people flocked to hear him. The Lyallpur Canal Colony, as one of the areas directly affected by the Colonies bill, was worked up more easily by the agitators than most other places. Amongst those concentrating on this area was Chowdhury Shahabuddin, later a knighted Speaker of the Punjab Legislative Assembly. Then he was a practising lawyer and took a very active part in the zamindar agitation.

Towards the end of March 1907 (or at the beginning of April) the Zamindar Association of Lyallpur sent an invitation to Lajpat Rai — and followed it up with repeated reminders for an occasion when a cattle fair was being held at Lyallpur. Shahabuddin called upon Lajpat Rai personally to press the invitation on him. On April 21 Lajpat Rai arrived there accompanied by Rai Bahadur Sukh Dayal (afterwards a High Court Judge in Jammu and Kashmir), Bakhshi Tek Chand, Ram Bhaj Dutt Chowdhury and Jaswant Rai.

Lyallpur and Rawalpindi became the storm centres. Ajit Singh had addressed audiences at Rawalpindi a few days before the Lyallpur meeting. Conspicuous amongst the local leaders at

Rawalpindi were Hans Raj Sawhney and his brother Gurdas Ram Sawhney, both distinguished members of the bar and both active leaders of the Arya Samaj. Actuated by patriotic impulses, the Sawhney brothers were keen on politics, and attended annual meetings of the Indian National Congress. What is more to the point, they were among the ten guarantors of The Punjabee, which might be an added reason for the paper to take a keen interest in the 'Pindi affairs' — For some months the Deputy Commissioner of Rawalpindi, Mr. Agnew, has been subjected to scathing criticism in the news and editorial columns of The Punjabee. One of Ajit Singh's meetings at Rawalpindi was presided over by Gurdas Ram Sawhney. His brother, Hans Raj, and two other members of the bar, Jariki Nath Kaul and Khazan Singh, also spoke at this meeting which had been convened by yet another leading light of the Rawalpindi bar, Amolak Ram.

All five of these gentlemen were asked by the District Magistrate to show cause why they should not be disbarred for having participated in the meeting.

This notice caused a tremendous stir throughout the Punjab, for Lala Hans Raj and Lala Amolak Ram were much respected leaders of the province. Lajpat Rai arrived in Rawalpindi a day prior to the hearing of the notice and learnt that the town had decided to observe a hartal whilst the court heard the notice.

The atmosphere in Rawalpindi seemed extremely tense. The notice to the five lawyers excited so much interest that on the day fixed for its hearing a huge concourse — estimates put it at 20,000 — was seen at the court compound. A sort of anti-climax came when the District Magistrate — who arrived a couple of hours after the normal starting time — announced that "under instructions from the Punjab Government" further proceedings were being stayed. Lajpat Rai records "the crowd received this by cheering, and the news travelled quick like lightning."

Lajpat Rai was pressed to address the crowd — or at least to accompany it in a procession through the streets. He declined, though agreeing to address a regular public meeting in the evening.

While still in the Bar Room he heard that "the mob had forced its way into the bungalows of the Deputy Commissioner and the

District Magistrate". Though messengers rushed to stop such activity it was believed agents provocateurs were at work to incite violence.

Things moved fast on both sides — rumours fastest of all.

"We were still in the court when we learnt that the military had been sent for to suppress the rioting and to arrest the rioters. We were told also that a Pathan regiment had shown some unwillingness in getting ready. A Pathan came to me saying that, such and such regiment awaited my orders. I laughed and put him off — I suspected that man to be a spy. The military put down the rioting and cast a large number of people into the lock-up, including some very prominent citizens and some educated young men. We were getting all the news but what could we do?"

The public meeting to be held in the evening was disallowed and given up. The next day's round up included Lajpat Rai's host — Amolak Ram and the other notice case lawyers. Bail was refused and Lajpat Rai rushed back to Lahore to move the Chief Court. Even there very unusual things happened. We read in Lajpat Rai's account:

> "The judge decided that the application should be heard by a division bench, and that in the meanwhile the Government Advocate would ascertain from the Rawalpindi District Magistrate why the bail should not be granted. Before the application came up for hearing, the District Magistrate concerned came to the court with a letter from the Officer Commanding at Rawalpindi addressed to the Chief Court Judges which presumably said- that if the arrested leaders were let out on bail there might be a revolt among the Indian troops. The counsel for the accused were not permitted to see this letter though they applied for a copy. After formally hearing the arguments the judges decided not to allow bail."

The 'Mutiny'

Because of the Mutiny a great fear broods over the European community in India.... The Mutiny — that nightmare of innumerable savage hands suddenly upraised to kill helpless women and children — has been responsible for the waves of hysteria which from time to time have swept the European community and for a while made it a pathological case for pity and sympathy.... And there can be no doubt that the dramatic and heightened fashion in which the Mutiny has been pictured to us has been responsible for deeds that would have been impossible to Englishmen in their right frame of mind.

To understand how the decision to deport Lajpat Rai under *lettre de cachet* was taken, we must first examine the psychotic condition of the Anglo-Indian mind in 1907, for the Lieutenant-Governor and the Governor-General could not altogether be proof when the mind of the community fell a prey to a pandemic contamination.

The Anglo-Indian ruler had become so used to smooth easy ways, and to managing things on the strength of prestige, that on finding opposition gathering strength daily and hostile forces confronting him, he soon became panicky. In certain situations the Anglo-Indian mind was prone to fall a victim to the psychological legacy — 1857-complex — of the 'mutiny' days. So in 1907 memories of 1857 began to haunt the Anglo-Indian mind. From 1857 to 1907 was exactly half a century. How ominous! Sure enough the same forces would be let loose again.

The Indian troops would again revolt and unnameable things be done alike to soldier and civilian, even to woman and child, in cold blood! The Anglo-Indian press too showed acute symptoms of the "mutiny complex". At the clubs and messes gossip was day and night busy only with this topic. Sahibs, burra and smaller fry, saw blue devils everywhere (reds were not yet born!) — the ghosts of 1857! They could swallow any story if it worked in the mutiny motif. Unscrupulous informers found this rather helpful.

The Anglo-Indian press could be seen drifting towards hysteria even before 1907. The 'tie-up' with 1857 made matters very much worse. The Anglo-Indian daily of Lahore was in a hysteric rage and in its columns were published mad letters that asked for flogging of the educated people involved in political agitation. C. F. Andrews, then new to the ways of Anglo-India — he had not so long ago arrived in India to work as a professor at St. Stephens' College, Delhi — was shocked and wrote a letter of protest. Some time later, even the Bishop of Lahore, Dr. Lefrov, had to protest against the tone of the Anglo-Indian press. Lord Minto himself admitted (in confidential despatches to Whitehall, as we shall presently see), that the tone of these writings was disgracefully low; but the Punjab Government refused permission for the prosecution of the offenders.

Doped daily by these rabid prints, the Sahibs were quite willing to believe that there were plans afoot for a repetition of 1857 — that quite a hundred thousand sepoys waited only for word from Lajpat Rai! The 1857 holocaust had started on May 10; for the dread half-centenary repeat performance too, May 10 became ominous. It distinctly had the 'ides of March' odour about it. As May 10 drew near, nightmarish shrieks could be heard hysterically insisting that something drastic must be done immediately. For that fateful date, it is said, the Sahibs at Lahore had made *bandobust* for their families to be given shelter in the Fort. The railway authorities too were said to have been asked to be ready to meet any emergent call.

Keir Hardie who visited India in 1907 found ample evidence of this pathological state of mind. At Delhi the municipal tax had been doubled. Keir Hardie recalls this and observes:

> "There was agitation and the tax was withdrawn. On May 10 there was a street fight between natives, over in five minutes. Reports were disseminated at the European Club that dissolute Eurasians and natives had risen and were butchering Europeans. In the native city business and pleasure went on as usual."

What amazed Keir Hardie most was, however, an Etawah happening in which Lajpat Rai's name figured. The episode afterwards came to be known as the 'Etawah hoax' and affords a helpful glimpse into the working of the Anglo-Indian mind in 1907.

It appears that at Etawah in the United Provinces the Hindu and Muslim parts of officialdom had for some time been working at cross purposes. The Hindus got the Muslim Kotwal transferred and succeeded in importing a Brahmin Deputy Superintendent of Police in his place. The Muslim-dominated departments and officials were therefore at loggerheads with the police. Nothing seems, however, to have happened (writes Keir Hardie) till the Lala Lajpat Rai affair arose in the Punjab. Shortly after the Magistrate (Mr. Rose) was informed confidentially by the *Tehsildar* (a Muslim) that they had reasons to believe that a subscription list on behalf of Lala Lajpat Rai had been circulated amongst the local Hindu officials, notably by Mr. Shyam Bihari Misra, Deputy Superintendent of Police, Mr. Pushri Prasad, Deputy Collector, and certain vakils, notably Mr. Jaswant Singh, a Punjabi pleader practising at Etawah and that these people had in addition been carrying on a seditious correspondence with the various sections of the Arya Samaj. It was stated that it was possible to intercept such correspondence and immediate steps were taken to do so. Keir Hardie tells us:

> "In due course nineteen letters were intercepted or at least were produced by Khalil (specially employed informer) as having been intercepted....most of them being of a very inflammatory and incriminating nature, though some were of a private nature, an important feature being the signature of one or other of the Hindu officials mentioned above. The Commissioner of the Division, Mr. Coble, then made further enquiries and assured everybody of the apparent genuine nature of documents. Mr. Sharpe, the Director of the Provincial Criminal Investigation Department, was summoned. He also agreed as to the seriousness of the case and advised a simultaneous search and enquiry at three other centres, viz., Unao, Kheri and Amritsar."

Meanwhile, however, a very extraordinary thing occurred. Mr. Rose had evidently been talking over the situation with the local commandant of volunteers, Capt. Adamson. There can be no doubt that all the local officers took a serious view of the case and were fairly hoaxed into the idea that the city was in the verge of rising and that the police were unreliable.

At all events the upshot of their discussions with the captain of the defenders of their hearths and homes was that the latter warned the volunteers at Tundla and Cawnpore to be in readiness to come to their rescue when wired for. In the interval, however, both Mr. Coble and Mr. Sharpe had arrived on the scene and they were followed shortly by the Inspector-General of Police himself. The latter for some unexplained reason took a completely different view of the case.... It is certain that he... after a very cursory investigation announced his opinion that the letters were all forgeries and he succeeded in eliciting from the Inspector responsible for taking up the case that Khalil was certainly a man of bad character with a reputation as a swindler but without any convictions against him.... An acute difference of opinion between the officials making investigations arose. Mr. Rose was said to have protested that he was prepared to put the matter to test in a court of law. However, the Government accepted the Inspector-General's view and a warrant of arrest was issued against Khalil, who absconded.

The Government reprimanded Mr. Braully and dealt more severely with Mr. Rose, perhaps because of the volunteer fiasco. The Anglo-Indian officialdom could be made to swallow almost any preposterous story readily if the name of Lajpat Rai was somehow worked in. It imagined the whole town of Etawah as ready for a rising. "The loyalty of the police had been tampered with." It is said the Government was asked to make use of the Regulation of 1818 and had almost agreed to do so. Keir Hardie says that deportation warrants had actually been issued.

The Punjab Government was in a like frame of mind when it got Lajpat Rai deported.

The initiative for the arrest of Lajpat Rai of course came from the Lieutenant-Governor of the Punjab, Sir Denzil Ibbetson, though it is not clear whose flash of genius it was that first thought of this new use for Regulation III of 1818. Ibbetson's own reactions to the stormy events of 1907 were reflected in a memorandum he drew up then. Minto sent on the gist of this to Morley, as we shall see later. The Indian Sedition Committee (1917), presided over by Justice Sir S. T. Rowlatt, examined this document and summarised portions of it in their report. After giving a short of regionwise summary of the minute, the Rowlatt report observed:

> "The Lieutenant-Governor held that some of the leaders looked to driving the British out of the country

> or at any rate from power either by force or by the passive resistance of the people as a whole, and that the method by which they had set themselves to bring in the Government machine to a standstill was by endeavouring to stir up a strong feeling of racial hatred. He considered the whole situation 'exceedingly' dangerous and urgently demanding remedy."

The remedy adopted was the deportation of Lajpat Rai and Ajit Singh, as leaders of the movement, under the provisions of Regulation III of 1818, The proposed Canal Colony legislation too was vetoed by the Government of India but the suggestion that the root of the trouble was agrarian was not accepted by the Secretary of State, Lord (then Mr. John) Morley. Speaking in the House of Commons on June 6, 1907, he said:

> "There were 28 meetings known to have been held by the leading agitators in the Punjab between 1st March and 1st May. Of these five only related, even ostensibly, to agricultural grievances, the remaining 23 were all purely political."

Maintaining that the agitation in the Punjab was essentially agrarian in character and that the underlying causes were economic, Lajpat Rai thus corrected Morley's facts:

> "The number of meetings held from March 1 to May 1907, was, at the lowest calculation, at least double of 28, or perhaps treble, and most of them related even ostensibly to agricultural grievances; the number of purely political meetings could not have exceeded ten or twelve."

Lajpat Rai's deportation was readily sanctioned by the Viceroy, Lord Minto. The 'Liberal' Secretary of State, 'honest John' (Lord Morley) was informed after the warrant had been issued. All the same, he defended it firmly in the House of Commons. What passed between the Viceroy and the Secretary of State may be seen partly in Lord Morley's Recollections and partly in Lady Minto's India, Minto and Morley 1905-10.

On May 2, 1907 Minto wrote to Morley:

> "Sir Henry Cotton not long ago asked you in the House, of Commons about some letters which appeared in the Civil and Military Gazette. They were disgracefully low in tone, just the sort of writing to stir up racial hatred. The Punjab Government decided not to prosecute and would not allow private prosecution. They may have been right, but it makes one's blood boil to know that a leading English newspaper could publish such productions. We have written to the Lieutenant-Governor suggesting that, though no definite action is to be taken, he should see the Editor and point out the harm that is being done."

Six days later, Minto telegraphed to Morley:

> "Telegram (deciphered) Minto to Morley. May 8.
>
> Three days ago we received a weighty and urgent minute from Ibbetson on the present political situation in the Punjab.... He describes a state of things giving rise to the greatest apprehensions. Everywhere the extremists openly and continuously preach sedition, both in the press and at largely attended public meetings convened by them, while well-disposed classes stand aghast at our inaction and will before long, in Ibbetson's opinion, begin to despise a Government which permits sedition to flourish unrebuked and submits to open and organised insult."

The campaign of sedition assumes two main forms. In the towns of Lahore, Amritsar, Pindi, Ferozepore, Multan and other places, has openly advocated the murder of high officials, and he and others have urged the people to rise, attack the English, and be free. In the country systematic efforts are being made, to corrupt the yeomanry from whom the army is recruited. Special attention is given to Sikhs and military pensioners; seditious leaflets are circulated to Sikh villages, and, at a public meeting at Ferozepore, where disaffection was openly preached, the men of the Sikh regiments stationed there were invited to attend, and several hundred were present. The Sikhs are told that they saved India for us in the Mutiny, that we are now ill-treating them, and that this is a judgement on them for betraying their country in her war of independence.... It is alleged that we wish to crush the flourishing indigenous industries of cotton and sugar cane; it is said that we have taken the people's money and given them paper in return, and the villagers are asked who will cash our currency notes when we are gone. The people are urged to combine to withhold payment of Government revenue, water rates, and other dues; to refuse supplies, carriages and other help to Government officers on tour, and Native soldiers and police are pilloried as 'traitors' and adjured to quit the service of the Government.

This propaganda is organised and directed by a secret Committee of the Arya Samaj, a society, originally religious, which has, in the Punjab, a strong political tendency.

The head and centre of the entire movement is Lala Lajpat Rai, a Khatri pleader, who has visited England as the Congress-representative of the Punjab. He is a revolutionary and a political enthusiast who is inspired by the most intense hatred of the British Government.

The Viceroy was as far away from truth in describing Lajpat Rai's political affiliations, as he was from accuracy when he called this Aggarwal a "Khatri" pleader.

The cipher telegram continues:

> "He keeps himself in the background, but the Lieutenant-Governor has been assured by nearly every Native gentleman who has spoken to him on the subject that he is the organiser-in-chief. His most prominent agent in disseminating sedition is Ajit Singh, formerly a schoolmaster, employed last year by the supposed Russian spy, Lasseff. He is the most violent of the speakers at political meetings; he has frequently advocated active resistance to Government and his utterances are largely directed towards exciting discontent among the agricultural" classes and the soldiery. After dwelling upon the objections to

prosecuting these men under the ordinary law and the impossibility under present conditions of producing satisfactory evidence of what has been actually said at a meeting, the Lieutenant-Governor made a formal official application for the issue of warrants against them under Regulation III of 1818, and laid stress upon the extreme urgency of immediate action, as the situation, instead of improving, shows signs of growing seriously worse.

The case was considered in Council yesterday, and warrants have been issued today for the deportation of Lajpat Rai and Ajit Singh to Mandalay, special measures being taken to avoid the possibility of popular demonstrations *en route*.

In my opinion, and in that of the whole of my Council, this action was imperatively necessary, and the present emergency is so great that I may be forced to issue an ordinance under section 23 of the Act of 1861 to regulate public meetings, chiefly with the object of obtaining full and accurate reports of the utterances of the speakers, and in extreme cases to prohibit meetings altogether. It is impossible in the absence of shorthand reporting of vernacular languages to get correct reports of speeches. We have to trust to oral reports of informers smuggled in, and do not consider that, in face of the multitude of witnesses who would be brought to contradict informers, we could obtain conviction for sedition.

Information received today shows that systematic attempts are being made to tamper with the troops in the Pindi division, but the troops themselves are quite satisfactory."

Following up the lengthy code telegram from which we have just been quoting, Lord Minto wrote to the Secretary of State on May 8:

"...I have had some long talks with Lord K. Kitchner and from what he has heard, no mischievous effects

> whatever would appear to have been produced on the troops, but the feeling in the country districts in the Punjab is evidently bad, as the 11th Bengal Lancers thought it advisable to recall some survey parties they had sent out, owing to the disagreeable attitude of the villagers.
>
> Though we have heard rumours from time to time of bad feeling in the Punjab, we were quite taken by surprise by Ibbetson's information... No one, I suppose, knows the Punjab better than he, and I should not think him in the least inclined to exaggerate. At the same time at the present moment I cannot see any danger in the nature of a rising from an unarmed population as long as the Army is loyal. We shall in all probability have further riots, and there may be bad ones, but now that we are warned we ought to be able to take ample precautions as to these."

There was bad news from the Frontier too, as we learn in: the next paragraph:

> "In the Peshawar district there is cause for anxiety owing to the possibility of the fanatical Mahommedan sympathy of the frontier tribes with the Mahommedan population of the province.... As far as danger goes it is, in my opinion, confined to the Punjab and the North, and Lord K. has taken every military precaution ...."

The neurotic condition of the Anglo-Indian mind at this moment is also revealed in this dispatch from Lord Minto:

> "My own feeling continues he is that a great deal of the unrest is due to the anniversary of the mutiny. We have been told to expect trouble between the 8th and the 11th. I think the mutiny broke out at Meerut on the 10th, and at Delhi on the 11th, and I feel pretty convinced that, putting political causes aside, recollections of 1857 are making the present year an exceptional one."

Two paragraphs later on the neurotic state of the Anglo-Indian mind is admitted more clearly:

> "The information I get from Calcutta points to a nervous hysterical Anglo-Indian feeling there which I can only call very" unpalatable, the beginning of much of the same feeling which it is not pleasant to read of in Lord Canning's time during the Mutiny. We are infinitely stronger now than we were then. On the other hand, the communication of ideas and native public opinion has become much more easy and universal than it was in 1857, and the mistakes our officers make are much more generally known, and are known by people who are much more aware of their own rights, and are far less ready to accept such mistakes as a matter of course. At the present moment we have to deal with a crisis which I earnestly hope will not last long and during which we must be very firm and very just. The factors that we have to control and to conciliate are so inflammable that we cannot afford to throw a chance away. Any general belief that we are undecided or weak would be fatal. But the more I see, the more convinced I am that we cannot continue to govern India with any hope of tranquillity until we give her educated classes a chance of a greater share in the government of the country...."

Morley promptly replied-just general observations that left action to the people on the spot Morley to Minto:

> "May 9 — If looks from your Punjab news as though we were approaching deep waters... Well, we must make the best of it. If rows go on, I dare say some stern things will have to be done. You may be sure of my firm support, even if the sternest things should unluckily be needed. It may turn out that you will want that support not only against sedition-mongers, but also against your law-and-order people, who are responsible for at least as many fooleries in history as the revolutionists are. I only hope that plenty of

> deliberation and comprehensive balancing of pros and cons may precede any strong measures.... If there be a scintilla of real evidence that seditious rags are infecting the Native Army, nobody would refuse suppression. Only you won't forget that in moments of excitement, such as this may become people are uncommonly liable to confuse suspicions and possibilities with certainty and reality... ."

About the mischief that the hysteria of the press was working:

> "You have no idea of the sensational headlines in some of our most widely-read prints! One would have supposed that Pindi was a scene of fire and sword, carnage and rape, as if it had been the siege of Magdeburg in the Thirty Years' War. Idiotic, isn't it?"

Morley gave his imprimatur to all sorts of reactionary and coercive measures; but the ghost of his former liberal self was not perfectly laid to rest and kept on pointing the finger of reproach, and whispering the names of various Czars and other tyrants. Some of this whispering one can overhear in the records of his thinking that Morley was sending to Minto. Thus, about the reactionary policy in India:

> 'The question is the Future. This like the Czar and the Duma. Are we to say: You shall have reforms when you are quiet. Meanwhile we won't listen to a word you say. Our reform projects are hung up.... People here who have been shouting against the Grand Dukes in Petersburg for bullying the Duma, will shout equally vociferously against you and me if we don't, in our own sphere borrow the Grand Duke policy...."

To understand the 1907 doings of the Government in the Punjab we have to watch carefully Morley and Minto and to some extent Ibbetson. Morley had a reputation of being liberal, almost a radical, but he bade goodbye to that reputation — except inasmuch as it was found useful in disarming opposition to the new coercive policy. Minto was conservative and reactionary, but usually free from, hysteria. He could not, however, altogether remain unaffected. Hysteria broke out as a sort of pandemic among the European community in India. At any rate he found that exaggerated accounts were helpful in getting things done entirely his own way, but with the Morley imprimatur, Ibbetson was, of course, utterly reactionary.

Some people even suspected that he was creating trouble deliberately to be able to get a free hand with all sorts of agitation. A more charitable view would be that taken by Morley, when Ibbetson, not long after the deportations, went on leave to England in shattered health and had to be operated upon by a surgeon. Morley thus put down his impressions of the Punjab Lt.-Governor:

> ".... Ibbetson came to see me — rather a wonderful recovery, it strikes me. He is clear-headed and firm of purpose according to his lights and experience: that he reads his experience-aright, I don't feel so sure. It cannot be easy for any man to waken up to new times, after a whole generation of good honest hard labour in old times. It is your hard lot to have to carry things by the agency of men whose feeling is inclined to be backward. Well, we must make the best of it. I talked to him a little of the difficulties — not considerable at present, but very real — of the S.S., and hope I opened his mind, though it is a hard mind, I suspect..... The plain truth is that if there were any solid and substantial reason for believing India is drifting into a dangerous condition, and if that can be decently established, then — so far as opinion in Parliament and the country is concerned — we can do what we please."

Morley had his doubts that any such "solid and substantial reasons" existed when all they had to offer him was hearsay and at best the oral reports of informers smuggled into public-meetings.

Minto had developed a clever technique of handling Morley, and it succeeded exceedingly well for a while. He talked of the articles of war, of shooting for sedition after summary trial,, and then as a concession he would be content with a press measure! Minto was very much aware of the success of this, technique. He wrote to his wife:

"June 6 (Shimla). I cannot help being amused at The Times which arrived last week. They think that everything has been done by Morley. He has backed me up splendidly, but he diet not initiate any action here: I have had to take the whole responsibility of everything. With regard to the deportation of Lajpat Rai, he (Morley) had not even time to express an opinion. The Ordinance 'proclaiming' certain districts was absolutely my own act. The power to 'proclaim' rests only with the Viceroy personally...."

Minto was not far wrong when towards the end of his term he wrote to his wife:

"As a matter of fact I believe I have gained my point in everything since I have been here, but it has generally been by not losing my temper when I should have been thoroughly justified in doing so, often by asserting myself in the most courteous language, and always by humouring the personality with whom I have had to deal."

The brilliant Morley was jockeyed into the Minto policy by the none too brilliant but rather astute Viceroy. Probably he himself began to suspect that the policy he had fathered was really the ugly progeny of somebody else. The putative father made some exhibitions of temper in the Recollections in which one could trace the history of the widening gulf between the Secretary of State and the Viceroy. As early as August 1907 Morley seemed to be getting fed up with Minto's men.

They have reads the jotting for August 23, "just sent me your press telegram of yesterday. It startles me that even hard Tchinovniks like your — and your — should so far forget that they are the servants and agents of Parliament in a free country, and should dream that a S.S. could live one hour after the assembling of Parliament who should have assented to these new provisions. I see that — says that this drastic power of muzzling an agitator will save the necessity of 'urging deportation'. He must have forgotten what I very explicitly told him, that I would not sanction deportation except for a man of whom there was solid reason to believe that violent disorder was the direct and deliberately planned result of his action. The very men who resisted you lib your Arundel reforms — the most admirable and prudent thing that has been done in our time! The very men, or the sort of men,, who urged us to take advantage of disorder at Lahore and Pindi, as a plea for dropping Arundel reforms! And then, at a time when the Cabinet is dispersed, the lawyers are dispersed, and my Council is half depleted, they give me a short week in which some of the most delicate and thorny points in the whole range of law and politics are to be disposed of. I dare say these executive gentlemen (who are so ready with compliments to one another for sagacity, experience, and all other virtues) can dispose of them in a week or an hour. But then they have the advantage of not having to argue and defend their proposals, I am not in so happy a position. I have often told you of my wicked thought that Strafford was an ideal type, both for governor of Ireland in the seventeenth century and governor of India in the twentieth century. Only they cut off poor Strafford's head, and his idea of government has been in mighty disfavour ever since. My decision will have reached you by wire before this, but I shall be much surprised if it is anything else than a flat veto. If a man's harangue provokes a riot, why don't they lock him up for riot? Have they not police enough? If not police, what then has become of the 'obligatory garrison'? It is all very well to say that these proposals are held by the Govt. of India to be necessary 'for the peace of the country'. But what is the use of saying that, when Parliament won't accept it? And one should think I was abusing the confidence of Parliament if I tried to make them accept it. The former proposal to pass a general Press law to be put in force exclusively on the initiative of the military authorities, was, I should guess, about as stiff a dose as ever was preferred to a British Minister within a hundred years. But this notion of turning a private meeting into a public one almost beats it And the notion of giving the Lt.-Governor or other authority the right of forbidding a speaker whose views he dislikes to open his mouth in a given area! Let go for an honest guillotine and have done with it. And let him try, in Gordon's phrase, to put himself in the skin of an unlucky S.S. who has to oil and grease the slider."

Later he talked of the administrative tandem with the horses in the comic but unhappy Pickwickian situation. "We both try to understand India in the same way, and look at our common business in the same spirit. Yet it is and must be from the necessities of the case, that one horse in the pair is sometimes tugging to the right, and the other to the left; or is it like the tandem in Pickwickike leader turning round to stare at the wheeler?"

When two years after Lajpat Rai's return from his exile in Mandalay, Minto again wanted his sanction for further deportations (in Bengal), Morley did not accept his suggestions readily (Nov. 9, 1909).

"I won't follow you into deportation. You state your case with remarkable force, I admit. But then I comfort myself, in my disquiet at differing from you, by the reflection that perhaps the Spanish Viceroys in the Netherlands, the Austrian Viceroy in Venice, the Bourbon in the Two Sicilies, and a Governor or two in the old American Colonies, used reasoning not wholly dissimilar and not much less forcible. Forgive this affronting parallel It is only the sally of a man who is himself occasionally compared to Stafford, King John, King Charles, Nero, and Tiberius."

A couple of months later, talking again of the policy underlying the deportations:

> "Jan. 27, 1910 — That policy did not work out brilliantly in Russia, and did not save the lives of the Trepoffs, nor did it save Russia from a Duma, the very thing that the Trepoffs and the rest of the 'offs' deprecated.

Whilst he affected airs of gravity on the floor of the Commons when saying that the disclosing of the grounds of Lajpat Rai's imprisonment would not be in 'public interest', as a matter of fact Morley had himself never been told, except in vague hints, what those precious grounds might be!

Again and again Morley had to take shelter behind 'public interest' in refusing to disclose the nature of 'other facts' concerning Lajpat Rai. One finds no clue to these mysterious unravelled 'facts' either in his Recollections or in Mary Minto's compilation — or in any publication by the Government or its apologists — though the passage of time should have rendered it safe long before now to disclose the nature of the dreaded happenings! All Morley could have disclosed would have been the silly stories of Anglo-India — its vision in delirium tremens of another Nana Saheb and a lakh of sepoys awaiting his word.

A European official who out of Christian charity visited Lajpat Rai in his captivity told him that he was believed to have weaned the troops groom their loyalty to the King and that he was taken for a second Nana Saheb.

Yet Lajpat Rai wrote the truth when he said in his representation to the Government of India that he never had an opportunity to mix with the troops. And the Government had certainly no evidence to the contrary. The idea was suggested, in fact, not before his deportation, but afterwards when the Government was known to be looking for some evidence against their victims. The first glimpse of this in the Minto-Morley dispatches — the official source-book of Indian history for this period — is in Minto's letter of August 29:

> Minto to Morley Aug. 29:
>
> "...... I am afraid as regards the Army we have not made the position quite clear ...... It is quite lately, since the arrest of Lajpat Rai, that we have become aware of the attempts to corrupt Native officers and soldiers ...... I have told you that we were entirely taken by surprise and the more we get to know, the worse things seemed."

This particular despatch is one of the most alarmist — even hysterical — of the Minto despatches as Minto was trying his best to get Morley to agree to an odious Press Law — the tone of the despatch and the mentality underlying it will become clearer by a further extract:

> "Here we have the evidence of everyday life, the constant information that comes to us from Native sources, the warnings of Native officers, the statements

> of our own Native informers. I fully admit a great deal of it may be unreliable. If it went home and were sifted we should be told that it was mere hearsay often emanating from personal prejudices. But we cannot disregard everything that is in the air. The mysterious story of the chapatties before the Mutiny might have been a warning, but not evidence. The facts that stare us in the face are the circulation of leaflets and seditious newspapers in the lines of native regiments..."

It is only lately that we have become aware of the tremendous efforts the agitators are making to trade upon the existence of the low rate of pay, the ravages of plague, and anything else they can lay their hands upon to corrupt the loyalty of the Native Army. We know that nothing is being left untried to bring this about...Of course the Articles of War give very great powers, but at the present moment I should be sorry to have a man shot for sedition, though his guilt were proved up to the hilt. So far I believe only two men have been tried for It by Court Martial. With things seething as they are, any extreme action might simply mean provocation. All we can do is to be overy firm, cool and cautious. We are fully warned, and we think certain precautions absolutely necessary to prevent further corruption. The next step of sedition in the Army, if it makes another step, must be Mutiny, and then we can take up the Articles of War in all their strength....".

The chapattis — the leaflets! Nana Saheb — Lajpat Rail Deportation to Burma then of the last Mughal Emperor — now of the Lion of the Punjab — if we may anticipate the adoring sobriquet!

Yet in this despatch there is no direct mention of Lajpat Rai having attempted to seduce the loyal troops; on the contrary, the trend of the writing shows that these attempts followed his arrest and deportation. In appraising these attempts, Minto was no doubt led to exaggeration by the alarmist state of the Anglo-Indian mind in the jubilee year of the 57 'mutiny'; it may be conceded, however, that the deportation of Lajpat Rai had aroused universal resentment amongst Indians and some of this resentment penetrated into the cantonments, though they were believed to have been perfectly inoculated against sedition or disloyalty.

To revert to the Minto despatch to Morley that we were quoting. This interesting despatch contains an interesting story about Habibullah and Lajpat Rai:

> "We have had some curious information too of communications from Lajpat Rai and other agitators with the Amir. As regards the Amir, I attach no value to it at all, he probably puts such letters in his wastepaper basket, if he has one, but it shows how immensely important his friendship is to us ..."

Yes, how immensely important, and therefore how completely it justified the enormous expenditure on the Amir's visit, which looked very extravagant even to Curzon!

5

Rise of a Revolutionary

Election as Congress President

For the third time the question confronted him — should he permit his name to be canvassed for the presidentship of the Indian National Congress? The old difficulty now no longer existed, he being anxious not to break with some of the Moderate leaders and the Moderates wanting somehow to keep him out. The Congress was fast becoming a mass movement.

The Moderates now counted for little. The Amritsar session, even though it drew up no radical programme, had been too much of a mass show for their taste. With the death of Gokhale, Lajpat Rai's ties with that group which were more of personal esteem than of a common political outlook had snapped.

He was not troubled by the 1907 compunction — whether the Moderates would find him unacceptable, whether his nomination would embarrass Gokhale. He need not worry, as in 1914, whether the Moderates would manipulate and manoeuvre, taking advantage of his absence abroad to smuggle in one of their own group — for now a Moderate could not possibly be foisted on the Congress. Now there was no fear that he would be treated as the nominee of one faction pitted against that of its rival.

But though the Moderates were fast becoming extinct in Congress politics, there were fresh problems to face. He had hardly been three weeks in India when Mahatma Gandhi published his first manifesto expounding a programme of non-cooperation, a programme to which the Khilafat leaders in consultation with Gandhi had already committed themselves. In a way non-cooperation admirably expressed his own feelings and his own political philosophy; but some of the items of the programme drawn up by the Mahatma he certainly found it hard to endorse. And more important than any of the items was the question — would the people respond to an appeal for a whirlwind mass campaign of the kind that Mahatma Gandhi envisaged? In other words, was the moment ripe? The individual items did not matter so much, but everything depended on a sound estimate of the practicable tempo.

His own political affinities in the past put him very close to the Maharashtra and Bengal nationalists but Gandhi was a new force. For Gandhi's saintly personality, his courage, simplicity and truthfulness? Had the very highest regard, and he had begun to look upon mm as the perfect type of leader for the Indian masses — as one who could in his personal living just be one of the masses and yet lead them prophet-like even as Moses led his people out of Egypt. He had watched with the keenest interest Gandhi's emergence in South Africa and his activities on his return to his own land. He had seen him at work in England when the war broke out, and admired his zeal and earnestness and organising talent, without altogether sharing his politics.

Later on he had controversy with him in public print over the doctrine that formed the very core of the Gandhian political philosophy — the doctrine of ahimsa. But in spite of these differences in outlook he had spoken in the very highest terms of Gandhi's personality and work. Especially since the Rowlatt Act days he had felt drawn more and more towards Gandhi and he had clearly indicated this in messages that he addressed to his countrymen before he left the United States. "He (Gandhi) is just the leader after our own heart," so he had said.

Yet, Gandhi's leadership had not so far been tested in any really big campaign that might justify his being accepted as the

Field-Marshal for the war that he now offered to wage. And Gandhi seemed determined to know whether those more experienced than himself gave him their cooperation or withheld it. There were indications also that if the veterans did not fall in, there might be tough time in store for them. The choice certainly seemed no easy affair; and for one who had been away from India for five years it was particularly difficult.

Lajpat Rai stuck to his old avoidance of party grooves. It looked again as if a new set of rival grooves was forming. In the third week of April, Gandhi issued a manifesto, setting forth his programme as President of the Home Rule League, and Tilak issued another on behalf of his National Democratic Party. Lajpat Rai was in no hurry to seek an affiliation with the one or the other.

At the end of May 1920 the All-India Congress Committee met at Banaras and for the first time considered non-cooperation. Tilak though he happened to be in Banaras kept away from the meeting. The Banaras meeting decided that the programme be considered at Calcutta at a special session of the Indian National Congress. In fact it had been understood at Amritsar that a special session would be required to consider the Government's decision on the report that was being prepared by the Hunter Committee on the Punjab happenings.

This report had already been published — also that of the Sub-Committee of the Indian National Congress — and the Government had made known their decision. Meanwhile the peace treaty of Sevres had been signed and the Muslim misgivings about the Khilafat had come true. Both these combined — the Punjab and the Khilafat wrongs — had given rise to the non-cooperation programme. Since the Amritsar session, Rules under the Reforms Act had been framed and published and, in the opinion of many, these had taken away a good deal from the Montagu Reforms which the Amritsar session had already declared "unsatisfactory and disappointing". All these happenings could be considered by a special session of the Indian National Congress, and a special session was called to meet in Calcutta in the first week of September 1920.

The constitutional machinery of the Congress was soon set to work to choose the president for a session necessitated by a combination of extraordinary circumstances that confronted India and her National Congress. Lalaji's name suggested itself most naturally to many people, because such recognition of his great career of service and sacrifice had long been due, and because the people looked forward to what may be offered out of the rich experience he had garnered for them in his years of exile. Besides, this particular session was to consider the question of the Punjab wrongs more than anything else and the greatest Punjabi would therefore be a most appropriate choice for the presidential chair.

Other names too were proposed-amongst them that of Tilak himself. On July 24 there was a pressing telegram from Motilal Nehru, President of the Congress for the year, saying: "Tilak definitely declined; none other more suitable than yourself." On July 27, Nehru wired again from Dumraon (where the parties to a very big lawsuit kept him and C. R. Das busy as opposing counsel): "You are duly elected President Special Congress. Congratulations." But he still vacillated particularly because the election had revealed no unanimity, not even an absolute majority. But from no quarter was there opposition to his name of the sort that had been seen in 1907 or 1914. He took counsel with several friends and did not decide for yet a few days. Amongst his papers is a letter from Kalinath Ray, editor of the Tribune, Lahore, and another from his old friend Mul Raj — both dated July 28 and both strongly urging acceptance.

"The days of absolute majorities are drawing to a close," observed Ray, "and in the present case even persons wholly in favour of your election may have been deterred by considerations wholly irrelevant to your claims."

And Mul Raj pointed out that the President's job would be no sinecure and enumerated briefly what seemed to him the great forces "all determined to smash it (the Congress)" but, characteristically advised, "It is perhaps best. In the words of our friend Lala Harkishan Lal to leave the matter to Higher Powers." And above all, the wishes of Bengal nationalists, for whom he had great regard and who after all were to be the hosts, were conveyed in a telegram dated July 29:

> "Bengal majority entirely favours your election. Should accept - Chaudhary." (This was Sir Ashutosh

Chaudhary who had a short while earlier retired from the Calcutta High Court Bench and was already taking a conspicuous part in Congress doings in Calcutta).

So he agreed to preside over the special session to be held in Calcutta in a month's time.

Tilak's death at this time (August, 1920) added to the complications. It plunged the whole country in mourning; but it meant a peculiar loss to those who still stood aloof from the new programme of non-cooperation. They felt sorely in need of his sound judgement and sturdy leadership. A leader of the Lokamanya's stature would at any time leave behind him a great void; at such a critical moment the void inevitably was amongst the most outstanding features of the political scene. Ever since their first meeting at a Congress session in Lahore, more than two decades earlier, Lajpat Rai had felt drawn towards Tilak.

With the passage of time invisible bonds forged by the attraction exercised by a forceful personality had ever grown stronger. The staple of their political creed might well be identical, but in policies of the moment differences were bound now and then to arise, even very sharply, as happened at Surat in 1907. What was remarkable was that Tilak's fascination never dimmed even when these differences looked most acute. At Surat Lajpat Rai had refused to be a partisan and had lost caste with some of Tilak's followers; but Surat left behind an indelible print of a picture that remained a source of inspiration and that he ever recalled with joy — that of Tilak dominating the Surat scene. Tilak on his part showed large-heartedness and rare understanding by the way he continued to cooperate with Lalaji as if there never had been a hiatus.

From no other Indian leader had Lalaji received as much support during his stay in the United States as from Tilak. He had ever avoided formal political affiliation; but his political creed undoubtedly was that of Tilak. Especially after Gokhale's death he had found himself very close to the Maharashtra group led by Tilak; but with the chief gone, would his ties of affection and loyalty to the Maharashtra group continue? Amongst the group itself the question of course arose as to who was to be its leader henceforth, and some were inclined to look outside Maharashtra and to turn to the Punjab leader whose angle in politics they knew had always been closer to that of their chief than that of any other Indian leader of the front rank. Soon after Tilak's death it was becoming apparent, however, that though Mahatma Gandhi insisted that if the Lokamanya had lived he would have blessed his movement, the Tilak group were not taking kindly to the new leader from Gujarat or to the new gospel that he was preaching. This added to Lajpat Rai's difficulties in committing himself definitely in regard to Gandhi and non-cooperation. He had still to watch things closely for some time.

Even in his presidential address at Calcutta he did not commit himself either for or against the non-cooperation programme and commended to future presidents the advantages of not taking sides in a certain type of controversy.

> "The President should not try to anticipate the decision of the Congress on a question on which the country is so sharply divided as it is on the question before us....
>
> "I have my personal opinion on the question involved in the programme of non-cooperation but during the session of the Congress, I will conduct the proceedings without taking sides." (As President of a "special session", it was easier for him to act up to this precept, for his tenure ended with the session itself).

Although there was very little time left — barely a month — when he made up his mind to accept the call, the presidential address was an affair of close on 50,000 words of sustained vigour. It was a marathon performance and a masterly one in its own way. Manuscript oratory was never in his line, for he always needed a live and continuous communion with his audience. Luckily he had been endowed with a memory that solved the problem for him. He delivered his 50,000 words with but the scantiest reference to the printed text — a performance that amazed many among his audience.

Of this address an easy three-fourths was devoted to the Punjab's long tale of woe under the O'Dwyer regime, culminating in the Martial Law terror. All that had been agitating his inner being ever since the news of the Punjab's humiliation and agony had reached him found vent in this address. He started with certain happenings during the early days of the O'Dwyer regime. He recalled what had come to his personal knowledge as a director of the Punjab National Bank when a banking crisis had arisen!

"While relief was promptly and freely given to European establishments, every Indian establishment was allowed to go under for want of timely aid — and presumably for 'moral effect'..... The banking crisis made us realise, as perhaps we had never before realised, the absolute helplessness to which we had been reduced by the present system, of government. We felt the situation keenly which had made it possible for the foreign capitalists to impose upon us not only their system but also their terms and their business, by the use of the very moneys that were realised from us by the government in the shape of revenues. When the Industrial Commission visited the Punjab, these and other facts were related to them by Lala Harkishan Lal in his evidence and on some Commissioner asking him if he realised what he was saying, he replied by an emphatic 'yes'."

In this strain he surveyed for his audience the entire O'Dwyer tenure to show that "it was all through a regime of terrorism and frightfulness and that it was only carried to its logical conclusion in the months of April and May 1919". "In the words used by Mr. Montagu (referring to General Dyer), the ideas which Sir Michael O'Dwyer had set before himself were 'terrorism, humiliation and subordination' and they reached their climax in the promulgation and administration of Martial Law." He examined the Martial Law doings and gave it as his verdict that "of all the persons who had anything to do with the introduction of Martial Law in the Punjab and with the events that preceded and followed it, Sir Michael was the chief culprit" "Indeed I may venture to assert that no man in the whole history of British rule in India has done such a great disservice to the British Empire and has brought such disgrace on the good name of the British nation as Sir O'Dwyer."

He drew up a regular charge-sheet against O'Dwyer. Under a round dozen counts, charging him with deliberately intensifying the "divide-and-rule" policy, and fomenting communal and rural-urban dissension, with having used his authority in illegal ways in the interest of his campaigns for recruitment and war funds, and for having sheltered those guilty of the "most brutal and diabolic deeds" as his tools in this work. Coming down to the culmination in the promulgation of Martial Law he accused O'Dwyer of having misled and deliberately deceived the Government of India to get their sanction, and with deliberate manipulation of the continuance of Martial Law.

The charge-sheet further made him responsible for the promulgation of barbarous orders and infliction of barbarous punishments under the Martial Law orders, which had his express or tacit consent. He further charged him with "being an accessory after the event", the Jalianwala massacre, because of his unqualified approval of that massacre. The last count in the charge-sheet was about O'Dwyer's having extorted, on the eve of his exit from office, through "illegal and near threats" addresses appreciative of his services — which addresses he had put to dishonest use in his own defence in England.

And he proceeded to marshal his evidence in support of the charges he made. The greater part of his address consisted of this evidence, for which he freely drew upon O'Dwyer's own utterances and upon his personal knowledge of certain happenings so far as the early part of O'Dwyer's reign of terror was concerned. For the later period he found material in the way O'Dwyer carried on his recruiting and levying of Voluntary' contributions for war funds; in the Czarist methods used in creating and handling 'conspiracy' cases, and above all, of course, the Hunter report and the Congress Sub-Committee's report on the Martial Law disorders, and two authentic source-books, were a rich, not easily exhaustible quarry.

O'Dwyer later on won a libel case against Sir Sankaran Nair and claimed to have vindicated himself. The fact is that Sir Sankaran was severely handicapped by his having been party to most of O'Dwyer's misdeeds, indirectly as a member of the Government of India. Shimla had proved too weak for O'Dwyer, and the fact that Sir Sankaran had in a way become party before he threw up his job in disgust was enough for O'Dwyer's purposes. All that O'Dwyer's 'vindication' amounted to was that the Government of India had not stayed his hand. But if he were keen on a genuine vindication he should have filed a libel suit against the Congress

Sub-Committee, or perhaps even sought permission to sue the majority of the Hunter Committee, and above all he should have sued Lajpat Rai than whom nobody ever made more serious charges against him or in more emphatic words. Through Lalaji's address the Punjab that O'Dwyer had terrorised voiced her arraignment of his misdeeds and that arraignment was never challenged.

Besides the Punjab wrongs, the special session had to consider two other important questions — the Turkish Peace Treaty and the Rules framed to work the Montagu Reforms. About the Reforms he was rather brief but categorical, summing up his reaction to the scheme in one sentence.

"It was one of partial elation in 1918, it sank into one of depression in 1919, it changed almost into one of despair in 1920."

Whatever 'elation' might have been created in his mind when the joint report of the Secretary of State and the Viceroy appeared vanished when the Report finally crystallised into a statute and now the Rules framed to work it had rendered that statute still more hopeless. He asked his people "to make up their minds that what they want is the whole loaf and not merely half of it I could have no objection to take even the half, provided I was sure that the half offered was not selected by the bureaucracy.

The bureaucracy is so adept in the art of mixing and cooking that the half which they propose to retain contains all the nourishment of the whole, leaving the other half worse than chaff. They manage it so skilfully that in the process of doughing they mix many a germ of disease in the half which they propose to let you have. It will be a marvel of good fortune, if with all the distinctions of Hindus, Mussalmans, Sikhs and Christians, of urban and rural, of Brahmins and non-Brahmins, of residents and non-residents, of British subjects and those of Native States, of military and civil, made in the rules and regulations, we are still able to evolve a national spirit and with a will to live and prosper as a free nation."

On the Turkish treaty he spoke very strongly and very wisely. The merely religious aspect of the question did not detain him long.

"In the words of Mr. Leland Buxton it does not in the least matter what Professor This or Doctor That thinks the Muslims ought to believe. What does matter is that the vast majority of Sunni Muslims do believe that the Sultan of Turkey is their Khalifa and the interests of Islam require him to be the head of a large, powerful and independent State. The Mohammedan law-books define the boundaries of such a State."

On the purely religious aspect the last word must be with the followers of the faith:

> "We may then take it for granted that the interpretation put upon this matter by the Central Khilafat Committee is correct It was a matter for our Mohammedan countrymen to decide and they have decided it. There could be no doubt the pledges given to the Indian Mussalmans by the British Prime Minister had been cast to the winds when the time for a peace settlement came; equally there could be no doubt that the Indian Muslims were gravely perturbed that the Turkish Peace Treaty violates the fundamentals of Islam, prevents from fulfilling their religious obligations, makes it impossible for them to maintain friendly relations with a nation which is the cause of it."

On the political implications of the Peace Treaty and their indirect bearing on the problem of India (not merely for India's Mussalmans) he had a lot to say:

> "But there are in my judgement other issues also involved in the Turkish Peace Treaty which deserve consideration. I maintain that any further extension of the British Empire in Asia is detrimental to the interests of India and fatal to the liberties of the human race. The British have frequently used Indian troops to conquer various parts of Asia and Africa. For a long time there was an unwritten law which every European Chancellery considered binding on itself that non-European troops were not to be used in any European war. This was abolished in the last war. African troops and Indian troops were used during

> and after the war by the Allies in Europe. Black troops were in occupation of Germany and some time stationed in Ireland. I do not, of course, resent the abolition of the invidious social bar. From that point of view, I may even welcome it, but surely it widens the scope of militarism."

The extended scope might one day realise possibilities not foreseen by many:

> "If the British Imperialist has no scruples in using Indian troops in Egypt, Persia, Arabia, Mesopotamia, Syria and Central Asia, why will he have any in using the troops he raises in these countries against us? The Hindu-Muslim problem will become ten times more troublesome and dangerous, if this turns out to be true."

Conversely, "if the Muslim population of these countries continue to resist British attempts at occupation which they are likely to do for years, the Indian Army will be in constant requisition to fight their battles in those regions, which means a constant and never-ending drain on our resources, both human and economic."

He had no illusions that the League of Nations was going to usher in a new comity of peoples — "Gentlemen, there is no such thing as the League of Nations. Great Britain and French are the League".

He spoke very firmly of the Khilafat wrong and he spoke with all the vigour that he could command of the Punjab wrong; but, as we have said, he kept quiet over the corollary of these two, the non-cooperation programme advocated by Mahatma Gandhi to get these wrongs redressed. Stalwarts were arrayed on both sides. Gandhi was supported by the Ali brothers and a number of, Muslim leaders, and eventually by the President of the Amritsar session of the Congress, Pandit Motilal Nehru, too. The Pandit wanted a small alteration — that the boycott of schools and courts be gradual — and having secured this, accepted the non-cooperation resolution which was moved by Gandhi himself. Bipin Chandra Pal moved an amendment and C. R. Das seconded it. In fact the task of leading the opposition to Gandhi's programme fell to Das's lot Tilak was dead. Lajpat Rai was content to have a Speaker's neutrality. So Das led the Bengal and Maharashtra nationalists in opposing the programme. In the Subjects Committee the resolution was passed by a very narrow majority of seven votes; but in the plenary sitting Gandhi won the day convincingly. There was elaborate recording of votes. The pandal had to be cleared for the purpose and the telling operations, personally superintended by the President, lasted six hours. There were 1855 votes cast for Gandhi's resolution and 873 for the amendment. Lajpat Rai expressed some misgivings in the closing session; for the rest he returned from it as 'neutral' as he had gone to it.

With the principle of non-cooperation he was in hearty agreement; with the Calcutta programme too in a way, he had not much fault to find. It was at what might seem details that he jibbed, but he found it necessary to be very frank about his compunction. The titles, decorations, etc. received from the Government would not be given up by the "loyalists', but it was all to the good that others should get out of this crowd and make its stock go down in public esteem. The people would lose nothing and gain a good deal, if a large number of practising lawyers boycotted the courts. He had himself no intention of ever setting up as a lawyer again, and from his experience he knew what mischief the British judicial system had done. To other critics of Gandhi's programme in the nationalist camp, the boycott of legislatures was the item which formed a most formidable obstacle, but this item had been originally suggested by Lajpat Rai himself and only then appropriated by Gandhi.

He saw no reason to change his mind after the Calcutta session. The boycott of education he could not swallow easily. He had been a worker in the.cause of national education, according to his lights, since he entered public life as a young man. In India and abroad he had devoted much time to a careful study of problems connected with national education. Few among the top leaders had given these problems half as much thought as he had expended on them. The result of his experience and his study he had embodied in The Problem of National Education in India the manuscript of which he had entrusted to an English publisher before he returned to India. He had some bitter experience and disillusion from the institutions that he had devotedly helped in building up and no one could feel more keenly the harm that a wrong system of education was inflicting on the people; still he could not hail the abolition of schooling for the young as a boon for the nation.

More than the merits of the different items of the programme, what worried him was the question — was the moment ripe? Mistakes would not matter if a whirlwind campaign with real and determined backing from the masses materialised; the most perfect paper programme would be a fiasco if it did not catch the popular imagination. He preferred therefore to wait a while and watch how things developed. He did not plunge into the movement; but he would not criticise or condemn those who did. "I have my doubts about the country being with us in the self-denying ordinance ..... I will do nothing to hinder the progress of the movement I wish you every success, and if you gain the popular ear you will find in me an enthusiastic supporter," so Gandhi reported (after Tilak's death) Tilak's attitude towards non-cooperation. Lajpat Rai's attitude at the moment was no different. On one thing he was perfectly clear in his mind — the impossibility of 'Swaraj within a year'.

He was not among the optimists who believed that if they worked the Calcutta programme for a year or so. Governmental machinery would be brought to a standstill and the British will to rule India be paralysed. The struggle for swaraj he well knew would have to be hard and long, and the Calcutta programme could at best be a preparatory stage. 'Swaraj' while you waif may be a very catchy slogan for demagogues, but he did not think it wise for leaders to base national politics on such headlong optimism, or on slogans that would raise hopes with little prospect of fulfilment.

Non-cooperation Movement

Back in Lahore he quietly settled down to the work he had taken in hand before the non-cooperation session. He worked for his Urdu daily, the Bandemataram, and he went ahead with the scheme he had already announced for starting the Tilak School of Politics. He went about raising funds for this School, and though he was not seducing students away from their colleges, he rather thought if some of them 'non-cooperated', his School might get a better opportunity of giving them sound political' training.

In the Punjab the non-cooperation campaign did not seem to start in right earnest The Punjab Congress Committee did not show enough enthusiasm for it, and so am ad hoc non-cooperation committee was set up with Saifuddin Kitchlew, K. Santanam, and Sardul Singh Caveeshar as secretaries. These and Rambhaj Dutt Chaudhary and Sarala Devi were the leading lights of non-cooperation. A few college students began to assist them to some extent a little later. Santhanam and Caveeshar tried hard to win over Lajpat Rai and Harkishan Lal for they knew without these stalwarts a real vigorous campaign in the Punjab was not likely. Harkishan Lal the inveterate scoffer would listen to their earnest pleading, and put them off with wit and banter which left them guessing whether in the end it was going to be 'yes' or 'no'. He would laugh all serious argument off, and 'yes' and 'no' alike seemed eternally in disgrace. Lajpat Rai wished well by the movement but seemed to hold himself back yet awhile.

Mahatma Gandhi came down to the Punjab; for a few days the college boys were greatly excited and their strikes made the managing bodies anxious. Large crowds also flocked to see and hear the Mahatma. But the visit did not succeed in winning over Lalaji for the non-cooperation campaign. After the Mahatma had gone, a vast majority of the students who had struck resumed their normal studies; just a handful chose to hold out The net gains of his visit were small. The Punjab still seemed to be 'watching' as Lalaji certainly was.

Students — individually (or in small groups), not as a community — came along to seek Lalaji's advice whether they should non-cooperate. His usual reply would be that a student should weigh the pros and cons for himself and then decide. He did not attach much importance to the liberal education being given in the colleges but a student must discard it only if he felt strongly and had the will to be firm about it and not be just carried away in a moment of impulse. If he happened to be a medical or engineering student or the parent of such a student that sought his advice, he definitely discouraged the idea of non-cooperating. Mere graduates perhaps were useless, but, the country, needed many more doctors, engineers and technicians. To law students he wholeheartedly commended non-cooperation.

Occasionally those came to him who had definitely 'non-cooperated' with their college teaching. They approached him with misgivings, for he was not with the movement. But to their surprise they found him friendly and helpful with advice; and his Tilak School extended a welcome to them. He wanted them not to non-cooperate with all education. He knew that generally the students had non-cooperated against their parents' wishes.

He provided a rented hostel for them and drew generously on the funds of the School in finding stipends to maintain them. To this School came non-cooperating students not merely from his, own province; a few came from the UP; some from the C.P. and Maharashtra, one or two even from the far south So things dragged on till the regular annual session of the Congress was due at Nagpur. Now he must either actively join the movement or definitely keep away from it.

Even though in the Punjab the movement had not quite caught on, he could see there was good scope for it. In many of the other provinces the response had been a delightful surprise to him.

He was in a way being drawn towards the movement, and his neutral friendliness was not without its own humours. Alongside the Congress session an all-India students conference was being organised at Nagpur. He accepted the invitation to preside over this conference. It was the Calcutta situation over again: the Congress passing the non-cooperation resolution which he could not accept with this difference that the organisers of the students conference knew beforehand what they were up to and also that it would not be quite the thing to suit their President!

He did not, however, shirk talking plainly to them on students' non-cooperation and he seemed to be thinking aloud:

> "In my concluding address at the Special Congress at Calcutta, I said that I was opposed to that item of non-cooperation which related to the boycott of schools and colleges. Immediately after returning from the Congress, I addressed a public meeting at Lahore and

I told the students and others that I would welcome the abolition of all the arts and law colleges. Whenever students approached me for advice, my advice was given under the following heads:

Law college: leave at once.

Medical, engineering and technical colleges: don't leave.

Arts college: consider the situation well.

We are all agreed that the present educational system does tend towards strengthening the bureaucracy and that we should do what little we can, considering our present political responsibilities in a way to establish institutions which might be free of official control both on the side of finance and on the side of education. But I do not know whether we are agreed that national schools and colleges now established will be included to carry on the more important work of political propaganda in the country. We cannot afford to do that. We are out to obtain swaraj in the shortest time possible and we cannot give our time and energy to the solution of a problem which requires both time and money. I have therefore been saying to my friends that we shall not incur any responsibilities and we shall not undertake any duties which will in any way militate against the work we have in hand. If we do that we shall be frittering our energies in enterprises the results of which might not be achieved very soon. We cannot devise a national system of education without a, national Government ... Having made that clear, I am perfectly willing to ask and encourage every student in any arts or law college to leave that college if he feels the call of duty, provided he has no delusions in his mind that provision is going to be made for his education, either locally, provincially or imperially by anybody. Provision' may be made in some places as it is being made, but he should not expect it.".

Answering the question 'what are those (non-cooperating) students to do?' he said:

> "There is a great field for work — the work of propaganda, organising the nation, reviving industries, making an honourable living without being traitors to our country. Put your hand to any work you find handy.... I know... that sentence of Mahatma Gandhi was ridiculed — that people ought to go and construct roads or work in factories..... An honest, independent, patriotic road-mender is infinitely superior to a Deputy Collector. I want the youth of the nation to go forth into the villages, factories, workshops and to work with their hands and feel the spirit of comradeship with fellow-workers who are waiting for their inspiration to come from you."

The students paid little heed to his word of warning and decided on unconditional "boycott" of all "Government and Government-aided colleges and colleges affiliated to the Government-chartered Indian universities", and in the next resolution looked "to the national leaders to bring into existence in every province at an early date national colleges conducted on national lines affiliated to the national universities .... and to start educational institutions for general and Industrial training of Indian youth....."

He had done his duty by sounding the note of warning and left the conference to take whatever decisions it thought fit, as he was needed in the many consultations of the Congress leaders.

In the Congress itself, luckily, a spirit of accommodation prevailed. During the preceding three months everyone had realised that Gandhi had to be accepted, and Gandhi too had realised how seriously handicapped he was if Lajpat Rai and C. R. Das did not join hands with him. He was anxious to enlist their support as they wished to see a united front. Both parties honestly and sincerely wanted unanimity and were willing enough not to be too exacting about matters of mere detail.

Lalaji's objections to the educational boycott enjoined in the Calcutta resolution were paid heed to and a fresh formula was evolved to meet them. In the Calcutta resolution we read:

> "Gradual withdrawal of Wldren from schools and colleges owned, aided or controlled by Government, and, in place of such schools and colleges, establishment of national schools and colleges in the various provinces."

At Nagpur this had to be amplified:

> "By calling upon the students of the age of 16 and over to withdraw without delay irrespective of consequences from institutions owned, aided or in any way controlled by Government, if they feel that it is against their conscience to continue in institutions which are dominated by a system of Government which the nation has solemnly resolved to bring to an end, and advising such students either to devote themselves to some special service in connection with the Non-cooperation Movement or to continue their education in national institutions; By calling upon the trustees, managers and teachers of Government-affiliated or aided schools and municipalities and local boards to help to nationalise them."

Lalaji was satisfied that the abolition of schooling had been averted, that a necessary distinction had been made between minors at school and grown-up lads at college, and the impossible responsibility for starting a system of national education not rashly undertaken, as it had seemed to be in the Calcutta resolution. If only medical and technical education could be expressly excepted, his stand would be completely endorsed, but this did not seem easily feasible; as he himself told the students' conference he knew medical and engineering education had been harnessed for imperial ends to British militarism. He was quite satisfied with what he got.

C. R. Das had been principally opposed to the boycott of legislatures. The general elections were over before the Nagpur session. Thanks to the boycott, more than 80 per cent of the voters had kept away from the polling booths. At Nagpur while talks for a compromise and a united front were afoot in the late hours of the night, C. R. Das told Muhammad Ali that he had decided to accept non-cooperation. Overjoyed,' Muhammad Ali kissed the Bengal leader on the right cheek and the left. Next day, the principal resolution, reiterating the Calcutta resolve and laying down the programme of non-cooperation as finally amended after give-and-take, was moved by C. R. Das and seconded by Lajpat Rai This was indeed a great triumph for Gandhi — and one the credit for which went to Gandhi and Das and Lajpat Rai alike. The official historian of the Congress has summed up the occasion with the aid of a somewhat grotesque image:

> "In Calcutta... the stool of the non-cooperation was resting on but one leg. At Nagpur it stood on all its four legs with perfect equipoise. Gandhi and Nehru, Das and Lalaji were all for it ..."

Things had partly been shaped behind the scenes, for not all misgivings could be set at rest by clever phrasing. The Punjab contingent as might be expected had discussions with him and this too helped. However, this happened, the chief thing was that the re-union had come and that it was not a mere patch-up but a hearty re-union.

Besides the non-cooperation resolution, Lalaji was commissioned to second another one also which made an equally fundamental change since it affected the creed of the Congress. Even since 1908 no one could enlist himself as a member of the Congress without first subscribing to the British Empire — a sort of oath of loyalty which the Moderates had prescribed, largely to keep out some of the extremists who openly stood for severance of the British connection. Now that the Moderates had gone out of the Congress, there was no reason for this legacy to continue. It went ill with the non-cooperation programme any way. The resolution removing this anomaly was moved by Gandhi and seconded by Lajpat Rai. The Congress creed was now changed to 'Swaraj by all peaceful and legitimate means', instead of 'responsible Government within the British Empire by constitutional means'! There was a change in the goal, not merely in the means.

In a forceful speech Lalaji gave the history of the creed and explained how the Surat split had been partly caused by differences over this issue. Even then, he said, it had struck him as unreasonable that a man with Sri Aurobindo's sincere and lofty patriotism should be kept out of the Congress.

> "Not that I believed at that time we had either the means or the will to work for complete independence but I thought that none of us had the right to exclude from the deliberations of this Congress anybody who pitched his ideal so high."

Replying to those who drew distinctions between 'Empire' and 'Commonwealth', he asked if there was a British Commonwealth. "Not yet," replied Holford Knight, one of the three fraternal delegates from British Labour. Talking of the pledges of British statesmen, Lalaji said: "We may place every faith in the words of an English gentle had believed themselves to be unchallengeable. The Congress team in the Lahore municipality became a most inconvenient affair for the bureaucracy. The example of Lahore was followed elsewhere too.

The students who had come out of the colleges brought in their train some rather awkward problems. Village work was all right for a while, but after that they wanted to complete their education. They insisted on arrangements for their studies.

A Kaumi Mahavidyalaya was improvised to educate the college boys who on completing their studies would get their degrees from a Kaumi Vidyapeeth of which Lalaji was made the chancellor. A school department with stress on handicrafts was also started. (Lalaji's grandson — the only child of his daughter — was amongst the first to join this school). Some schools sprang up at other centres too. Lalaji's own school at Jagraon, the Radhakishan High School, was 'nationalised' — and in due course depleted of students.

All these problems meant hard work; and the hardest of all was the raising of the crore for the Tilak Swaraj Fund. Here the Punjab must find its quota, happen what may.

For this Lalaji toured about incessantly, often visiting and addressing half a dozen out-of-the-way townships in a day and levying and collecting the quota from each one. Nine lakhs for the Punjab was a large amount, but Lalaji was a beggar on a grand scale and he did not rest till he had raised this amount.

Lalaji worked with the speed of a whirlwind. The normal tasks of course could not be neglected his responsibilities as editor of the foremost daily of the Punjab and various other routine jobs, big and small. There were besides frequent calls from outside the Punjab. The other provinces had claims on him as one of the half a dozen national leaders, and the National Working Committee had to meet at short intervals, and it met all over India. In one of these tours the Ali brothers accompanied him, somewhere the laundry got mixed and a huge salwar of the Big Brother which when fully opened out looked more like a canopy than a garment long remained a souvenir of that tour and of the then prevailing intimate collaboration between Hindu and Muslim leaders.

Historical Bardoli Decision

During the three months that elapsed between Lalaji's arrest at the Punjab Congress meeting and his conviction on February 20, 1922, great changes had occurred in Indian politics. The seeds had been there at the time of his arrest but their subsequent career on germination might not have been very easy to foretell. These developments sprang from two factors — the Congress resolve to launch a campaign of civil disobedience, and the outbreak of mob violence in spite of Congress injunction to the contrary.

'Civil disobedience' had of course been from the outset visualised as a culmination of the progressive non-violent non-cooperation, though it is possible the author of non-cooperation had cherished hopes of a settlement with the Government before non-cooperation had to be taken to the grim stage of refusing taxes. These hopes not having been realised, the people of Bardoli — a small taluk in Gujarat — under the guidance and presidentship of Vallabhbhai Patel had resolved in October 1921 on a campaign of civil disobedience.

The author of non-cooperation had planned that this experiment would start at Bardoli under his personal supervision to serve as a model for local leaders elsewhere. The Working Committee in a resolution passed on November 3, 1921 had laid down certain tests which, if fulfilled, would empower Provincial Congress Committees to take up individual and even mass civil disobedience. Within a fortnight of this came the riots in Bombay —

with a toll of more than 50 dead and 400 wounded — on the occasion of the hartal called to mark the popular boycott of the Prince of Wales's visit to India, The leader of non-violent non-cooperation flinched. But besides the spectacular fast the net result had been the laying down of further restrictions for the launching of civil disobedience, and the drawing up of an elaborate pledge of non-violence for volunteers.

But the movement was by no means to be abandoned — it was definitely to be accelerated. More and more volunteers were to be enrolled, and though the final launching of a campaign of civil disobedience in a particular area would no longer rest with the Provincial Committees, those bodies were expected to continue active preparations for such campaigns, if possible even at a quickened pace. The Bombay riots had retarded preparations for the battle of Bardoli, but clearly there was no apprehension of its being dropped with a euphemistic announcement saying it had been "indefinitely postponed". The atmosphere was kept tense with the expectancy of zero hour.

This is where Lalaji had left things at the time of arrest. Every moment the country was expecting big happenings. He had not pinned his faith on "Swaraj within a year", but a bold bid for it in the very near future he certainly did look forward to. In his message to his countrymen at the time of his arrest he said:

> "When I left the shores of America, I knew that I would not be allowed to remain outside the jail for a long time; and on my departure from there, I had told my friends that I would be satisfied if I were allowed to work amongst my people even for six months. But now through the grace of God, I have been enabled to work with you for about 19 months, and I go to jail with a glad heart, and with the firm belief that whatever we have done, we have done according to our conscience and our God. I have no misgivings or fears in my mind. I am convinced that the path we have chosen is the right path, and our success is sure. I also believe that I shall soon return amongst you and resume my work; but even if that is not to be, I assure you that I shall have nothing to

be sorry for when I return to my Creator. I am a weak and frail man, and do not claim to possess the splendid spirituality of Mahatma Gandhi. Sometimes I am not able to control my anger, nor can I say that I have never harboured feelings which I ought not to have entertained. But this I can truthfully assert that I have always kept the interests of my country and nation before my mind, and my actions have been directed with a sole eye to the interests of my country. I know that I have made many mistakes in the discharge of my duties, and have sometimes indulged in criticism which might have given offence to some of my countrymen. For all that I beg forgiveness. I hope that they will forgive me, especially my Moderate and Arya Samajic brothers.

My countrymen, I now bid you goodbye. I go to jail in the firm belief that the honour of my beloved country and nation is safe in your keeping. The Bandemataram and the Tilak School of Politics are my two children; and those also I leave in your keeping."

The all brothers had been arrested even before Lalaji, although they had let themselves be persuaded by the Mahatma to express regret for certain statements they had made. Then, one by one, had gone the other front-rank leaders — C. R. Das, Abul Kalam Azad and Motilal Nehru. The Mahatma no longer had the advantage of their criticism and advice. Now leadership had become really a one-man affair.

The Congress met at Ahmedabad in December 1921, and formally appointed the Mahatma executive head of the Congress — if you will, its dictator. But this was clearly understood to be a war exigency. The Mahatma was given these extraordinary powers to launch the campaign and make the best of it. The Congress resolutions appointing him virtual dictator ended with significant limitations to the dictator's authority:

"In view of the impending arrests of a large number of Congress workers this Congress whilst requiring the ordinary machinery to remain intact and to be utilised in the ordinary manner whenever feasible, hereby appoints until further instructions Mahatma Gandhi as the sole executive authority of the Congress and invests him with the full power to convene a special session of the Congress or of the All-India Congress Committee or the Working Committee, such powers to be exercised between any two sessions of the All-India Congress Committee and also with the power to appoint a successor in emergency.

This Congress hereby confers upon the said successor and all subsequent successors, appointed in turn by their predecessors, his aforesaid powers.

Provided that nothing in this resolution shall be deemed to authorise Mahatma Gandhi or any of the aforesaid successors to conclude any terms of peace with the Government of India or the British Government without the previous sanction of the All-India Congress Committee to be finally ratified by the Congress specially convened for the purpose, and provided also that the present creed of the Congress shall in no case be altered by Mahatma Gandhi or his successors except with leave of the Congress first obtained."

The Mahatma took the rudder and proceeded to sail. On February 1, 1922 he addressed a famous ultimatum to Lord Reading, a seven-day notice demanding the release of all sent to jails if no violence could be proved against them, and besides an assurance of full freedom to carry on a non-violent campaign for the redress of the Khilafat and Punjab wrongs and for the achievement of swaraj. Failing this, at the expiry of the ultimatum civil disobedience was to be launched to begin with at Bardoli.

Then started a new chapter somewhat abruptly. There was a sporadic outbreak at Chauri Chaura, an unknown small village (in Gorakhpur district, UP), which has since become a historic name. Twenty-two constables were done to death.

Bombay (November 17), then Madras (January 13) and finally Chauri Chaura on the 5th of February just two days before the Bardoli 'ultimatum' expired!

The Mahatma flinched once again. After this second and sudden jolt he began to rethink civil disobedience. Had he started rethinking soon after Bombay? Had this continued even after the Bombay decisions following the Prince of Wales riots? Was the 'Vishnu roop' just the beginning of this rethinking started by manifestations of violence? Whatever the answers to these questions, the next event relevant to this narrative was that of February 12, 1922. The Congress Working Committee met at Bardoli, and on Mahatma Gandhi's advice indefinitely suspended mass civil disobedience.

The decision was based on the manifestations of violence in Bombay and at Chauri Chaura. All activities designed to court arrest, all processions and public meetings, etc., in defiance of bans imposed by authority, were to be abandoned and Congressmen were instead asked to devote their energy to a constructive programme in which hand-spinning was the most important item.

The zero-hour expectancy ended in this anti-climax!

Bengal Pact

Some time later it was suggested that the sea-side might do Lalaji good and Karachi was selected as being dry and salubrious. There he stayed for a while as the guest of Jaswant Rai who since The Punjabee days had settled down there to a prosperous business career. On December 8, 1924 Lalaji received at Karachi a telegram from Motilal Nehru which read: "Abul Kalam Azad proposes important consultation Delhi 11th. Please join health permitting. Nehru." This was followed up by another telegram from the Pandit: "Can reach Lahore on 12th wiring Das."

They met at Lahore for an exchange of views, this being necessitated by the slender likelihood of Lalaji's attending the forthcoming Congress session. A few days later he left again for Sindh to give the bracing climate of Karachi a fuller chance. For a few days he stopped at Hyderabad. During the previous visit he had talks with Jairamdas Doulatram, Choithram Gidwani and the other political workers there, mainly about the problems arising out of the riots and the consequent search for a formula of adjustment. Lalaji found the Hyderabad friends very receptive to his point of view. At Lahore, before setting out for Karachi a second time, Lalaji had received letters and telegrams from Jairamdas stressing the need of his presence at Kakinada particularly for the proposed Hindu-Muslim conference. "Dr. Choithram and I.... request you to arrange... a meeting of Hindu Congressmen before the 22nd, if the 22nd H. M. meeting cannot be postponed", and this letter was followed up by a telegram in which Choithram, myself appeal you attend Cocanada or Hindu-Muslim question will go wrong".

Not intending to go to Kakinada, he met these friends at Hyderabad before they left for the Congress meetings. He rather liked that band of workers, particularly Jairamdas being impressed as much by his sincerity and devotion as by his methodical ways. Lalaji talked to Jairamdas and other friends about the political issues of the day, and about the peculiar problems of his own province and theirs. These exchanges alternated with chats on Indian history; he recollected that whilst working on his history of India during his imprisonment, he had wanted certain details of the first Muslim invasion of India and that he had not been able to get a copy of the Chachnama. He was keen on reading the Chachnarna account in full. The English translation of this source-book having gone out of print, they could not lay their hands on a copy forthwith but promised to be on the look-out for one. Some time later they did secure a copy and sent it to Lalaji.

In spite of all temptations beckoning him to Kakinada he stayed on in Karachi. But when the Congress session started, he was impatient always for news. Early in the afternoon he would set out for a drive and for a stroll along the Clifton. On his way he would stop the car outside a newspaper office to get the latest news. The editor would come out all smiles, and when asked about the news would smile vacantly again and eventually say there was nothing of any consequence.

This went on for some days before it dawned on them that this gentleman's politeness did not permit his telling us plainly that his paper had no arrangements for a news service, and he had himself to wait for the day's news till the other evening papers came out! However, certain items of consequence to Lalaji did come in the news during this stay at Karachi. Three stand out from amongst these — one preceding the Congress session, one part of it, and one following soon after.

The first of these was the 'Bengal Pact' entered into by C. R. Das to get Muslim support in the politics of Bengal. The news of this pact came as a shock to Lalaji. He did not like much some of the clauses of the pact. He definitely thought it was short-sighted to think of a separate Bengal settlement especially at the moment when a national pact was being hammered out; for, the National Pact Committee, on which Lalaji had worked, had submitted a draft which was coming up for consideration at Kakinada. A separate Bengal pact in a way torpedoed the national one. Faced with two rival drafts, the Kakinada Congress withheld its own imprimatur and just let both be circulated.

To Lalaji far more serious than the merits of the formula adopted or the moment chosen was the fact that Das had done all this while deliberately keeping him out, and leaving him to get the news from the newspapers after the event, when all the time he (Lalaji) believed that they were working in very close mutual consultation. Like many others Lalaji suspected that in the talks leading to the pact Abul Kalam Azad had a hand — an inference that today might seem more or less borne out by the Maulana's glowing tribute to Das's statesmanship as seen in this pact. If the misgiving proved true it was something serious, for had not Abul Kalam Azad been discussing altogether a different kind of pact with Lalaji, and in the discussions had he not definitely condemned what Das's pact now upheld? Abul Kalam was there in Calcutta sure enough; could Das have ignored him completely in entering into a pact with the Calcutta Muslims? Das at any rate had met Lalaji at Lahore only a short while before, and though they had talked a good deal about the Hindu-Muslim question he had given him no inkling of a local pact in the offing.

Even if his pact had been conceived after their meeting, Das certainly had known that Lalaji was at work on a national pact and the least that he could do was to let Lalaji know how his hands had been forced by local emergencies. Even that small courtesy Das had not conceded.

Abul Kalam may or may not have taken a hand in the pact-making. If he did, it was not fair-play, but what Das had done definitely pained, Lalaji as personal injury; it went so violently against his own code of friendship and loyalty, and Das was such a dear friend. In his political life his most intimate contacts had been with the Maharashtra and Bengal nationalists. When after long years of absence from his country he picked up the old threads at the Calcutta special session, Das was the head of the Bengal nationalists, and these and the Maharashtra group had stood together. At Calcutta Gandhi had not been able to convert either Lalaji or Das. They had both held out till Nagpur and then they had both made a settlement with Gandhi.

Again while still in prison, both had begun to revolt against the orthodox programme of non-cooperation. Das had come out earlier and openly started the revolt; Lalaji had gladly given him all the help he could from his cell in prison. Since his release he had believed that Motilal Nehru and Das and he were working in the closest collaboration.

Even more than to Nehru he had felt attached to Das who was for him the symbol of all his old and precious ties with Bengal, and who besides in all the stages in the political detour towards Gandhian non-cooperation and away from it had been so near himself - much nearer than the Allahabad Pandit who had accepted non-cooperation at Calcutta itself before either Das or Lalaji had done so, and who had come round to the Councils programme somewhat later than either of them.

Lalaji recollected also that Das had not been quite fair to him in circulating the confidential letters he had sent him from prison. In one of these he had with utmost frankness laid before Das all the misgivings created in his mind by talks with certain Muslim friends in the Lahore Central Jail, and though the letter had been meant strictly for Das himself he had heard reports that Das had not at all treated it so.

Some time earlier Joseph Baptista, the Bombay trade union leader with a sharp tongue and Maharashtra fondness for play upon words, had perpetrated the witticism that the verdict of history would be that the 'Dasses were Asses'. Now Lalaji recalled that half in despair, half laughingly, and for days he could be heard repeating it to himself. The 'pact' proved a great strain, for though he was free to say that it had come as a surprise to him and that he did not approve of it, he could not give free vent to all his feelings; he had to restrain himself where C. R. Das was concerned.

From the Congress session itself, what amazed Lalaji, was the audacious proposal made from the presidential chair by Muhammad Ali that the 'untouchables' should be split between Hindus and Muslims — and this in the name of and as a contribution towards unity! This naturally perturbed Lalaji. So on getting up one morning he announced it as a solemn resolve taken on a sacred day — it being Guru Gobind Singh's birthday in fact — that he was going to start a nation-wide drive for the speedy removal of untouchability. He wrote out a longish statement to explain the background and implications of his resolve and then handed it to me to make out a telegraphic summary for the press, adding that this would enable him to see my aptitude for journalistic work. He could not promise Swaraj in a year, but the eradication of untouchability could be substantially achieved in twelve months. Civil Disobedience having receded, he had to turn to "constructive work" and, here, as he put it, universities could wait, untouchables could not.

The last of the three outstanding items of news at Karachi came on the 12th or 13th of January and was easily the most alarming of all the news that Mahatma Gandhi becoming a victim to appendicitis in the Yeravda prison had to be operated on by Col. Maddock in the Sassoon Hospital at Poona. Soon after the operation was declared successful, but that by no means ended anxiety. Lalaji decided to set off for Poona, and we took the boat to Bombay.

In spite of the strain put on him by these happenings, the sojourn in Karachi had been definitely good for his health. He did some reading or writing when he felt like it or attended to his correspondence, but did not have heavy work to do. The climate was salubrious, the weather fine, Clifton was a pleasant drive and the beach a delightful sight. Best of all, not many visitors turned up, and few came repeatedly, excepting T. L. Vaswani — with whom he occasionally exchanged notes about the Gito — and one other gentleman keenly interested in physical culture, who liked to give Lalaji tips regarding his health and presented him with a pedometer as he attached some importance to knowing how much work one's legs had done during the day. Of his own choice Lalaji occasionally called on Jamshed Mehta or Abdullah Haroon or Hatim Alavi, and sometimes, before the afternoon drive went round to some of the prosperous businessmen, Punjabis, Sindhis or Marwaris, to collect funds for the Servants of the People Society. But there were no crowds to face, no visitors keen on darskan butting in at inconvenient hours, and no public functions, except the grand garden party given by the citizens of Karachi in his honour.

In Bombay he stopped for a day, met a few friends and proceeded to Poona. N. C. Kelkar and his friends of the Kesari group received him with all the cordiality and warmth that his ancient friendship with Maharashtra entitled him to. His first anxiety being to see Mahatma Gandhi he hastened to Sassoon Hospital. The patient greeted him with a smile which in itself allayed half the anxiety. By then of course cause for serious misgiving was already gone, and though the patient was very feeble in health, his progress was quite satisfactory.

Lalaji was very happy to be in Poona and to recapture memories of the stalwarts who were no more and whose friendship had meant so much to him — the Lokamanya and Gokhale — the memories of his first visit to Poona in 1905, and of Gokhale's fundamental change? And who was this Olivier who had been entrusted with the India portfolio? Did Lalaji know him personally? What were his antecedents?

Lalaji knew Olivier but casually, possibly through the Webbs, for he was a Fabian and, it was said, had tried to govern Jamaica liberally. But Lalaji had no big hopes of him or of the Labour Government. He had noticed also that his friend, Wedgwood, had been in a way punished by being fobbed off with the Duchy of Lancaster. The suggestion was thrown out that it might be worthwhile someone going to England to- gauge precisely the new possibilities. Would Lalaji care to?

Lalaji had no illusions about the Labour Party. The Deshbandhu had no expectations of big things from Ramsay MacDonald. He thought rather differently of Lloyd George — whom the Deshbandhu himself perhaps resembled in certain ways, in quick and decisive leadership, in a daring with which each brushed aside all inconvenient commitments once a particular course of action had been chosen; both had an amazing capacity for taking unexpected decisions and springing surprises. Of all the British statesmen, Das thought, Lloyd George was the one person really capable of doing big things; and he added he rather felt one day he would stage a comeback at the head of Labour. After all, his social programmes even in pre-war days had shown such leanings, and once he made up his mind, he would know how to awe the working-class crowds better than any of the leaders thrown up by the Labour Party. This prophecy was not fulfilled, but Lloyd George did on several occasions, after the Liberal Party had been all but liquidated in the years that followed, seem to be seriously seeking an alliance with Labour. "Lib Lab" was a new coinage that went round for some time.

C. R. Das talked also a great deal about the ending of dyarchy and was optimistic about achieving this speedily. Not that he supposed that when his majority in the Bengal Council threw out all official proposals the end would be achieved; but it seemed there were some talks going on for certain measures which might technically change the provincial dyarchy into something else.

On his way back from Russa Road Lalaji wondered whether, encouraged by Das's pact with Muslims, the Bengal civilians too had started dangling before him the prospect of a separate constitutional advance for Bengal. Das with his great gifts of leadership and his tremendous sacrifice made so cheerfully, might yet be unwarily led into a trap by those more practised than himself in the craft of high diplomacy — that impression on Lalaji's mind seemed to be the net result of the Russa Road chat. He had not been able 'to have it out' with him as he thought at Karachi that he would try to remove the load off his breast. But perhaps the load vanished in another way.

He now adjusted himself to Das's 'way of doing things'. While admiring his great qualities and valuing his friendship dearly, he knew that this friendship henceforward must be put on a different basis, if he was no more to undergo the sort of disappointment that the Bengal Fact had caused him. The friendship certainly did not die. When a few months later repression started afresh in Bengal and Subhash Bose, without any charges brought home against him, was imprisoned under a mere executive fiat, Lalaji felt much moved, and as soon as he got the news he sent the Deshbandhu a telegram, putting himself entirely at his service.

The homeward journey too was punctuated by halts — at Banaras, Allahabad and Delhi. At Allahabad his principal object was to meet Madan Mohan Malaviya and to exchange notes with him — as he had done with others since his release and more particularly during this tour.

It happened to be an ardh kumbh year and pilgrims were flocking to Prayag for this six-yearly event. Lalaji arrived there in time for a Vidwad Parishad convoked by Malaviyaji on this occasion at the Sangam (the confluence of the sacred rivers that makes Prayag holy). The Pandits from Kashi and other places had assembled there to consider the problems of 'untouchability' of those who were being claimed back on behalf of Hinduism and to give a vyavastha or verdict based on scriptural authority. Being neither a Brahmin nor a Sanskrit scholar, Lalaji had the franchise neither of birth nor of learning to have a say in this assembly. He just watched and listened. He too knew a thing or two about the Smritis — though he had read them in (or with the aid of) translations — and could confront the pandits with authorities that would not be easy to challenge or explain away. But he could never frame half a sentence in Sanskrit, and the Parishad recognised no other language.

Nor was his less than nodding acquaintance with the sacred language of much help to him in properly following the proceedings. But it required no Sanskrit for one to make out that Malaviya whom all his political co-workers regarded as the conservative of conservatives in social questions was by many in this assembly taken for a rank revolution-monger! Again and again the text-flinging became riotous and it looked as if all the time half a dozen crazy badminton rackets were promiscuously battering half a dozen shuttlecocks. When the august assembly was in a high mood, a dozen or more of its distinguished members would be seen rising in their seats and shouting at the top of their voices — *vayamapi panditah* (we too are pandits).

It was fortunate for the Hindu fold that the 'untouchables' never heard the Pandits in assembly, for their conservative wing in one sitting's speeches might have driven out more untouchables than had been weaned away by the proselytising activity of Christian and Muslim missions in a few centuries. It speaks volumes for the unique patience and optimism of Malaviyaji that he was trying to carry even these Pandits along on the road of reform.

With the work being directed by the Shuddhi Sabha headquarters at Delhi, with Swami Shraddhananda at the helm, Lalaji was probably acquainted well enough already, though he had no intention of taking a direct interest in it. The chief attractions of Delhi, therefore, were the new MLA's in khadi who began to pour in for their maiden session. It would be a sight to watch them at their new job and also there would be a further opportunity of meeting some of the leaders whom he had missed in his recent wanderings - in particular those from the south. At Pandit Motilal's invitation he attended some of the early Swarajist meetings for important consultations to which N. C. Kelkar and Vithalbhai Patel and A. Rangaswami Aiyanger besides, of course, the leader, Motilal Nehru, used to be the principal participants.

The khadi-clad, Gandhi-capped MLA's were a new excitement for the large retinue of the Assembly Chamber, but on the whole they took the liveried salaaming all right without embarrassment and yet unapologetic about their own white homespun livery.

One of the early things they wanted to do, after the swearing-in and other preliminaries were over, was to demand the release of Mahatma Gandhi. The Congress President, Muhammad Ali, has said that he was looking for the 'key to Yeravda'. The Swarajists thought they might try and succeed where the Maulana did not appear to have much chance. On February 5 the question was to be debated in the Assembly; that morning Lalaji went to Pandit Motilal's Western Court rooms. His visitor's pass had been arranged. While yet they conferred, the news came that the Government had ordered the Mahatma's release, and where they had been thinking of slashing speeches for the-day's battle, they soon got busy with appropriate greetings to their leader on his release, and in these messages some of them could not help claiming the credit for their party to have found 'the key to Yeravda'.

The Delhi sojourn provided occasion also for a discussion with Hakim Ajmal Khan and Dr. M. A. Ansari regarding the deterioration in Hindu-Muslim relations.

The sea-side stay in quest of health and the subsequent wandering about in many provinces beginning with the dash to Poona and ending with the return to Delhi and Lahore had been worthwhile. Perhaps this gave him a much better opportunity to study the Tie of the land' after the ebbing away of the non-cooperation campaign than attending the Kakinada session could have provided. This had also settled his priority no. 1 — the untouchables — for work in the immediate future. The present writer had accompanied Lalaji throughout on this important tour, Lahore to Sindh and back again to Lahore.

Fight against Untouchability

The drive against untouchability conceived at the end of 1923 had for its immediate provocation the outrageous proposal in Muhammad Ali's presidential address to the Kakinada Congress to split the 'untouchable' community between Hindu and Muslim missionary organisations. The suggestion really emanated from a wealthy Mussalman willing to give away a large amount of money for work on behalf of Islam in this 'field', and had been conveyed to the Congress by its Muslim president as a proposal that would eliminate one effective cause of friction. Before long it became known that the unnamed wealthy Muslim philanthropist behind the scenes was none other than His Highness the Agha Khan whose men and money in fact were already making vigorous inroads into Hinduism in the worst of proselytising traditions.

Jugal Kishore Birla's munificent offer of Rs. 5,000 a month had relieved Lalaji of the immediate worry of a begging campaign and he straightway set up an Achhut Uddhar Committee for work in the Punjab in which the Sanatanists might collaborate with the unorthodox. But the work was not to be confined to the Punjab, Lalaji set up an all-India committee with himself as president. The head office was set up at Sabzi Mandi, Delhi.

The Servants of the People — the number of whose branches with new additions now ran to nearly a dozen — were out, almost the whole lot, to various districts for the Achhut Uddhar drive in the Punjab and the U.P. The number of whole-time workers under this organisation at one stage ran to nearly one hundred. The work was confined mostly to the Punjab, Delhi and the UP, but the Servants of the People had its own centres outside these areas too. A remnant of Lalaji's much earlier work in this field was a stretch of land on the Ravi not far from the Shahdara railway station, near the baradari that he had bought for creating a colony where some depressed class families might be settled and where a centre might be set up for educating them to better ways of life and to economic betterment through small industries. Other things had intervened, in particular his long exile. Now he thought many times of working out a scheme and putting the land to its proper use — a colony of the untouchables.

This time however all the emphasis was on propaganda work through public meetings, lantern lectures, conferences, etc., amongst the caste Hindus to banish from their minds the idea of untouchability. The baradari land was eventually sold by the Servants of the People Society after Lalaji's death and the money realised went to the Society's Achhut Uddhar Fund. A part of the land remained with the Society and on this was set up on a modest scale an ashram run by the Village Industries Association.

Under Mahatma Gandhi's guidance the Congress had adopted the removal of untouchability as one of the planks of its constructive programme. Lalaji devoted his time and energy to working out this item, as it was one that appealed to him most in that programme. With him this was neither theological nor proselytising activity. In fact his approach was in no way different from what Mahatma Gandhi had preached.

Still critics who accepted the constructive programme sometimes found fault with Lalaji's Achhut Uddhar activity as communal work, presumably because it was not done under the Congress auspices. The little known fact was that Lalaji had offered his services to the Congress Working Committee to work on their behalf this item of the constructive programme. He had offered further that he would not burden the general funds in any way, but would himself raise all the money the work needed.

The Working Committee never accepted or acknowledged the offer. But some time later Deshbandhu Das conveyed to him that the offer had been considered by the Committee but the President (Muhammad Ali) could not swallow some of the names suggested by Lalaji for constituting a board proposed by Lalaji for their work, and he mentioned that of Malaviyaji as amongst those objected to. The Deshbandhu said he would talk things over again with the Maulana, but Lalaji never afterwards heard from the Working Committee or the President or the Deshbandhu. Reliable reports reached him, however, that the Maulana had remarked that the Congress could not permit a 'second Shraddhananda' working under its own auspices. Anyway, he gave Lalaji no chance to make the Congress professions regarding untouchability good. There was nothing surprising in that, for was not Lalaji's resolve a direct counterblast to the Agha Khan's suggestion that Muhammad Ali had presidentially commended? It is significant that Mahatma Gandhi started the Harijan Sangh a good while after he had completely cut adrift from the influence of the Ali brothers.

The Birlas had in the first instance promised money only for one year, but the fact is that they continued it till Lalaji's death and on a reduced scale even after that for a while. Then the Harijan Sangh was started and they had to divert their grant — and to enhance it For the Punjab the Harijan Sangh was a sort of continuation of Lalaji's work, because gradually he had withdrawn his life-members from the Achhut Uddhar Committee, as they were needed elsewhere.

In Swaraj Party

"Now, which of you three is going to make room for Lalaji?" was the somewhat abrupt question with which Shamlal Nehru greeted the three Swarajist Assemblymen from the Punjab - Duni Chand (of Ambala), Raizada Hans Raj and Dewan Chaman Lal whom he found chatting in the Assembly library. Shamlal obviously looked full of important news. He had just come to know that the rules for eligibility to the Legislative Assembly were about to be amended, and that it had been decided that the existing rule which disqualified anyone who had been in prison with a sentence exceeding six months would go.

"Anyone of us, and willingly," was the Punjab trio's reply to Shamlal's query. They were all delighted that Lalaji would become eligible.

This unofficial forecast came early in 1925 during the Delhi session of the Assembly. Lalaji had hitherto been ineligible not merely because of his sentences of imprisonment, but also for his having been disbarred by the Chief Court. In 1917, during his war-time exile in the States the authorities had banned the circulation of some of his books and on the strength of this arbitrary ban, the Chief Court, without hearing him, had removed his name from its rolls. Of this additional disqualification few even among his close friends seemed aware and the term in prison was generally believed to be the sole obstacle. The question naturally arose whether a seat could be found for Lalaji if the obstacle disappeared.

The very day Shamlal had brought the news. Raizada Hans Raj sent a letter to Lalaji offering to make roam for him. During the next few months he repeated his offer several times leaving it to Lalaji to avail himself of it at the right moment.

In the course of that very session the amendment in rules was notified and it did not go quite far enough. The six months' limit was raised to one year, and as Lalaji had served an aggregate sentence exceeding that period, it did not seem quite sure whether he would be eligible. Raizada himself consulted some of the eminent lawyers in the Assembly — amongst them M. A. Jinnah — and they could not give a reassuring reply. Later on, during the Shimla session, Sir Alexander Muddiman, the Home Member, was informally asked, and his interpretation made clear Lalaji's way to the Assembly; for, according to Sir Alexander it was not the aggregate of the different sentences but the length of each single sentence that was to be taken into account. None of the sentences awarded in Lalaji's case went beyond a year and he might therefore be deemed eligible.

Shortly after, Lalaji was taken ill at Solan. On his recovery he told Raizada Hans Raj that he had satisfied himself about the interpretation of the amended rule and made sure that he was eligible. The Raizada wrote out his resignation and came down to Lahore to place it personally in Lalaji's own hands.

About his other disqualification, some of Lalaji's friends sounded the Punjab authorities and ascertained that they had no intention of obstructing Lalaji's return, possibly it was presumed that in any event the disqualification could easily be removed by a representation to the High Court. Since it could be taken as a certainty that there would be no rival candidate to dig up this inconvenient fact and bring it to the notice of the returning authority, Lalaji felt sure that his way to the Assembly Chamber was now clear. So Raizada Hans Raj resigned and in bidding farewell to his constituency through the press, he thankfully recalled that he had been returned unopposed, and he confidently hoped that Lalaji would be returned in like manner. Thanking his colleagues in the Assembly the Raizada expressed the hope that Pandit Motilal would find in Lalaji his "best friend and a true colleague".

When the dates for a by-election were gazetted Lalaji had to be summoned from Delhi telegraphically to Jalandhar to file his papers. Lalaji and the Raizada were the only ones to file nominations. Lalaji had to preside over the Hindu Conference being held on December 6, 1925 in Bombay and thither he proceeded on the withdrawal day. That day (after Lalaji's departure) the Raizada withdrawing, Lalaji was returned unopposed. In The People (December 13) he offered his thanks to Raizada Hans Raj and to the constituency; even to the authorities for "having put no difficulties in my way".

His concluding words were:

> "As to my programme in the Legislative Assembly, I must take some time to formulate it."

We have deliberately given a somewhat detailed recital of these minutiae, for in the subsequent controversy the question loomed large whether Lalaji was pledged to join the Swaraj Party by assurances given at the time of his election. In strict accord with the party code the correct thing for Raizada Hans Raj would have been to place his resignation in the hands of his leader and not in those of Lalaji. The fact is that in his repeated offers to Lalaji, during the best part of a year, the Raizada never laid down any conditions and never demanded any assurances.

In correspondence as well as in talks his offer to resign had all along been entirely free from even a remote suggestion of any accompanying conditions. When he finally desired, the Raizada's resignation, Lalaji did so in the full assurance that the seat was being vacated for him without any conditions for him as "Lalaji", and not for a member or prospective member of this or that party.

On the Raizada's side the only public statement was the one in which while thanking his fellow-Assemblymen and his constituents he expressed the hope that Pandit Motilal would find in Lalaji his "best friend and a true colleague". The hope that he expressed conveyed his own desire and not an assurance extracted from or given by Lalaji; and, even so, he did not explicitly say that he expected Lalaji to join the Swaraj Party Was the "hope" in any way based on any "assurance"? For an answer we should record two further details - a little talk that preceded Raizada Hans Raj's statement, and a letter written in the sequel. After Raizada Hans Raj had written out and signed his resignation and placed it in Lalaji's hands he begged leave to say something — that he held Pandit Motilal in very high esteem and that it should pain him if he (Lalaji) should in any way inconvenience Panditji. Lalaji in reply said that Motilalji should find in him his best friend and true colleague. The talk was all too brief and in broad and rather vague terms.

Later on when Raizada Hans Raj issued his statement to the press, he sought really to repeat Lalaji's own words — though he did not explicitly say so. Seeing in this a possibility of misconstruction and misunderstanding, Lalaji wrote to Raizada Hans Raj that if in any way it was suggested that there was any condition or obligation accompanying his offer or his own acceptance thereof, he was quite willing not to avail himself of the offer, and though the vacancy had already been caused he undertook to have the Raizada re-elected, and to foot the bill for these proceedings. Raizada Hans Raj does not seem to have taken any further steps one way or the other — neither withdrawing his press message nor explaining it to Lalaji, nor availing himself of Lalaji's offer to have him re-elected. Shortly after they had to meet at Jalandhar for the nomination ritual; both filled in the papers and filed them but neither said anything about the press statement or the letter. After Lalaji's departure, Hans Raj filed his withdrawal and secured for Lalaji an unopposed return.

Lalaji was returned early in December 1925. He attended the Congress session at Kanpur at the end of that month without having committed himself to joining the Swaraj Party, in fact at Kanpur he was very near parting company with Pandit Motilal. In The People for January 17, he said:

"I am not a member of the Swaraj Party; I need not become one, as being a Congressman I am a Swarajist for all practical purposes."

When he was sworn in, he had not yet joined the party. In fact before joining the party on January 25, he had already attended several sittings of the Assembly. Five years prior to his formally joining the party he had accepted Pandit Motilal's invitation to join the Swaraj Party, and in doing so, had written to him as leader of the party:

January 20, 1926 My dear Panditji,

I have to thank you for the invitation you have extended to me to join the Swaraj Party in the Legislative Assembly. Last time when I met you I said that personally I had made up my mind to accept your invitation; but that before giving my final consent I would consult my Lahore friends and would give you a final answer on Monday next. Since then, I have consulted my friends, and this letter is the result of that consultation. While joining the party, I would like to make my position quite clear, so that there be no misunderstanding about it now or hereafter. As I read the roles of the party, I do not think my position is in any way inconsistent with them.

(A) I believe in council work. I am opposed to the boycott of councils and the assembly. I am not in favour of the Swarajists accepting offices in the gift of Government.

(B) I don't believe in wholesale obstruction and have never believed in it.

(C) I wish to retain my freedom of action on communal questions. I understand that communal questions shall not be decided by a party vote.

(D) In disputes between labour and capital, I am a labour man; but as I understand, the majority of the Swaraj Party is also of the same way of thinking.

Subject to these observations, I shall be glad to be a member of the party.

Yours sincerely,
Lajpat Rai

He told Motilalji, besides, that his joining the Party would not make his newspapers, The People and the daily Bande mataram, controlled organs of the Party; these were to remain as independent of party affiliation as they had hitherto been.

The assurances and formalities apart, what was Lalaji's political stand about the time he joined the Assembly? In July 1925, he had started his weekly; The People and though even before that he was writing frequently for the press and airing his views, now he was doing so every week and there could be no room for anyone to say that it was not known where he agreed and where he differed. When the withdrawal of non-cooperation started with the Chauri Chaura anti-climax he had begun to re-think politics and even from jail he had sent out articles (his authorship of which was not much of a secret) giving the trend of his thoughts. This was clearly a Swarajist trend — that is, he desired Congressmen to capture the legislatures. Even from prison he had helped C. R. Das in laying the foundations of this party. When he came out, even while convalescing, he had done his bit for the Swarajist candidates. In the Punjab the entire campaign had been his care. After that, when he went to England he had been in the closest contact with Motilalji, and had carried on talks with the Labour Government on behalf of the Swaraj Party. But he had not joined the party, had never been subject to its discipline and had valued and exercised his freedom to criticise it wherever he thought fit. He was an unofficial Swarajist in the sense that:

(1) he believed in a council programme and was not with the "no-change" school; and

(2) he did not believe in acceptance of office, and therefore was not with the Responsivist school.

To a hurried lumper he might easily appear to be nothing but a Swarajist, and yet to one rather scrupulous about essential detail his differences with Swarajism were clearly expressed, and you might even say, underlined in his writings, week after week. Starting as a heresy, and for a while being treated as such by the 'no-change' orthodoxy, Swarajism had in turn settled down into an orthodox church and developed its own Athanasian creed which demanded that "whosoever will be saved" must swear by "obstruction, continuous, uniform and consistent." This formula Lalaji had at no stage been able to accept. Like "Swaraj within a year" and by a named date it seemed to him obviously much too unpractical and to his ears almost had a ring of insincerity about it. In practice the Swarajists had often strayed far from the letter of the formula.

They had installed V. J. Patel into the Speaker's chair and their everyday practice in the legislature was by no means consistently governed by the obstructionist canon. Obstruction in fact was just one of the weapons in their armoury. But they put certain rather severe limitations of their cooperation - they would not accept 'office', and in its original wide signification this had meant that even committees of the house were under taboo. By the time, however, Lalaji arrived on the scene, the taboo was already slackening its grip, for the Swarajist leader himself, quite wisely (as Lalaji thought), had accepted a seat on the Skeen Committee on Indianisation of the Army. This was a significant departure from the Swarajists' avowed creed — a serious violation of the taboo, and one that many expected would inevitably lead to other violations. In fact some feared (others hoped) that this might be the thin edge of the Responsivist wedge.

At times Lalaji felt that the Swarajist leadership was becoming too exacting in the name of discipline, that it was forgetting all too soon the indulgence it had asked for its own 'heresy', that of late there had been too much talk of "amputating the diseased limb", whilst the orthodox non-cooperation still could not convince himself that the entire Parliamentary limb calling itself the Swaraj Party was anything but a malignant growth on the body-politic. In criticising what seemed to him the intolerant attitude of the leadership, Lalaji seemed at times to be taking the side of the Responsivists though he was so little in sympathy with the quintessence of responsivism in the 1925 context, viz., the desirability of accepting office in a dyarchical Constitution.

He himself had expressed misgivings about his having chosen the wrong moment for his parliamentary debut. For, as he put it, the "situation was uncertain and obscure". In 1925 the discipline and solidarity of the Swaraj Party was being sapped by dissension, and an over-stressing of discipline was only making matters worse. Things came to a crisis with the Tambe episode. Shreepad Balwant Tambe, the Swarajist Speaker of the G P. Legislative Council, was offered an executive councillorship and he accepted it. His action was trebly open to objection. It was wrong of a Congressman to accept office in the diarchical system.

It was a bad parliamentary precedent that a Speaker should be thus seduced by the Government. And it was beyond doubt a clear act of gross undiscipline, for Tambe had never cared even to inform the national executive of the Swaraj Party about the offer and of his own intention. Pandit Motilal was naturally much upset. What made matters worse was that Jayakar and Kelkar and certain other important Swarajists offered, if not exactly an apologia, at least an extenuation of Tambe's conduct.

To them it was practically on the same level with V. J. Patel's appointment to the Speaker's office and Pandit Motilal's nomination to the Skeen Committee It might be that the conduct of Pandit Motilal and of V. J. Patel was not censurable technically as a breach of the party's rules, but the crux of the whole thing (the two dissenters urged) was that the rules had not kept pace with the real evolution of the party's principles and tactics. These had been in a flux and from obstruction simpliciter the party had, without openly admitting so, already travelled a considerable distance towards responsive cooperation and it was high time the party rules and leadership gave due recognition to the fact.

La Affaire Tambe filled the political forum all through October. On November 1, the national executive of the Swaraj Party met at Nagpur. Pandit Motilal maintained that Tambe's was not an isolated action but that it had the backing of many others and that in the Central Provinces — where, the Swarajist successes at the elections had outshone those in all' other provinces, the leader of the party himself had encouraged attempts at securing office. It was plain that the C. P. Swaraj Party was not of one mind regarding the Tambe episode, and a goodly part were in favour of the

Responsivist heresy. In Bombay, Kelkar and Jayakar set afoot a move to get responsive cooperation accepted by the local Swaraj Party. The death of C. R. Das a few months earlier had been a severe blow to Swarajist leadership. Motilal had to face the storm so soon after. He must have missed in counsel the uncanny intuition of C. R. Das, and in action his gigantic dynamic force. The AICC met at Nagpur and the meeting ended in a patched-up truce. But, within a few days this was followed by resignations of Kelkar and Jayakar from the Executive, because they complained that the leader had violated the truce by persisting in attacks on Responsivists. They resigned so that they might be free to air their views.

Thus, the storm still continued to rage when Lalaji was returned by the Jalandhar constituency.

Though he was himself opposed to experimenting with offices, Lalaji's sympathies lay very largely with the Responsivist group. There were ties of personal esteem — a legacy from Tilak's days, and Kelkar and Jayakar and the Maharashtra group in general more or less shared his outlook regarding the need for a Hindu organisation. But more strictly relevant to the questions at issue was the fact that the talk of "uniform, continuous and consistent obstruction" was to Lalaji even more abhorrent than that of office. Besides at a time when a big campaign like that of non-cooperation was not in progress, when the leaders themselves were groping in the dark and policies and principles seemed to have been thrown into the melting pot — at such a time he felt it was not wise to stifle all difference of opinion in the name of 'discipline'. Rather, freedom for a cold scrutiny of all doings seemed more than ever needed so that a clarification might be possible. Jayakar complained of the 'hectoring' tone of the leader of the Swaraj Party and there were many who, whilst not sharing Jayakar's responsivism, felt that the leader was invoking 'discipline' too often and all too readily, and who did not like to see him set up in the role of a political sawbones ready to lop off whatever he suspected of being a "diseased growth".

The Responsivists were thus getting a certain measure of sympathy and support from Lalaji even though he himself was neither enamoured of their label nor convinced that the acceptance of office under the diarchical Constitution would be a wise step.

In fact he was not completely reconciled even to the acceptance of the Speaker's office, though here experience soon allayed his apprehensions for which the credit we suppose should go to the genius of V. J. Patel who filled the office with dignity and yet made himself useful to the cause to an extent beyond the best expectations.

This feud inside the Swaraj Party was thus leading to an internal crisis when Lalaji arrived in the Assembly. Not being a partisan, and in fact not being even a member of the party, he was for a while of use as a moderating influence. After filing his nomination papers he had proceeded to Bombay to preside over the Hindu Conference, for which M. R. Jayakar had been chosen Chairman of the Reception Committee. Pandit Motilal and the President-elect for the next Congress session. Sarojini Naidu, were also present in Bombay, and after much discussion in which Lalaji's was an effective role a truce was arranged.

But the "cease-fire" did not mean a settlement. It afforded an armistice; whether a settlement was possible could only be decided at the Congress session at Kanpur at the end of the month.

And a settlement formula seemed as far away as ever when the Congress assembled at Kanpur and Sarojini Naidu took over from Mahatma Gandhi. At the end of his term, the Mahatma retired from the political arena devoting a whole year to his ashram and to the direction of his pet constructive programme. The Congress organisation he now handed over to the Swarajists — completing the surrender he had started some months earlier. This surrender had begun with a bare tolerating of the Swarajist heresy of a parliamentary programme; and even for their being tolerated within the pale, the Swarajists had to pay a price in the form of especial support of the khadi programme.

At Belgaum, when Gandhi presided, they effected a settlement with him by accepting the 'khadi franchise' for membership of the Congress. When a few months later the AICC met at Patna, it was clear that the Swarajists regarded the franchise as unworkable, to put it bluntly, as a nuisance, and some of the no-changers indulged in plain-speaking and said that the Swarajists had never been sincere in accepting the franchise. Gandhi himself was in the mood to yield further, and even waiving aside the question whether the AICC had any jurisdiction to tamper with the resolution passed by the plenary session, sacrificed his pet, the spinning franchise, as a peace-offering and as a gesture of generosity. At Kanpur he completed the surrender by handing over the Congress machinery to the Swaraj Party.

Hitherto the Swaraj Party had managed the elections on its own, with the barest sufferance from the Congress; now the elections were to be run fully with the Congress imprimatur. The parliamentary programme had hitherto been an affair of the Swaraj Party only; now it became the care of the Congress as such. The Swarajists thus got the entire Congress prestige, machinery "and funds at their disposal The Congress now accepted the responsibility of whatever they did as a parliamentary party, and of course this also meant in a way that for their doings they were now accountable before the entire Congress. The Swarajist camel was now in possession of the Arab's entire tent. The surrender completed, Gandhi retired to Sabarmati to devote himself to the charkha and the promotion of the homespun.

But the principal resolution of the Kanpur session not merely installed the Swarajists in power in the Congress, it also laid down a programme for them. And here controversy again popped its head: will it be an obstructionist programme or a responsivist one?

All attempts at finding a via media failed. Pandit Motilal would not tolerate the Responsivist label, nor would he brook any formula that might expressly or by implication tolerate acceptance of office. Within the limitations thus set it did not seem possible to satisfy Kelkar and Jayakar.

As in 1907 at Surat and in 1920 at Nagpur, Lalaji was the question-mark of the Congress session. He had not even joined the Swaraj Party; for his unopposed election to the Assembly he had not had to ask for party nomination or to appeal in the name of that party or its programme, and in his writings in the press since his election he had quite freely criticised some of the Swarajist doings and doctrines. The Responsivists got a certain measure of support but he was not attached to their group and had not accepted either their label or their faith in capturing office. In his home province there was no question of office for the Swaraj Party; nor were there any Responsivists among his Punjab lieutenants and friends. In fact, their full pressure was exerted in favour of a settlement with Pandit Motilal. The Responsivists, on the other hand, were bound to feel let down by him should he settle with Nehru.

When the Swarajists first went to the Legislative Assembly, with the support of the Independent Party, they had offered terms of settlement to the Government. This had happened on February 18, 1924 and all the "innocent souls" in the Congress believed that the Swarajists would just present that demand — an 'ultimatum' as some chose to call it - and be done with the Assembly for good. The demand had been presented and for the best part of two years there had been no indication that it was going to be accepted; meanwhile those who had been anxiously waiting for the final exit of Congressmen from the Assembly had with surprise and with misgivings watched the progressive dilution of the original obstructionist programme, till it had come down to acceptance even of a nominated seat on the Skeen Committee.

Now that the next general election was in sight, the Swarajists once again began to think of the much deferred break over non-acceptance of the "National Demand". The draft resolution for the Kanpur Congress laid down that they should walk out of the Assembly and go to the country and devote themselves to the furtherance of the constructive programme. Such a gesture, it was believed, would impress the voters' imagination and thus secure for the party even more glorious triumphs at the polls than those of the 1923 elections.

Such a programme was not much to Lalaji's liking. It seemed he would rather go with Malaviyaji and Jayakar and Kelkar, and then there break with the Swaraj Party — which would now mean with the majority party of the Congress itself. But pressure was brought to bear upon him, particularly from his Punjab friends, to avert such a happening. Within the framework of the draft resolution Pandit Motilal was willing to consider modification of detail, and friends urged that Lalaji must come to a settlement with Motilalji. At Nagpur too the Punjab contingent had insisted that he must settle with Gandhi. But there was this difference — he himself was anxious to arrive at a settlement with Gandhi; for, he accepted the principle of non-cooperation, and was all for starting a big non-cooperation campaign; only certain details were unacceptable to him. His own inclinations and commitments led him much further away from the Nehru programme in December 1925 than they had done from the Gandhi programme four years earlier. Negotiations led to a breaking-point again and again, but common friends tirelessly ran to and fro and again and yet again brought Panditji and Lalaji together to arrive at a settlement. At Lalaji's insistence the draft resolution was changed in several of its provisions; in particular it was provided that the Swarajist members of the Legislative Assembly and the Council of State shall vote for the rejection of the Finance Bill and immediately after leave their seats. Till then they could function as they had hitherto done under their party rules. Also it laid down that:

> "It shall be open to the Special Committee to allow the Swarajist members ... to attend the legislatures when such attendance is in its opinion essential for some special or unforeseen purpose".

In other words, of the budget (or New Delhi) session only the fag-end was being risked, though the brief, much less important session at Shimla would be under interdict, and if in all likelihood the special committee deemed it of unusual importance it would ask the Swarajist Assemblymen, to attend it. This was the compromise resolution that Pandit Motilal moved and Lalaji supported. Malaviyaji moved a briefly worded amendment which reads:

> "That the work in the legislatures shall be so carried as to utilise them to the best possible advantage for the early establishment of full responsible Government, cooperation being reverted to when it may be necessary to advance the national cause and obstruction when that may be necessary for the advancement of the same cause."

Jayakar, while seconding the amendment, announced his own and Kelkar's resignations from the Assembly and Moonje's from the C. P. Legislative Council.

A break had thus come — not with Motilal Nehru, but with Kelkar and Jayakar — and this was no small wrench to Lalaji. Perhaps if his own Punjab lieutenants had not been so keenly insistent he would have acted differently. But Lajjavati and Santanam and Achint Ram had in beseeching him done their utmost and it was not so easy for Lalaji to ignore their earnest entreaties. Perhaps if these lieutenants had fully taken into consideration their leader's commitments with Jayakar and the Poona group, or realised how ill at ease he would feel after a break with them, they might not have been so insistent. The Kanpur resolution in its final form had enough elasticity to be deemed not completely inconsistent with his own assessment of what the political situation required, but he would not have liked to break with Jayakar and the Poona group.

On the merits of the resolution he wrote in his paper that the Kanpur session had "brought back the Congress into its own" as all political work was henceforth to be done "in the name and under the guidance of the Congress. The Swaraj Party had been dominating the legislatures; outside it had no organisation worth the name." On the anomaly of such a self-contained party with no one except the electorates to give account to, his comment ran: "A good many Swarajists did not care at all for the Congress Committees, they paid no subscription, attended no meetings and did nothing to further the cause of the Congress. The only authority they looked to and cared for was their leader. In fact, the Council Swaraj Party had members who were not Congressmen. The Kanpur resolution has changed all this."

In current controversy the two concrete recurring issues were — obstruction and office. On the first of these he reiterated his stand: "I am very strongly opposed to the boycott of Councils and also to the policy of wholesale obstruction in the Councils. I believe that the Councils should be worked for what they are worth in the same way in which they have been worked by the Swaraj Party during the last two years."

And on the acceptance of offices: "I am still of opinion that Nationalism requires that there should be at least one party of Indian politicians who would not accept any high office in the gift of the Government. In doing so, Indian Nationalists are only following the historic example of Irish Nationalists."

The Kanpur resolution was in no way opposed to such an approval. But it could be asked, "What is the meaning of that part of the resolution which requires the Swarajists, after the next session, to come out of the Councils and appeal to the country?"

Lalaji's interpretation (and justification) of this provision was: "As I understand it, the object is to make a striking demonstration. A helpless people like ourselves who have no material sanction behind their demand cannot altogether banish demonstrations of this kind from their programme. In the history of Indian Nationalism this has been done several times, even long before Mahatma Gandhi's movement was born. Sir Pherozeshah Mehta once left the Council with all his followers as a protest against the Government attitude . . . Mr. Shastri left the Council after the Viceroy had rejected his resolution about the administration of Martial Law in the Punjab. The Swarajists are going to the country for the new elections. Their chief work in the existing Assembly has been to unite with other parties in putting forward their minimum demand for the change of the Constitution. I see no objection on principle to the course contemplated by them. They want to show to the Indian public, and to the world in general, that they have done everything possible to come to terms with the British Government and the Government has invariably treated their advances with contempt."

Assessing the gains of the Congress, Lalaji wrote: "I think the one permanent gain of the Congress session has been that the Congress has come into its own. So far as political work is concerned, it has been no nest for the last three years. The whole of the political work was done by the Swaraj Party. Consequently the latter loomed large and the Congress was overshadowed by it The Swaraj Party will now be practically abolished. The Congress Executive will control and guide the policy of those who seek election to the Councils and the Assembly in its name and under its prestige. This is a decided advantage both from the tactical and practical points of view;" and he added "though it is not entirely free from risk."

However, convincing this might have sounded, the fact is that the leaders of neither of the two schools in conflict were satisfied, and, on neither side could be seen the requisite good will and trust needed for making a compromise a success. Lalaji himself had been pressed rather overmuch by his own Punjab lieutenants -

particularly by Santanam and Lajjavati not to part company with Pandit Motilal, and somehow to evolve or accept a compromise. The sequel showed that such pressure had not yielded an enduring settlement.

One notable little event was an innovation at this session — the ceremonial hoisting of the national tricolour. Hardiker's Hindustani Seva Dal was by now regularly functioning and Lalaji was chosen for unfurling the flag and taking the salute.

But as could have been anticipated, the Maharashtra group were sore. And not long after Lalaji had to complain about the sour comment he was getting from them. He wrote in The People:

> "My Maratha friends appear to be very angry with me. Ever since the Kanpur Congress, the Maratha has been at me in some way or the other. In every issue it has some fling at me. I have never replied and do not intend to do so now. My respect for and attachment to Messrs. Jayakar and Kelkar has not in any way been affected by the differences in our policy. The Poona Maharashtrians and myself have been lifelong friends and it will pain me immensely if ever I have to say anything unkind about them. I must resist that temptation to the best of my capacity. I am confident that we shall work on the same platform and with the same mutual goodwill as we have always done in the past. The present differences are only temporary. I do not think sarcasm and ridicule ought to be employed against friends and that is my only reply to the lasting in the Maratha".

He was being invited to preside over a Hindu Conference in Burma. He accepted the Invitation but asked the organisers to put off the conference till after the New Delhi session. But (as he wrote later on in The People) "the desire to see Burma, and be finished with it prevailed." This was somewhat natural as he had never been to Burma after 1907, and then, being kept in captivity had only aroused his curiosity about Burma without an opportunity to satisfy it. Possibly also he wanted to work off the rather melancholy effect produced on him by the Kanpur developments and on second thoughts he hastened compliance with the Burma summons. Accompanied by Achint Ram from Kanpur, he proceeded to take the steamer that was leaving Calcutta on New Year's Day.

He met his old Burmese friends, and made new contacts among them and of course he met and heard the Indian settlers there and gave them what advice he deemed fit regarding their problems. Above all he visited Fort Dufferin and the PWD Bungalow inside that Mandalay fort in which he had been kept a prisoner.

He saw the pagodas and the images, the ancient ones as well as the new shrine, then being built for the relics that the British authorities at Peshawar had presented to the Burmese priests.

His jottings published in The People had some interesting observations about the Burmese manners and morals, the picturesque costumes even of men and the extraordinary long hair of the women folk — streaming down to the ankles — "and are even longer than that." He heard that when some time ago the patriot priest Uttama was released from prison... "young Burmese ladies, made him pass through a double row of themselves on a path covered by their hair, which they stretched along the path." This beat all the emotional doings of crowds for their leaders that he had witnessed in his own country!

The Indian community was rather perturbed over the legislation then pending regarding expulsion of non-Burmese. With his keen sense of realities and his customary candour he summed up the situation facing them: "The Indian has had his time. He is no longer essential. The country can be governed and managed without his help and cooperation. In fact, the Anglo-Indian rulers, merchants and manufacturers would be happy if the Indian is eliminated from Burma altogether." He frankly said that "the problem of Burma must be decided in the interest of Burma and the Burmese and not of anybody else." He advised the Indian community therefore to "remain there only as Burmans", completely identifying themselves with the Burmese, so that they would not have to ask for special representation and the Burmese not to treat them as aliens. This counsel of perfection was never adopted and the result was seen in the sufferings of the Indian community when in 1942 they were forced to flee to India before the on-rushing tide of a Japanese invasion.

From Burma he returned to New Delhi to attend the Assembly session which started in the latter half of January 1926. A few days later, as we have seen, he formally joined the Swaraj Party. During this session he made a notable contribution by participating in several important debates — when the first Indian Trades-Union Bill came up, and when a resolution on employment came up, and yet another (Mr. Shafee's) regarding political prisoners and exiles. The last-mentioned touched the personal chords, recalling what he had undergone and claiming that no one else in the House was better qualified to speak on the motion out of personal experience.

"Practically, all the three clauses have applied to me at some stage or other of my life. In 1907, I was deported under Regulation III of 1818. In 1921 I was convicted of a crime which the Government of India afterwards declared was not a crime. The same year I was again convicted of a crime which the Government Advocate said had not been proved. When I wanted to return from America I was treated as an exile by the refusal of a passport."

While yet this session was on, the Hindu Mahasabha met at Delhi under the presidentship of Raja Narendranath. Lalaji took a leading part in its proceedings In fact the Mahasabha policy was then being shaped mainly by Malaviyaji and Lalaji Raja Saheb as President had been, in the first place, their joint choice. A strong section in that organisation favoured the idea that the Hindu Mahasabha should nun candidates on its own ticket in the general election due in a few months Lalaji (and Malaviyaji) opposed this policy, and following his lead, the delegates decided against the proposal except to a very limited extent, that is, where the local contingencies absolutely demanded that the Mahasabha should be represented by its own nominees.

In March while the Assembly session was still in progress, the AICC met at Delhi, and substantially altered the walkout provisions of the Kanpur resolution. The course now decided upon was that the walk-out should not be put off till the rejection of the Finance Bill. The Kanpur Resolution was sought to be amended. Lalaji objected that the AICC had no jurisdiction to amend the resolution passed by the plenary session. The objection was accepted but the sponsors of the new move thereupon shifted their ground and said that they interpreted the Kanpur resolution as laying down the latest date and that an earlier walk-out was not contrary to its text. Lalaji took exception to the 'interpretation', but was outvoted. At Kanpur he had insisted that the walk-out should be resorted to only after the throwing out of the Finance Bill.

That provision now having been abrogated, he was in a way free to absolve himself of the Kanpur commitments. In actual fact the AICC resolution cut short the party's attendance in the Assembly only by a few days — it was already near the fag end — Lalaji wrote in his paper that if he had his way he would have put off the walk-out till the August session, but the die has, however, been cast.

6

Writings and Speeches

The Hindu-Muslim Problem is the Problem of India

The Hindu-Muslim Problem is the problem of India. We have heard and read much of Hindu-Muslim unity. It is always a matter of controversy between the Anglo-Indian [British person in India] and the Nationalist. The former asserts, and the latter denies, the impossibility of Hindus and Muslims uniting together to form one nation. The amount of unity or disunity existing at a particular moment is also always an issue. Yet it is a fact that from 1919 to the end of 1921 Hindus and Muslims of India were fairly united. It was during this period that for the first time in the history of India a Kafir preached from the pulpit of the biggest and historically the most important and the most magnificent mosque of Northern India. It was during the same period that the Malechhas fraternised with the Hindus on the occasion of their religious festivals.

It is also a fact that the amount of unity achieved in this short period, has since then melted down, and for the last three years Hindus and Mussalmans have been at daggers drawn with each other to an extent never before known under British rule. All attempts to stem the tide have so far proved ineffectual. All efforts for finding a solution have been fruitless. It cannot be denied that at the moment of writing, the relations between the two communities are strained almost to the breaking point. Communal riots and scuffles are of more frequent occurrence than ever before. Mutual distrust and suspicion has reached the Nth point. Even in Congress circles, in spite of much hugging and cooing, the relations between the leaders of the two communities are not free from distrust and suspicion. Hindu-Muslim unity is always put in the forefront of the Congress programme, but so far the leaders have failed to successfully grapple with the situation and find out a suitable solution. The explanation is obvious. Either they have lost influence with the masses, or they are not sincere. I cannot accept the latter alternative, and thus it is only the former that is left to us to adopt.

Before Mahatma Gandhi was released, the whole country looked to the Yeravda jail for the cure of the disease that had overtaken the body politic during his incarceration. All hopes were concentrated on one person, and that person being in jail, it was expected that his freedom would mean the freedom of the country from Hindu-Muslim quarrels. Both parties had faith in him. His leadership was acknowledged by all. There was not the least possible suspicion of his motives. He was the very personification of love, forbearance, trust, and goodness. So it was believed that the "key to the Yeravda jail" was the key to Hindu-Muslim unity. Providence in its own wisdom supplied that key, and the Mahatma was released. It is now more than six months that he has been released. His health was very delicate when he was released, so delicate that he could not leave the hospital for about six weeks or so after his release. Yet with characteristic selflessness he immediately set himself to study the situation, to probe into the causes of this unhappy change. He left nothing unexplored. He met and heard the stories of both sides, and also of those who professed to belong to no side. He made independent enquiries, and thought and meditated.

Eventually he issued a statement which, sweet, reasonable, and highly conciliatory though it was, failed to satisfy anyone. When I say anyone, I exclude that class (a fairly large and influential body) for whom his word is law and who will not question anything he says. If any distinction were to be made between the amount of satisfaction the statement gave to the Hindus and the

Muslims, it will not be wrong to say that it gave less satisfaction to the former than to the latter. There is, indeed, a general impression among the Hindus that in apportioning blame and responsibility he was not impartial. There are classes of Hindus (most influential, energetic, and active) whom his statement mortally offended, and who have not hesitated to retaliate with words and resolutions of protest and anger. Whatever one may think of its justifiability or otherwise, this represents a frame of mind which no one who is anxious to bring about lasting peace between: the two communities can ignore.

The solution which the Mahatma suggested, and the cure he prescribed, have, I am afraid, appealed to none. Even his diagnosis is not so masterly as one had a right to expect from him. He has laid great stress on mere symptoms and has not gone deep into the underlying and predisposing causes. He had something to say about Mian Fazl-e-Husain and Swami Shraddhanand, but he did not go into the forces that went to make the one and the other. No one doubts his honesty of purpose, his deep love for all, his desire for peace, and his anxiety to bring about such a complete unity among Hindus and Muslims as to make their united demand for Swarajya irresistible and to make Swarajya itself, when attained, durable and progressive. But with all this the document is rather disappointing, and the solution suggested is on the face of it superficial, though noble and magnanimous in appearance. The events of the last six months are enough evidence of its utter failure both as a palliative or [and] as a curative remedy.

Yet amidst all these disappointments and disconcerting events and circumstances, and in the midst of [the] resulting chaos, there is one fact which emerges boldly and which gives hope to all well-wishers of India. However, divided Hindus and Muslims may be, however bitter their relations with each other, they are still united in their demand for Swarajya, in their opposition to the Government, and in their hatred of the subjugation imposed upon them from without. It will stand to the eternal credit of Mahatma Gandhi that he has brought politics home to the masses of India, that he has created a wonderful and never to be effaced awakening in them, and that he has produced a consciousness which marks the beginning of a real nationhood. With this solid and permanent achievement to the Mahatma's credit, there is no reason to despair of the future. His statement may not be as satisfying as one would have wished it to be, but he is still at the wheel and is hopeful as ever of being able to lead us through to the desired goal. But the one essential condition of success is that there must be no ignoring of facts, and no clinging to shibboleths blown away by the wind of experience. If he will apply his mind to the removal of the real causes of Hindu-Muslim disunity, and keep himself open as to methods and means, he may yet succeed. Even if he does not, others may, given the right attitude, the right mind, and the readiness to apply the right remedy.

After the above was written on board the ship during my voyage to India, I have had further corroboration of statements made in what I have seen, read, and observed since my landing at Bombay on the 18th of October, 1924. The two shocking [pieces of] news which I heard immediately on landing were about the Kohat tragedy and Mahatma Gandhi's fast. The most disconcerting feature of the former was the total emigration of the Hindus from Kohat, out of fear of further Muslim attacks. I am not at present prepared to assert what the respective liabilities of the communities were in regard to this tragedy, but I have no doubt in my mind that the Government has throughout shown such utter inefficiency and incompetency as stands unique in the history of British rule in India. I am not very much enamoured of British rule, or for the matter of that [for that matter] of any foreign rule, and in spite of my great admiration for British character, I have been a life-long critic of the British administration. Yet I always believed that the one justification for British rule in India was its ability to protect the minorities, and to guarantee peace and security to them under any circumstances.

The spectacle of a whole community of about 3,500 men, women, and children marching away from their homes to distant places under Government transport arrangements and with Government help, for fear of being annihilated by an infuriated majority, is, however, a conclusive proof of the falsity of this belief, because it can only mean one of the two things-either the insincerity or the inefficiency of British officials, at least in the North-West Frontier Province. I will assume here for the purposes of this argument that the Hindus of Kohat were in the first instance to blame, and that they had provoked the Muhammadans for a fatal attack on them; still, it was the duty of the British Government to keep the Hindus in Kohat, to protect them from further molestation by the Muhammadans, at any cost, to restore order and peace, and then to proceed to try and punish the guilty persons. Practically what happened at Kohat was that the authorities considered themselves overpowered and incapable of granting the necessary security to the Hindus. We have often heard of lynch law. What is lynch law? It is nothing else but the prevention of the ordinary course of justice and the preventing of the authorities from proceeding according to law. Was not the happening at Kohat an illustration of the same tendency?

The law demands that every accused person should be fully protected from molestation by the accusers, until a court had found him guilty and sentenced him legally. Assuming that the Hindus of Kohat were in the position of accused persons, it was the duty of the government to arrest them, and keep them in safe custody until they could be placed before a court of justice and regularly tried. The British Government admittedly failed to do this at Kohat. Even assuming that the Hindus wanted to go away for fear of their lives, it was the duty of the Government to dissuade them, and provide sufficient military security to enable them to stay in their homes. No one wants to leave his home and property in the way the Kohat Hindus did, unless he felt that his life was no longer safe. This particular incident has disclosed a new phase of the communal strife, which should be particularly noted by those who want to patch up and create an appearance of unity without going to the root of the problem.

As regards Mahatma Gandhi's fast, it is an open secret that the desecration of Hindu temples, one after another, at Amethi, Gulbarga, Kohat, and, other places, and the tragedy of Kohat, gave him such a shock that he considered it his duty to undergo a penance for his misunderstanding and mishandling the Hindu-Muslim situation during the last three years. For the first time he felt miserable at the thought that he, who had striven his best to obtain Hindu cooperation for the saving of the Muhrnmadan "temple" Khilafat, had to see desecration of Hindu temples by tens, in most cases without any provocation, at the hands of Muhammadans. The sense of helplessness and disappointment generated by this shock impelled him to impose a purificatory penance of twenty-one days' fast on him [self], in the hope that whilst he purified himself of any sin that he might have committed unconsciously, he would be able to create an atmosphere which might give opportunities of improving Hindu-Muslim relations.

My first feeling was one of disapproval. On reaching Delhi, however, I felt that the impulse which forced him to take the vow could not perhaps be satisfied otherwise. Similar was my feeling about the Unity Conference. I don't think the Unity Conference has solved the problem or could possibly solve it, but on the whole it has been useful in paving the way for the right understanding of the problem with its various complications and implications. Mahatma Gandhi is now resolved to devote the best part of his energies, time, and attention to the solution of this problem. From the bottom of my heart I wish him success, but he will not succeed unless he devotes himself wholeheartedly to the understanding of the real causes that underlie the present situation, and scrupulously avoids proceeding on assumptions and presumptions engendered by affectionate relations with friends, and well-meaning but ineffectual professions of devotion on their part. He must adopt a scientific attitude towards this question, and proceed by scientific methods to find out the root causes of trouble and its possible solutions.

I have resigned my position of leadership in the Congress in order to be free to express myself. I am going to speak the truth plainly, and untrammelled by any delicate feeling about the responsibilities of leadership, and unaffected by what anyone might think of me. Anybody may criticise me, but I will not enter into controversies. I have considered it necessary to say all this before I start giving expression to my views on the subject.

The Unity Conference and the Relativity of Rights

In the discussions at the Unity Conference held at Delhi, one thing struck me very forcibly. That was the fact that so many of the ablest and most patriotic Muhammadan young men, as well as a few Hindus, were obsessed with the idea of "absolute rights."

Time after time it was said that the Muhammadans had an inherent right to slaughter cows, and that right could only be curtailed by their own voluntary sacrifice. It was on the basis of absolute right that draft resolutions had actually been prepared by a number of young men who counted among them some of the most brilliant and self-sacrificing workers in the Congress organisation.

And yet, as I have pointed out more than once, the idea of absolute rights is a fallacious one, and has really no foundation in law. Pandit Motilal Nehru, the President, also took pains to explain the same point of view. I am not quite sure, however, that the explanations were quite satisfactory; and as the idea seems to me to be shared by a large number of men, I would like to deal with it at some length.

I contend that there is no such thing as an absolute right vested in any individual or in any community forming part of a nation; that all rights are relative, that no society can remain intact even for twenty-four hours an the basis of absolute rights, that the idea of absolute rights was exploded long ago, because it was found to be not only wrong in theory but pernicious in practice. I have no desire to encumber this paper with quotations from the writings of great thinkers and legislators of the West. The point seems to me to be so simple as not to require much labouring. All organic relations depend upon the mutual obligations of the members composing the organism. No part of the organism has any absolute right.

Firstly, all the rights of an individual are subject to the equal rights of others, which fact creates duties and obligations on the part of the different members of a society towards each other. In a well ordered social organism no one has a right to do anything which will unreasonably clash with the legal interests of anyone else. Nay, in order to secure goodwill and progress, the more advanced members of a social organism have sometimes to go further and sacrifice their interests for the commonweal; or for the benefit of the other members of the community.

The protection of the poor, solicitude for providing for the necessities of those who cannot look after themselves, the widows, the orphans, the blind, the lame, the aged, the minor, etc., all fall under this category.

There was a time in the history of Europe when great emphasis was laid on the rights of man. That was the time of the French Revolution. Thomas Paine's "Rights of Man" was a typical reflection of the mentality of that generation. Within less than fifty years it was found that the theory was entirely fallacious and pernicious. Mazzini's "Duties of Man" was a complete and convincing reply to Paine's "Rights of Man." The French Revolution was based on the Rights of Man, and the Constitution with the declaration of the rights of man. The American Constitution makes the same attempt. In actual practice, however, the rights are subject to great limitations in both.

Take, for example, the liberty of speech and the liberty of the press which are guaranteed by both the Constitutions. Can anyone in his senses contend that either the French or the American Government is in the least deterred from curtailing these rights whenever it thinks it best in the interest of the nation to do so? I happened to be in the United States during the [First World] War, and I saw with my own eyes how the so-called fundamental rights guaranteed to the people by the Constitution were taken away by them under one pretence or another, either by Federal Legislation or by the action of the Government.

Everyone seems to have the right not to be forced to fight against his will. Yet during the Great War, this right was denied by all the several governments concerned, and everywhere people were forced into the army against their will. Everybody knows what a great fight the conscientious objectors had to make against this curtailment of their so-called rights, and the sufferings which they were made, in consequence, to undergo. An individual may have an absolute right to think what he wishes, but the moment it comes to the expression of the thought in speech and action, his right is hedged round by conditions and limitations. This is the legal and the constitutional aspect of the question.

As regards its ethical aspect, it is absolutely clear that it is nobler to emphasise duties rather than rights. People who insist on rights rather than duties become selfish, proud, and self-centred. Those who emphasise duties, are quite the reverse. The highest development of humanity and of the spirit of service requires greater emphasis being laid on duties than on rights. That is the teaching of almost all the great religions of the world, if properly understood and rightly interpreted. That is the teaching of Buddha, Christ, and Gandhi. It is also the lesson of actual day to day experience. It is certainly productive of infinitely greater good in a community if its members are inspired by the ideal of doing nothing which may be painful to other members, even if this means the denial to themselves of some of their so-called rights. Anyway one thing is certain. No member of a society can be allowed to exercise his rights in such a way as to clash with the just rights of others. The two rights must be so adjusted and co-related that they might be exercised without doing injury to each other.

I was really astonished to find that some of these young men who have been in the closest touch with Mahatma Gandhi, should have been found harping on this doctrine of rights, because, as already stated and as was pointed out at the Conference itself by Mr. Rajagopalachari, his teaching is obviously based more on the doctrine of duties than on that of rights. I would advise my young countrymen to think over this question a little more deeply, to read the literature on the subject a little more carefully, and to free themselves from the obsession of this pernicious doctrine of rights. Unless this is done, there is no hope for unity in India.

We must always remember that we are a sort of polyglot nation, much less homogeneous than any of those European or Western nations who have had to fight for their freedom. Such a country can never win its freedom, or having won freedom, can never maintain it, unless the various communities composing its people are inspired more by the ideal of duties than of rights. No unity is possible if everyone insists on his pound of flesh, and without unity there is no freedom.

Religion Must be Rationalised as Much as Possible

All those who aim at creating a United India, should remember that India is a land of many faiths and many religions; that these faiths and religions, again, are divided into sections and subsections; that these sections and subsections practise numerous religious observances ceremonials and rituals; and that some of these rituals and observances conflict with one another. It is impossible for any Government to guarantee to all these religions, sections, and subsections, full and complete freedom in the matter of the observance of all their rituals and ceremonials, especially when they are in conflict with one another. Some of these ceremonials and observances, moreover, are inhuman, cruel, and immoral. To insist upon, and to emphasise, the right of every community, small or large, to a strict and full observance of all their religious rituals and ceremonials is, therefore, a clear impossibility, besides being directly opposed to the idea of a United India. The British Government, in spite of its professions of religious neutrality, have, from time to time, interfered in the matter of religious practices; for example, they stopped by legislation the inhuman practices of Sati and infanticide which Hindu orthodoxy contended was a part of its religion.

It is not my purpose here to enter into details, but a student of the religions of India will easily be able to confirm my statement that the advent of British rule in India, followed by a diffusion of Western knowledge and Western sciences, and accompanied by a revival of the study of Sanskrit and Arabic, led to a number of religious reform movements being started, in order to purge the religions of India of all such superstitions and excesses as had been engendered in them by centuries of ignorance and blind faith. In the light of their new knowledge, people found that many of the rites and ceremonials and observances practised in the name of a religion were not sanctioned by the scriptures of that religion, and were opposed to the spirit of the founders and the early expounders of that faith. It cannot, however, be denied that there are communities in India who still believe in the necessity and efficacy of various kinds of rites and ceremonials which are positively inhuman and immoral. Society cannot interfere with the beliefs of anyone, but no progressive society can allow such practices to be carried on with impunity even in the name of religion, as are revolting to the sense of humanity and morality of the vast bulk of its members. Even allowing the largest possible liberty in the matter of religious observances, no nation can for all time tolerate such practices.

From a political point of view it is all the more necessary that religious differences be narrowed down. It is obvious that if everyone in India is, as of right, entitled to practise, in the name of religion, whatever he believes to be a part of his faith, no unity is possible. The idea of a United India demands that emphasis should be laid more on the points on which different religions agree than on the differences that divide them. The idea of a United India necessarily demands, therefore, the rationalising of religion and religious practices to the farthest extent possible. The claim that everyone has a right to full and unrestricted observance of all that he believes to be a part of his religion cannot possibly stand the test of analysis. Not only is everyone's right limited by the just rights of others, but insistence on the observance of conflicting ceremonials has to be actively discouraged, and all such ideas based on false notions of religion as increase hatred, estrange one community from another, and create barriers between different communities, and thus make communal consciousness more acute and bitter, have to be gradually eliminated.

Unfortunately for us, even religious reform movements in India have in some cases taken a wrong turn. They have brought into prominence the observance of very many rites and ceremonies which do not form an integral part of the religions concerned and have nothing to do with Dharma. Communal consciousness, again, has come to be synonymous with the observance of such petty ceremonials as perpetuate differences and form a solid wall separating one community from another. The Arya Samaj, the Muhammadan Reform Movement, and [the] Sikh Reform Movement, all illustrate this tendency; and it cannot be denied that Mahatma Gandhi himself and the Khilafat Movement, of which he was the strongest pillar, have also accentuated this feeling.

Mahatma Gandhi's personality is to a certain extent, a puzzle. In practice he is a liberal of liberals and a broad-minded humanitarian. He declares untouchability to be inhuman and is pledged to root it out, in spite of the fact that tens of millions of Hindus regard it as an essential part of their religion. In theory, on the other hand, he sometimes seems to be supporting narrow-mindedness, even superstitious sectarianism in some of its aspects. This has brought about a reaction, and has given a new life to those Pandits and Maulvis who, before his advent, were fast losing influence among their respective communities. The result is that within the last three or four years, Hindu sectarians have become more bigoted than they were ever before, and Muhammadan and Sikh sectarians still more so. The reactionaries amongst the followers of these religions have again come into power, and are exercising a baneful influence in keeping the communities apart from each other, and in bringing into prominence very many petty observances practised in the name of religion, and calculated to divide instead of uniting the several communities.

I have no intention of offending anybody's susceptibilities, but if the existing conditions are properly analysed it will be seen that sectarianism and narrow-minded bigotry have been very much strengthened within the last three years. The Khilafat Movement has particularly strengthened it among the Muhammadans, and it has not been without its influence and reaction on the Hindus and Sikhs. We do not ignore the important part which communal representation under the Reforms scheme has played in bringing into existence strong communal consciousness, thus making the relations between the two principal communities more acute and bitter than ever before, but our present concern is with this particular aspect of the matter.

If we really and honestly want a United India, we, i.e. the different religious communities in this country, shall have to make a clear distinction between essentials and non-essentials in religion. Full religious freedom does not mean or imply full and unfettered liberty in the matter of observances and practices which affect the just rights of other communities or otherwise injure their feelings. The assertion of such a right, either individual or communal, and the belief that the British Government will enforce the practice of such a right, has done a great deal of mischief in India. Take, for example, the case of the North-West Frontier Province. In a village where the population is 99 per cent Muhammadan and only 1 per cent Hindu, the assertion by a Hindu of his right to carry his idol in procession along the streets of the village where many mosques are situated, would be an extremely foolish act. The assertion of the right of sacrificing cow by a Muslim in a place like Ayudhia, Mathura, Bindraban, or Hardwar would be of the same nature.

Unhappily the British rule has encouraged both Hindus and Muhammadans to assert such rights, and to fight if they are denied. The philosophy of individualism and the idea of absolute religious freedom, both of which, as I have already pointed out, are wholly wrong, and which in India are at the present time directly traceable to British rule, have taken such a firm root in the minds of Indians that they are playing a havoc in all phases of our national life; and consequently the first step towards the creation of a real national life would be a widespread propaganda carried on to educate public opinion in matters of this kind on right lines. To me it is an unpleasant paradox in this connection, and a puzzling commentary on the present situation, that men and women who break every day of their lives almost every canon of Hinduism or Islam by acts of omission or commission, should not only pose as leaders of their respective communities but should actually be accepted as such.

The sum total of my reasoning is this, that one of the causes of the present tension between Hindus and Muhammadans has been the unfortunate revival of the idea of absolute freedom in the matter of religious observances. As I have already said, no one can interfere with or question the belief of another. Such belief is entirely the concern of the individual so long as it does not enforce itself in action. But when we come to observances, we have to consider the environment in which we live, and in the interest of peace and neighbourly goodwill, to avoid social collision, have to sacrifice a certain amount of our freedom.

In a country like India, to inculcate the idea that every religious practice so far observed or presumed to be sanctioned or enjoined by one's faith, is holy and sacred and unchangeable, is, in my humble judgement, mischievous, and requires to be counteracted. At the present stage of its development India requires more of rationalism and toleration than orthodoxy and bigotry. Unhappily, during the last decade we have created an atmosphere which smells more of orthodoxy and bigotry than of rationalism and toleration. The Non-cooperation Movement itself has materially contributed to the creation of this atmosphere. It was unfortunate that the Khilafat Movement in India should have taken its stand on a religious rather than political basis. There were political grounds to support it. It was still more unfortunate that Mahatma Gandhi and the leaders of the Khilafat Movement should have brought religion into such prominence in connection with a movement which was really and fundamentally more political than religious.

The desire to seek religious sanction for the various items of the non-cooperation programme was another great blunder. It led directly to the revival of a sectarian zeal, and to the re-enthroning of influences and forces which were antagonistic to the idea of a united India. Non-cooperation, which was based on the idea of Hindu-Muslim unity, thus became one of the forces favouring disunity. Never before did I see educated Hindus, Mussalmans, and Sikhs attaching so great an importance to insignificant and petty things in the name of religion as they do now.

Shastras and Shariats have been studied and requisitioned only to create an atmosphere of narrowness and bigotry. I have seen young Muslim gentlemen being vigorously attacked by Maulvis for daring to shave their beards, and all India saw the spectacle of a Muslim President attempting to stop the playing of instrumental music at an annual meeting of the National Congress. We have heard of many more amusing claims being put forward in the name of religion, which could never have been imagined before. The last four years, by the way, have brought into existence a legion of Maulanas, Pandits, and Gyanis whom no one had ever credited with any religious sanctity or spiritual prestige.

I mean no offence to anyone, but I am stating these facts to illustrate my point. Take, for instance, the playing of music before mosques. In my experience of the last forty years I had never felt that the question was of any importance at all, and yet I had been a constant reader of newspapers, and a faithful observer of events. It is similarly a matter of pain to me to notice that some of the most broad-minded Hindus, who have travelled all over the world, should feel the necessity of observing any sort of untouchability towards Muhammadans. You cannot expect India to be ever politically united as a single nation, as long there are Indians who believe that it is against their religion to drink water or eat food touched by a non-Hindu. I remember a great Samaj leader once denouncing Congressmen for having sold their religion for the sake of unity; and the selling consisted, in his opinion, in their freely eating and drinking with the Muhammadans.

The fact is that a large number of Hindus and Muslims who profess a desire for Hindu-Muslim unity and who talk of a united India, do not realise that unity has a price which they will have to pay before it can be achieved. I do not maintain that either Hindus or Muhammadans should sacrifice the essentials of their religion for the sake of unity. For me, personally, the essentials of Dharma are very few indeed, and they are such as make for unity not only in India but throughout the world. But I have no right to, and do not, expect that the large body of Hindus and Muhammadans will share my views on this point. I must, however, say frankly that unity is a dream never to be realised unless Hindus and Muhammadans, Sikhs and Christians, make up their minds to be more liberal and rational in their religious and social life than they at present are.

The narrow religious atmosphere which at present dominates Hindu and Muhammadan and Sikh communal life is fatal to the idea of a united India, and the sooner the leaders of all these communities realise the truth, the better for us all. I cannot subscribe to the proposition that either Hinduism or Islam is so narrow as to make it impossible for the followers of the two religions to become politically united. To be frank, we will have to follow Europe in this matter if we really desire political freedom. Religion must be divorced from politics. Social life must be broadened, and political life based only on broad national policy: I don't mean to say that religion should be divorced from our lives or that our political structure be divorced of religious influences in the higher sense of the term. Healthy religious influences are undoubtedly necessary for the development of character, personal as well as national. I say nothing against religion or Dharma in this sense, but I do mean that [the] ceremonial aspect of religion should only be the concern of individuals or of communities, and should not be permitted to create barriers or political distinctions between the followers of different religions, or between different religious communities as such.

Since writing the above, I have re-read Mahatma Gandhi's articles on Hinduism and on Hindu and Muslim unity. His views on Hinduism are fairly liberal, however much one may differ from his explanation of the caste system and from his interpretation of the worship of [the] cow. In one of his articles he says: "I hold that we may not dignify every trifle into a matter of deep religious importance"; and further: "In all non-essential matters, a Hindu must yield for the asking." As an instance of non-essentials he remarks: "One can easily appreciate the Mussalman sentiment of having solemn silence near a mosque the whole of 24 hours." In the whole of his writings I have failed to come across one sentence where he administers similar admonition to the Muslims. His pleadings for the protection of [the] cow are couched in a different style. I have come across other observations, somewhere, to the effect that he would not have either of the communities give away even a little of their religious faith for the sake of unity.

Narrow Sectarianism Holds us Back from Obtaining Swaraj

The observations made in the last article raise several cognate questions, which may profitably be discussed before we come to the political and economic aspects of the problem. Are the Hindu and Muhammadan religions and cultures so fundamentally different, or to be more exact, so antagonistic, as to make their followers naturally and instinctively hostile to each other? If so, what chances are there of our being able to bring about a unity between the two? It is said that Hinduism is not a dogma, that it is almost impossible to define it, that it is a system of life of which caste is an essential feature; and that as long as caste is there, it is impossible to make it sufficiently tolerant and progressive, so as to make unity and cooperation with other religious communities either easy or even possible.

Yet it is an admitted fact that in spite of a rigid caste system and a rigid code of social morality, Hinduism is the most tolerant of all the great religions of the world. Hinduism does not ridicule or despise other peoples' beliefs or faiths: nay it does not question other peoples' right to follow their own faiths and attain spiritual satisfaction thereby. It lays no exclusive claim to be the only royal road to salvation. It is not out to convert other people and thereby save them from hell or perdition. In fact it expressly lays down that for different people, in different stages of physical, mental, and spiritual developments, there are different ways of approaching God and obtaining satisfaction and salvation. To its own followers it allows the fullest freedom to believe what they like and to worship as they please.

Even its rigid social code and its caste system are in the melting pot. While formerly Hindu society allowed its members to go out of it, nay actually expelled and outcasted them on the slightest pretext and on the flimsiest possible ground, at the present moment it is prepared to make all kinds of allowances for the disregard of its social code by its members, and is anxious to keep them within its fold. There was a time when high-caste families, rich, influential, and cultured, were outcasted and thrown out of Hindu society on the most intangible grounds, out of sheer suspicion and bigotry. Now even open beef-eaters are tolerated, excused and honoured. There are numerous men and women in Hindu society, honoured and respected members of it, who openly defy and violate the most important canons of its social code-men who have not only married out of caste but even foreigners, men who eat prohibited food and make no secret of it, who take prohibited drinks without any efforts to conceal the fact, men who ridicule the Vedas and are atheists. We find that amongst these latter are some of the most notable leaders of Hindu society.

How can we explain this strange change? To what is this due, and what does this signify? To my mind the change indicates the realisation by the society and its members of a higher Hindiusm which is above forms and formalities — a culture that is more of the mind and of the spirit than consisting in eating, drinking, or even marrying, along certain accepted lines. It is this realisation which makes men and women who have risen above forms and formulas to still feel proud of Hinduism, to be anxious for its assured continuance in their country for the benefit of their children and their children's children.

It is this realisation which explains the phenomenon of beef-eaters, husbands of foreign women, scoffers of the Vedas, in short, extremely unorthodox and outwardly un-Hindu people, championing the cause of Hinduism, standing shoulder to shoulder with the orthodox in the defence of their temples, shrines, festivals, customs etc., and resenting as strongly as the latter, the attacks of non-Hindu missionaries, preachers, and proselytisers on Hinduism and [the] Hindu community.

But there is another reason also which explains the phenomenon. The material and political prospects of his class are bound up with those of the rest of their community. It was not so very long ago that many of these people dissociated themselves from the great bulk of the Hindus, while some of them openly said, rather with pride, that they were not Hindus. The recognition by Government of the communal system changed the situation. They found that except as Hindus they had no status, and their children would have none, unless they chose to adopt Islam. This they were not prepared to do. So, willy-nilly, they had to declare themselves Hindus and seek elections from general non-Muslim constituencies, basing their claim on their championship of Hindu rights.

Unlike Hinduism, Islam is a faith of dogmas and doctrines. Every Muhammadan must believe not only in the existence of God without a second but also that Muhammad (Pbuh) was His Prophet, and that Holy Quran is His final word. He must also believe, according to the orthodox school, that Muhammad (Pbuh) was the last of the prophets and whatever he said and did is binding on all his faithful followers.

There have been expounders of Islam who have tried to raise it to a kind of high occultism, but their efforts have not met with any considerable success, and Islam remains, to all intents and purposes, with the majority of its followers, what it has been all through centuries past. My Muslim friends will pardon me if I venture to say that too great an insistence on dogma has been the bane of Islam, the cause of its political downfall, and that unless it is given up, it will stand in the way of Islam ever regaining its lost position as a world-wide political factor. Islam is as much divided and sub-divided into sections and factions as Christianity once was and perhaps to this day is.

The division and sub-division of Hindu society into sects have one redeeming feature. The general tolerance of Hinduism prevents them from destroying each other. History shows that this cannot be said of Islam.

Religious intolerance of the severest kind has been a handmaid of chivalry, bravery, zeal, learning, and piety among the Muslims throughout Muslim history. Three out of the four first Khalifas were murdered by their fellow Muslims. The pages of Muslim history are full of similar acts done by religious zealots or political adventurers. One would have thought that recent events in Turkey and Egypt would have chastened Islam at least in this respect. But the stoning to death of an Ahmadia by the orders of the Government of Kabul, and the approval of that barbarous act by some of the most prominent and educated leaders of Muslim India, have shown that the canker is still there and has not lost an iota of its original violence.

Egypt and Turkey, however, seem to be in a different mood. It appears that they, at any rate, have realised the necessity of marching with the times and making a clear distinction between essentials and non-essentials. The Indian "Maulanas" may call them "bad Mussalmans," but they do not care, as long as they can retain and protect their political freedom. A religiously "bad Mussalman" (a Turkish Nationalist told me that an Indian Mussalman once called him a bad Mussalman because he occasionally took a peg [an alcoholic drink]) is an infinitely better person than a Mussalman who bows his head to a foreign power and who prates of his "Sharia" to perpetuate his bondage. The "bad Mussalmans" of Turkey are in my eyes infinitely superior to those pious Mussalmans of India who, though professing great regard for the most insignificant and minor details of "Sharia" and "Hadis," are willing tools of a foreign bureaucracy, and are purchasing places and preferments for themselves and their fellow Mussalmans by resorting to various questionable means.

It is a sign of the times that while [the] Mussalman's piety finds such eloquent expression in its fights with Hinduism, it is dumb and powerless in the presence of leaders who openly defy, by acts of omission and commission, some of the most sacred canons of Islamic Law. Is it not a fact that just as in the case of Hindus, Muslims accept as leaders, men who do not believe in the infallibility of the Quran, who disclaim any faith in "Hadis" and "Fiqah," who openly and undisguisedly drink wine, eat bacon, do not say prayers, and do not observe fast in the month of Ramzan, not to mention minor matters, such as their opinions about purdah, keeping [a] beard, etc.?

It comes to this: that while Hindus and Mussalmans are prepared to be led by men who openly flout all the sacred canons of their respective faiths, they are not prepared to relax by a hair's breadth the severity of their customs and rituals and observances, in order to live in peace and neighbourly goodwill with one another. A united India will mean freedom for both Hindus and Mussalmans, but they prefer the strict observance of the most futile and non-essential elements of their respective faiths to freedom. Is this not a sight for the gods to weep over?

I am firmly convinced that we cannot create a united India and cannot win Swaraj in any shape, unless the religious canker is removed. "Mazhab" (in its narrow sense), as my beloved friend Stokes often reminds me, is the curse of India, and as long as it rules supreme, there is no hope for India. The idea that we can remain "good Hindus" and "good Mussalmans" in the narrowest sense of these terms, and yet win Swaraj, is in my judgement, an absurd one. It has done a lot of mischief within the last four years. I still believe that we do not need to depart in any manner or degree from the true and essential spirit of Islam and Hinduism in order to be free and united. There are good and true Christians, Roman Catholics and Protestants, Presbyterians and Anglicans, Jews and Gentiles, in Great Britain, France, and Germany, but the earnestness of their religious faith does not prevent their being free citizens of their respective countries. A hundred years ago, who could have imagined that a Jew would one day be the Prime Minister of Great Britain, another a Secretary of State, and a third a Viceroy of India?

The Jews are perhaps the smallest religious community in Great Britain. They never claimed any special representation in Parliament or any specific share of Government posts. In fact about 150 years ago, the communal consciousness of the Roman Catholics and Protestants in Great Britain was as keen and exclusive as that of the Hindus and Mussalmans today. For a long time the Roman Catholics were excluded from Parliament and could not be employed in any Government office, and still they never claimed any special representation. Now all these disabilities have been removed, and Roman Catholics, equally with the Protestants, hold the highest positions in the State. In this matter the example of Great Britain has been followed in all the great countries of Europe and in the United States of America, and the result is what we see. I am certain in my mind that Turkey, Egypt and Syria are going to do the same thing; and if they do not, they will never be free. Does anyone expect India to be the only exception to the rule?

"Untouchables" and "Kafirs"

The considerations urged in the last article are so important and relevant that I will not apologise for laying further emphasis upon them. Every possible effort should be made (a) to integrate the different religions as much as possible by emphasising the points on which they agree, by eliminating non-essentials, and by restricting essential differences within the narrowest limits; (b) to remove all barriers to free social intercourse between the communities, which do not go to the root of anyone's faith.

Let us take the question of untouchability. I find no sanction for it in the Hindu Shastras. I find no mention of it in history. As far as the Hindu untouchables are concerned, most sensible Hindus are agreed that in their case, at least, it is senseless, inhuman, and intolerable, because of the fact of their being followers of the same religion and members of the same community as the so-called higher castes. Some of the advanced reformers like the Arya Samajists are prepared at once to raise them high in the social scale by investing them with the sacred thread and starting inter-dining and inter-marrying with them. Even the most orthodox are in many cases prepared to let them [walk?] on their floor, to admit them in common schools, and to remove all outward and palpable signs of pollution by touch. In their case, at least, untouchability is doomed, and will, I believe, disappear in a very short time.

The ultra-orthodox will no doubt foam and fret, oppose and resist. Here and there they will outcaste, and break social relations with, the reformers. But the number of the latter is so large already, and is growing so much larger and larger, as to reduce the orthodox to impotence. Take the case of Mahatma Gandhi or of Seth Jamnalal Bajaj or of Swami Shraddhanand or of Lala Hans Raj. Has the orthodox Hindu community the will and the power to excommunicate them and throw them out of the pale of Hinduism? I am not in favour of forcing [the] pace and wounding the feelings and the susceptibilities of the orthodox, but I know that in this respect at least orthodoxy is doomed. Its days are literally numbered.

In the case of non-Hindus, untouchability takes a different shape. In their case, no pollution by touch is recognised. But it is not allowed, to eat or drink food or water touched by them. This practice is also doomed. As I have said, I can find no authority for it in the Hindu Shastras. It was probably based on the idea of non-cooperation with foreign rulers who happened to be beef-eaters. It was good and effective as long as the Muslims in India were the enemies of the people or their conquerors, and the Hindus could hope to turn them out by establishing a Hindu Raj. It is no longer possible. The enemies of the 8th to 16th centuries form an important and integral part of the Indian population today. They are neither foreigners nor rulers. Racially they are, in the vast majority of cases, the bone of our bone and the flesh of our flesh.

Formerly, a Hindu who once drank water or ate food touched by a Mussalman was immediately lost to Hinduism, never again to return to its fold. Thanks to Guru Gobind Singh, Swami Dayanand, and other reformers, that idea has been exploded and exploded for good. Even born Muhammadans can now be admitted into Hindu society. Under the circumstances there is no excuse now for continuing or perpetuating this prejudice. But prejudices like these take time to die. Die it must; why not then hasten to destroy it by active efforts? I know that some distinguished Hindus will take exception to my statement, and may even denounce me for it. But I am out to speak what I believe to be the truth and the whole truth.

It is absolutely necessary for producing an atmosphere of neighbourly goodwill, and for creating a United India, that the existing prejudice should be given up. You cannot make a united nation of communities between whom such barriers in the matter of social intercourse are recognised and enforced. Moreover, the abolition of the practice will be useful to Hinduism in another way. It will remove all fears of forced conversion by making a Hindu drink water or eat food touched by a Muslim. It may be noted that I am advocating the removal of the restriction as a barrier and not the necessary introduction of interdining.

Take another case, an equally important matter. There was a time when in the eyes of the Muslims all Hindus were Kafirs, and it was implicitly believed that the property and the women of a Kafir were legal prizes of war for a Muslim. The times are changed, and with it the conception of a Kafir must be changed. No Hindu who believes in and worships one God, can by any stretch of language be called a Kafir unless the definition of a Kafir be that every non-Muslim is a Kafir. In the eyes of a large number of Muslims the latter is the right definition of a Kafir; and according to Ulemas, even those Muslims are Kafirs who, although believing in Allah and His prophet, do not follow other tenets of Islam as understood and interpreted by them.

For example, they pronounced Sir Syed Ahmed to be a Kafir, and they denounce the followers of Mirza of Qadian also as Kafirs. If they are right, then H. H. the Agha Khan is the biggest Kafir, and so are Ghazi Mustafa Kamal Pasha and Zaghlul Pasha also. If then their definition of a Kafir is right, there can be no peace between them and the rest of the world. In that case all this talk of Hindu-Muslim Unity is superficial, absurd, and hypocritical.. In the course of the non-cooperation campaign, some of the Ulemas cited particular "ayats" (sections) of the Quran to prove that Muslims could enter into lawful agreement with such non-Muslims as were friendly towards them, against those who were inimically disposed towards them, brought fire and sword into the home of the latter, and otherwise injured them. Now to be frank, this kind of special pleading does not appeal to my intellect. It is not a mechanical union of this kind that will make a nation of us. What is needed is a chemical union. Are the Hindus "Kafirs"? If they are, all talk of unity between Hindus and Mussalmans is absurd.

No Mussalman or body of Mussalmans in India or outside has any legal right or authority to bind other Mussalmans. Leaders come and go; there is no one in India who can speak in the name of the whole Muslim community. The pact of Lucknow had no value or binding force unless it was accepted by Government and embodied in law. No agreement made or arrived at a meeting of the Congress or Khilafat has any binding legal value. Anything agreed to by the present leaders or even the Jamiat-ul-Ulema can he questioned by any other Muslim, and with even greater force by the succeeding generations. Even an agreement embodied in law, or forming part of a declaration of rights, is of no binding value on the future generations of Hindus and Muslims. Laws change with the law-makers. A law made today may be of no value fifty years hence. Under the circumstances, agreements or pacts won't take us sufficiently far. What is needed is a "change of heart." All efforts of the present generation of Muslim leaders should be directed to removing the idea that the Hindus are Kafirs.

Ordinarily, the relations of Hindus and Mussalmans in villages and small towns are most cordial. The present tension is the development of the last fifty years. But what has happened during the last three years has beaten all record. Some people are of opinion that special efforts have been made to bring about the state of things to prove that India is unfit for Swaraj, and that no further advance is safe in the matter of political reforms. In certain quarters there is a tendency to throw the entire responsibility on the officials of the foreign Government. While sharing the belief that the latter have had a hand in it, I cannot help saying that Muslim Maulavis, Maulanas and Associations have had a much larger, in fact a lion's share, in it, though, of course, it is not meant that the Hindus are quite innocent.

The fact that wherever there have been riots between Hindus and Mussalmans, the latter have looted the former, desecrated their temples and assaulted their women, betrays the widespread diffusion of the idea that the Hindus are "Kafirs," that the Muslims are in a state of war with them, and that in fighting them, their property and women are "halal" for the Muslims. There are some persons who maintain that this has been the work of Goondas. I say, no! The riots have been inspired by cleverer brains than those of the Goondas, they have been encouraged and supported by influential people. It is only the actual outrages that have been committed by Goondas, fanatics, and poor people.

An esteemed Muslim leader has propounded the theory that the fact that the Hindus are rich and Muslims are poor, explains these riots. Assuming the explanation to be correct, how does he explain the irrefutable fact that poor Mussalmans do not loot their rich fellow-religionists? The real explanation is that the latter are Muslims and the Hindus are Kafirs. This notion has been rubbed into the mind of the Muslim masses and Muslim middle classes, by clever propagandists and influential leaders. It is the duty of the Muslim nationalist leaders to inaugurate and carry on an extensive propaganda to destroy this notion and to impress on the minds of their co-religionists the truth that Hindus are not Kafirs, and that even on the occasion of fights and quarrels, their temples, their women, and their property are inviolable and unassailable.

The History of Communal Representation

In this article I propose to trace the history of the evolution of the idea of Communal Representation and separate communal interests. It was in the seventies of the 19th century that the movement for the establishment of the MAO College at Aligarh was started, and it was about the same time that the Arya Samaj was founded. The idea of a united India was present to the minds of the founders of both when they met at Delhi on the occasion of the Imperial Durbar of 1877. But they soon found out that it was impossible to unite India on the basis of a common faith. The Indian National Congress had not then come into existence, and the idea at back of Sir Syed's mind was to found an institution which would enable Indian Muhammadans to make up for lost time in the acquisition of that Western knowledge which was, in his eyes, *sine qua non* of worldly prosperity both under the Government and otherwise.

Sir Syed was materially helped and supported in the development of his idea by influential Hindus. Rich Hindus and Hindu princes liberally subscribed to the funds of the Aligarh MAO College. But the idea of a denominational college necessarily carries with it emphasis on communal characteristics and communal glories. It unavoidably increases communal consciousness. So it was here. Again, the success and the popularity of Aligarh College depended largely on its alumni finding high and lucrative posts under Government. At first the great Syed's personal influence with the high officials sufficed for the purpose, but it was soon found that it was necessary to supplement it by insistence on communal claims. Thus comparative statistics of Hindus and Muslims in Government services became a characteristic feature of the deliberations of the Muhammadan Educational Conference even in its early days.

Sir Syed was a great religious reformer. By his liberal expositions of Islam and by his attempts to rationalise Islam, he drew upon himself the wrath of the Muslim Ulemas, and they raised a storm of prejudice against him. His strength lay in his alliance with the Government. Whether the idea of this alliance had taken hold of his mind even before the Indian National Congress was founded, cannot be definitely asserted. What is certain is that after the foundation of the latter it became a definite article of his political creed. Thus, the Aligarh School of Muhammadans became characteristically anti-Hindu and pro-Government.

On the other hand, the Arya Samaj activities in the Punjab brought into existence a community of Hindus who began to lay emphasis on the glories of ancient India and also on the outrages committed on Hindus and Hindu temples, etc., by Muslim rulers. These Arya Samajists borrowed their ideas of political freedom from the writings of Thomas Paine, Joseph Mazzini, George Washington, etc. They attempted to unite Hindus against non-Hindus, both Christians and Muslims. The DAV College stood for Hindu unity, Hindu progress, and Hindu consolidation.

Thus, came into existence the two classes of Hindus and Muslims who stood for sharply divided communal consciousness and communal consolidation, with only this difference: that while one preached the cult of political freedom, the other preached that of alliance with the ruling power. This difference became the foundation of that fire of estrangement which has since burst into flames, and now threatens to reduce to ashes all hopes of a united India. The Aligarh-educated Muslims on the one hand, and the Arya Samajists on the other, have since then been the doughty standard-bearers of their respective faiths.

The demand for communal representation and separate electorates on the part of the Muslims was the next natural step in their march towards exclusive communal progress. The Government, on its side, found a natural and welcome ally in Sir Syed and his school of Muslims, and began to encourage their demands for special representation both in the Legislatures and the Services. The "political importance" of the Muslims also assumed the rank of a war cry. Hindus all over India resented this, but none more vehemently than those of the UP and the Punjab.

To those who want to trace the development and growth of this idea, the early volumes of the "Comrade" will furnish an interesting and illuminating study.

What was at the root of the claim about the political importance of the Muslims? The fact that they had been the rulers of India for centuries, and also the fact that there still existed several independent Muslim states outside India. It is a well-known historical fact that Sir Syed himself was opposed to the Muslims of India sending any help to the Turks in the war with Russia in 1877-78. I don't know if he was a Pan-Islamist. I am inclined to think that he was not. In any case, he was strongly opposed to the idea of the Indian Muslims meddling with the affairs of outside Muslim States.

Indian Muslims, however, soon found out that Great Britain, like other European powers, was only as much interested in the independent Muslim states as it suited its imperial interests. Suspicions began to be entertained that perhaps the attitude of the Indian Government towards Indian Muslims was only a narcotic to prevent them from taking any active interest in the affairs of Muslim states outside India. The alliance of the educated Muslims with the Government had its natural influence upon the masses. The classes and the masses were both permeated with the idea that the Government was their friend, and anti-Hindu. There were European officials who rubbed it into their conscience [consciousness] as much as they could.

But the reaction was bound to come. It came in two ways. Firstly, the Muslims began to raise their demands so high that even the Government found it impossible to meet them. Secondly, the gradual fall and dismemberment of the Muslim Empires of Turkey and Egypt opened the eyes of Indian Muslims as to the value of British friendship. First came the occupation of Egypt; then came the rapid contraction of the Turkish Empire by the loss of its Christian provinces; next came the Italian war on Tripoli, which was a purely Muslim country. Finally came the war with Turkey, with the dismemberment of the Turkish Empire by the treaty of Severes. This brought about a complete change in the political views of some of the Muslim leaders, and gave birth to the non-cooperation idea.

It is not implied that during all this time there were no Muslim leaders who stood for alliance with Hindus for the purposes of political freedom, as against alliance with Goyernment and consequent political dependence. It must be said to the honour of Messrs. Badruddin Tayyabji, Rahmatulla, and Rasul, among the dead, and Maulana Abul Kalam Azad, M. A. Jinnah, Hasan Imam, and Mazhar-ul-Haq, among the living, that they always stood for political unity between Hindus and Muslims.

It was left for Lord Morley, the great Liberal thinker and statesman of Great Britain, to finally sanction, at the instance of the Indian bureaucracy, the canker of communal representation with separate electorates into the Indian system; and this arrangement was subsequently sanctified by the pact of Lucknow arrived at by the Liberal leaders of both the communities.

This, in brief, is the history of communal representation. I have said nothing as to its necessity or otherwise, and before I do that I want to comment briefly on the policy of the late Sir Syed Ahmed Khan, and also trace the growth of Pan-Islamism in India.

From Sir Syed Ahmed Khan to Iqbal

Sir Syed Ahmed Khan was unquestionably a great man. He was highminded, unselfish, and devoted to the interests of his community. He lived and died for it. His political creed consisted of three articles:

(a) Non-interference in the affairs of outside Muslim states.

(b) Concentration of all efforts on the betterment of the Muslims' condition at home, and

(c) Alliance with the British Government.

In his eyes, these three articles were more or less interdependent.

As long as he lived, he commanded the almost undivided allegiance of his educated fellow-religionists, though even then a few of the latter interested themselves in the Indian National Congress. After his death, there was a change. A large number of his former followers and pupils abandoned all the three articles of his faith. But an equally large number continued to believe in and follow his policy. The masses went with the former. Thus, a situation arose which may be summed up in two phrases: Pan-Islamism, and hostility to the British.

Under the influence of the Non-cooperation Movement, a sufficiently large number of Muslims joined the Indian National Congress; but in very many cases their nationalism seemed to be only secondary to their Pan-Islamism. Now it is obvious that the Indian Muslims must sympathise with their fellow-Muslims outside. The misfortunes of the latter must draw their sympathy; their glories must fill them with elation. This is only natural. Hindus cannot realise this fully, as there are virtually no Hindus outside India. While admitting this, I have no doubt in my own mind that Sir Syed's policy of concentration at home was the better of the two.

The advocates of Pan-Islamism have never realised that nationalism must precede internationlism, whether political or religious. People who are not free at home, cannot help others either to gain their freedom or to retain it. People who are poor, illiterate, destitute, and dependent at home, cannot very well give away what they have in order to help others. The sentiment has a veneer of nobility, but it is neither practical politics nor sound economics, and in my opinion it is not good religion either. There are some people who will laugh at these ideas, but that does not affect this truth. The events of the last three years have in my judgement conclusively shown that, at least in this respect, Sir Syed's policy was sounder than that of those who reversed it.

Note: Compare Muslim contributions to the Khilafat and Smyrna Funds with those to the Tilak Swarajya Fund, the Malabar Relief and the Muslim Education funds, etc.

The first article of an Indian's faith must be to love India above every other country on the face of the globe. Only then can he be a patriot. Divided allegiance and divided love cannot produce either good nationalists and patriots, or even good religionists.

There was a time when the ablest and perhaps the most popular of Muslim poets sang the two songs, one beginning with the line *Sare jahan se accha Hindustan hamara* (of all the countries of the world, our Hindustan is the best), and the other a Mussaddas ending with the refrain: "The same is my country, the same is my country." It will be interesting to insert here a few verses from these songs, showing the depth of patriotism and the height of nationalism which inspired their composer, and the broad spirit of tolerance that pervaded them. The first contained the following:

(*Translation*)

Religion does not teach mutual animosity.

We are Indians; our country is Hindustan.

Greece, Egypt and Rome have all been effaced from the world,

but our name and distinction is still living.

There is some reason why our life will not be extinct,

although changing time has been our enemy for centuries.

This song is often sung as a substitute tune for "Bande Mataram," and has been raised to the dignity of a national anthem. Take the following from the other:

(*Translation*)

The land in which Chishti delivered his message of truth;

the garden in which Nanak sang the song of theism;

the land which Tartars adopted as their home;

the land which made the people of Hejaz leave the desert of Arabia;

the same land is my native land, the same is my native land.

(The land) which aroused the wonder of the Greeks.

(The land) which taught Science and Art to the whole world, etc. etc.

The place from where the world heard the song of theism;

> the place from where the Prophet of Arabia received cool breezes, etc. etc.

In the footnote it is said that the first line refers to the flute of Shri Krishna, and the second is a hadis to the effect that the Prophet said: "he was receiving cool breezes from the direction of India."

> (The land) in whose atmosphere life is life of Paradise.
>
> (The land) which is Gautama's country, (and thus) is the holy land of the Japanese, (the land) which is a smaller Jerusalem for the lovers of Christ.

There is another song composed by the same poet under the name of the "New Shivala"-the temple dedicated to Shiva, which is full of the noblest possible sentiments of Hindu-Muhammadan unity. I used to often recite it in my exile in the United States of America, and translated it into English for an English magazine. My translation was versified by Dr. Ananda Kumarswami and published in one of the American magazines.

Equally remarkable and pathetic is a poem called *Sada-e-Dard* (a wail of pain) lamenting Hindu-Muslim disunity. Following the same line and even more pathetic and impressive is a poem called *Taswir-e-Dard* (a picture of pain). I cannot resist the temptation of giving a few verses here:

> (*Tr.*) Oh, Hindustan, the spectacle makes me weep.
>
> Thy story is the most instructive of all stories.

The next verses bewail the fact that the writer has been assigned by fate (the duty of) being a reader of mourning literature (Nauha khawan) on India.

> (*Tr.*) Oh! plucker of flowers (evidently referring to the foreign rulers).
>
> You have not left a trace of the leaves even.
>
> By your good luck, the gardeners are engaged in warring with each other.
>
> (This evidently refers to Hindu Muslim quarrels).

Then come the following verses:

> (*Tr.*) Oh, fool, think of your country;
>
> misfortune is about to overtake it as there are consultations in heavens to ruin it. See what is happening and what is about to happen.
>
> What is the use of repeating old stories?
>
> Oh! Indians, if you won't awaken in time, you will be effaced, and there will be no mention of you even in stories.

In a collection of Dr. Iqbal's Urdu poetry just published at Lahore, his poems are divided into three periods. The first ends with 1905. All the poems breathing the love of country and Hindu-Muhammadan unity belong to this period. The second ends with 1908. The third begins with 1908. It is remarkable that all the poems cited by me belong to the first period. The first and the second periods are comparatively free from sectarianism. [The] third period is full of sectarian religionism.

Compare these gems of Urdu literature and Indian nationalism with later songs in the days of Pan-Islamism, which begin with the verse:

> (*Tr.*) China and Arabia is ours (and so) is India ours.
>
> We are Muslims, the whole world is our native land.

In a still later poem occurs the following:

> (*Tr.*) Your hem is free from the dust of native land:
>
> Thou art the Joseph [to?] whom every Egypt is Canaan.

In a poem on patriotism or a love of country the poet sings of its evils and hints that the Prophet cut the roots of the tree of patriotism. This, he holds, is a new-fangled weapon of modern powers.

What a change! But even more remarkable are some of the folk songs composed during the best days of the Khilafat Movement, which have been sung and are still being sung by the masses of Muslims in the Punjab.

Let the reader imagine what an attitude of mind must have been produced in the minds of the younger generation of Mussalmans by writings and songs like these.

Dr. Muhammad Iqbal is no ordinary versifier. He is an accomplished scholar and a poet of the highest order, who is master of several languages. His writings and poems are to be found in every educated Muslim's home, nay, even in most cultured Hindu homes too. He has by no means been the solitary propounder of these views. I have selected him because, being an admirer of his, I have been a constant reader of his compositions.

Pan-Islamism and its Bankruptcy

Add to this the Fatwa of the Ulemas that India being a "*Dar-ul-Harab*" (a place of war), every good Muslim ought to leave it and migrate to a Muslim country. We know by this time how the Hijrat Movement ended; how much money was wasted over it and how much misery was wrought thereby. The best commentary on it was witnessed by me at Constantinople. On the third or fourth day of my stay there, I met two young Indian Muslims walking in the street. They accosted me first.

When I asked them how they fared in Constantinople, one of them burst out almost in tears and said that if he ever returned to India, he would give out a bit of his mind to tell his Muslim countrymen how mischievous was the teaching that India was "Dar-ul-Harab" (a place of war) and how false the idea that the whole world was the home of the Muslims. That boy was one of the Muhajarins of 1921. He had travelled all over Muslim Asia from Afghanistan through Turkistan to Russia, and then back to Angora and Constantinople. His experience was so bitter, and his condition was so pitiable, that he denounced Pan-Islamism in rather strong terms.

That was what I learned from other Indian Muslims also whom I met in Turkey and Egypt, and this is natural enough. A Bengali Muslim in Egypt denounced the Khilafat Movement in such strong terms that I cannot reproduce his language. Blood is thicker than water, as they say. No part of the Muslim world except Egypt is excessively rich and prosperous. Everywhere the governments have to look after their people, and the latter have to eke out their means of subsistence. How can they be expected to provide for foreigners, even though the latter are Muslims? The Amir of Kabul was perfectly justified in asking the Mahajarins to leave his country. Later on he was forced, perhaps, for diplomatic reasons, to ask some professedly anti-British Muslims to leave his territories. Similarly it is idle to expect the Turks to help the Indian Muslim Muhajarin when there is so much poverty in their own land.

The fact is that my visit to Turkey, Asia Minor, Syria, Palestine, and Egypt, has completely disillusioned me about pan-Islamism. I found it nowhere. Every country is busy with its own home problems, and they are sufficiently complicated and troublesome to keep them engaged all the time. Turkey is suffering from the aftereffects of a devastating war. The war has denuded the country of a great number of its male working hands, and this is one of the reasons that have forced their hands to abolish the Purdah system, and trust to their womanhood to produce food for them. The problem of expatriating Christians from Turkey and receiving the Muslims in exchange from Greece is a huge problem on their hands. The problem of safeguarding against internal enemies (Greeks, Armenians, and Jews, etc.) is sufficiently serious.

Internal and external fears compel them to keep an efficient army equipped on up-to-date lines. All this means a great financial strain. Over and above this, they are not quite united among themselves. As in other countries, so in Turkey, there are parties who think differently in politics. The abolition of the Khilafat and the expulsion of the Khalifa and other members of the royal family was a desperate step which they had to take in the interests of the present Constitution. They are making a most noble effort to consolidate their power, to reform their administration, and to raise their country to a first class position in the councils of Europe.

Under the circumstances, even those who do not see eye to eye with Mustafa Kamal and his party in matters religious and political, and who resented the abolition of the Khilafat, are opposed, out of patriotic motives to the reopening of the question, at least for some time to come. From my study of the conditions in Turkey (short and cursory as it was), I could only conclude that from first to last the Turks were intense nationalists. At the present moment their only concern is their country, which they want to preserve, manage and rule in the interests of the Turks. The Turks seemed to me to be a noble people, clean in their appearance and clean in their dealings with others. Their dress and their manner of living is almost wholly European, except that the men wear the fez.

About their religion, indeed, I know nothing, but anyone who has his eyes open can read the writing on the wall. There does not appear to be much of religionism in Turkey. They have abolished Purdah. I saw lady clerks working in the Post Office and other public offices without a veil. I saw thousands [of women] dressed in European dress with a Turkish over-mantle going about in public streets, and walking in public gardens without any veil. To me their dress seemed perfectly decent, which combined in a most appropriate manner the fashions of the East and the West. The Turks have issued strict regulations which aim at restricting polygamy to a very large extent, if not abolishing it altogether. I saw most drastic regulations being enforced against the use of any but the Turkish language. There are also very strict rules, subject to exceptions, against enlisting non-Turks in the army. I observed no prejudice against music, either vocal or instrumental. Even dancing is indulged in higher circles. I was sorry to see rather a general use of wine.

In short I saw nothing, either in Constantinople or in other towns of Asia Minor, which could show that the Turks were in any sense of the term more religious than the rest of the natives of Europe. Everywhere I saw signs of social and national distinctions and preferments. My impressions were confirmed by the Indian Muslim residents of Constantinople who met me. I was agreeably surprised to find that in the Al-Azhar University the quarters reserved for the residence of Indian students were called *Rawaq-e-Hanud* (i.e. a Boarding House for Hindus). In Syria and. Palestine also, the problem which absorbs the Muslim community is how to regain or maintain their freedom.

In Palestine the Muslims are in an overwhelming majority over the Jews. Christian Europe is creating a strong and well protected Ulster in Palestine, which leaves almost no hope of the Muslims ever regaining their lost position of supremacy. Everywhere one sees well-built and well-equipped colonies of Jews springing up, with their own highly efficient educational and philanthropic institutions, and with their equally efficient industrial concerns. They are fast buying lands of Muslims and Christians. Money is pouring in from America and Europe. The only "disconcerting" feature is that it is only the poorer class of the Jews and the oppressed members of the race that are emigrating to Palestine for permanent settlement. In Syria the Christians form a very important part of the population. In neither [of these] countries is there any communal rivalry or jealousy between the Muslims and the Christians.

I am afraid Indian Muslims are more Pan-Islamic and exclusive than the Muslims of any other country on the face of the globe, and that fact alone makes the creation of a united India more difficult than would otherwise be the case. I am inclined to think that in this respect at least, Sir Syed's policy was sounder than that of the Khilafatists. He did not believe in a religious Khilafat. He did not accept the Sultan of Turkey as a Khalifa, and he was opposed to the Muslims of India devoting much attention to the affairs of Turkey or other Muslim countries.

Hindu Revivalism and other Communalist Trends

What I have said about Pan-Islamism and the excess of communalism among the Mussalmans, should not be understood to imply that Hindus on their side have been quite inactive and innocent. One thing, of course, is patent. Hindus cannot be anything but Indians. They have no other country and no other nation to look to. They cannot, therefore, be accused of any kind of Pan-Hinduism, in the sense in which the term is used in relation to Islam. Hinduism and Indianism are, in their case, synonymous terms.

But in their own way, Hindu revivalists have left nothing undone to create a strictly exclusive and aggressive communal feeling. Early in the eighties of the last century some of the Hindu religious leaders came to the conclusion that Hinduism was doomed unless it adopted the aggressive features of militant Islam and militant Christianity. The Arya Samaj is a kind of militant Hinduism. But the idea was by no means confined to the Arya Samaj. Swami Vivekanand and his gifted disciple Sister Nivedita, among others, were of the same mind. The articles which she wrote on aggressive Hinduism are the clearest evidence of that mentality.

It must be remembered in this connection that Western knowledge, Western thought, and Western mentality took hold of the Hindu mind at a very early period of British rule. The Brahmo Samaj was the first product of it. In the early-60s the Brahmo Samaj was a non-Hindu body, and under its influence Hindu scholars, thinkers, and students were becoming cosmopolitans. Some became Christians, others took to atheism and became completely Westernised.

Thus, a wave of indifferentism about Hinduism spread over the country. The Arya Samaj Movement, and aggressive Hinduism, was a reaction against that un-Hinduism and indifferentism. Most of the early Hindu leaders of the Indian National Congress were in this sense non-Hindus. What did Mr. S. N. Banerjee or Lal Mohan Ghosh or Ananda Mohan Bose care for Hinduism? Even Mahadev Govind Ranade was but an indifferent Hindu. G. K. Gokhale was not a Hindu at all. I will not mention other names.

Thus, the political nationalist movement of India was brought into existence by high-minded Englishmen, enlightened and highminded Parsees, enlightened and highminded sons of Hindus (many of whom in their own mentality were either non-Hindus or indifferent Hindus) and a few enlightened and highminded Muslims. Born under these auspices, it was bound to be a movement of pure freedom. Pure freedom makes no distinction of race or religion.

As a child of the joint deliberations of Dufferin and Hume, it was, however, more a "safety-valve" than a movement of pure freedom. It was hardly three years old when its Godfather, the Marquis of Dufferin, changed his mind and decided to strangle it. The best way to strangle it, he thought, was to rob it of its national character and to raise the religious and denominational bogey. The latter proved to be a Himalayan glacier, under whose weight it was bound either to perish or to be cracked so badly as to remain mangled all its life.

That Himalayan glacier was the late Sir Syed's opposition to the Congress on denominational grounds. I do not mean to say that Sir Syed's fears about his community were absolutely baseless, but the cry which he raised was practically the death-knell of

Indian nationalism at the time. Sir Syed's attitude towards the Indian National Congress was influenced by the following considerations:

- That in India the Hindus were in a majority, and if a form of democratic Government was accepted as the political goal of India, the Muslims were bound to be in a minority.
- That the Hindus were both economically and educationally more advanced than the Muslims, and would monopolise much of Government influence for a long time to come.
- That a Hindu Raj might possibly mean the death of Islam in India, or at least a position of subservience for it.

I am inclined to think that he did not believe in the possibility of another Mussalman domination in India either with or without the help of foreign Muslim states, and he therefore favoured the idea of perpetual British rule in this country.

The founders of the Indian National Congress, on the other hand, were absolutely honest and sincere nationalists. They did not entertain any anti-Muslim intentions, but they knew that nationalism could take no notice of denominationalism. Sir Syed's opposition, however, forced them to take some notice of it. It was by no conspiracy against the Muslims that the Hindus of that period came to occupy a large number and proportion of higher Government offices than their Muslim fellow-countrymen, and were more prominent and influential in the public life of the country. They, therefore, refused to accept communal representation in services under the Government for each community. The struggle continued for a long time, until the Congress surrendered on the first point, though still refusing to recognise the second.

From a purely communal point of view, Sir Syed was right. From a national point of view his demand was fatal. The history of the several European countries shows that they had all to face a similar situation some time or other in the process of national evolution. What helped them to become nations was a decisive refusal to give in to the claims of religion. As a fundamental principle of their policy, they recognised the supremacy of State over religion, and gradually removed all religious distinctions so far as they affected the Constitution of the State including services under the State. In India we have adopted a different, in fact the opposite, course.

The acceptance of the principle of communal representation was a concession to religion and is the negation of nationalism. The supremacy of religion over State has thus been enthroned. Most Muslim leaders openly say that they are Muslims first and Indians afterwards, though in 1915, Mr. Mazhar-ul-Haq said from his place as President of the Muslim League that he was Indian from first to last. No one can be a true Nationalist who is not an Indian from first to last. He may be an Indian Hindu or an Indian Mussalman, but he must be an Indian all the time. A man who says he is prepared to sacrifice the freedom of India for the freedom of "*Jazirat-ul-Arab*" cannot be an Indian nationalist.

Leaders on both sides are emphatic that the present tension between the two communities is political and not religious. Muslims contend that the insufficiency and the unfairness of the Lucknow Pact are responsible for it. Hindus maintain that communal representation itself is at the bottom of the present trouble. Both are right in their own way. Whether the Lucknow Pact is unjust or unfair, it is certainly responsible for the Muslim demand for its extension to local bodies, government services, and the educational institutions.

People outside the Punjab have no idea to what extent the principle of communal representation has been or is being pushed in the Punjab. Practically all social relations between Hindus and Muhammadans, and Sikhs and non-Sikhs, have ceased. All three communities have their separate clubs, separate organisations, and separate colleges. Even in sporting clubs or social functions, all three communities insist on communal representation. In my judgement the trouble is both religious and political. I am certain that religion is being used for political purposes, but I am also certain that there is a certain amount of genuine religious element in it.

The very day when I wrote the above, Sir M. Hailey, Governor of the Punjab, made a speech in the Punjab Legislative Council which contained the following observations, which seem to me to be an absolutely correct description of the situation:

"We have a problem far more difficult than those I have described, because it deals with elements less tangible and factors less susceptible of direct approach or control. We have to find some remedy for the toxin of inter-communal dissension which today is vitiating our public and perhaps our social life. Let me be somewhat more precise here and use such frankness as is possible in one whose heartfelt desire is to allay and not to provoke discord. My reference is not mainly to communal rioting or open disturbance. There has been such in the past, but the province must take credit for the fact that it has of late escaped open violence which has been exhibited in the towns of some of our neighbouring provinces. Disastrous as open disturbance may be, sinister as are its effects in prolonging the alienation of rival communities, it is not the whole of the problem, perhaps not even its gravest feature. My reference is rather to the fact that in every sphere of life and activity, in social matters, in almost every question of administration, in the management of local affairs, in the conduct of education, even in the current discussion of questions of law and justice, the communal question intervenes."

Of course I do not admit for a moment that the Government and its officials have been, or are, so innocent in the matter as Sir M. Hailey would have us believe. In my humble judgement the communal situation in the Punjab, much of it at least, is of the making of the Government. This, however, is a different matter.

The Shuddhi, Sanghathan and Tanzim Movements

The aggressive Hinduism preached by the Arya Samaj was not political in its conception. That it has been strengthened by political considerations cannot, however, be denied.

This is an appropriate place for examining the origin and bearings of the Shuddhi Movement of which we have heard so much of late. The movement is as old as the Arya Samaj or even the Sikh religion. The Arya Samaj claims that the religion preached by it is universal religion, and aims at bringing the whole world under its banner. In this respect its claims are as ambitious and wide as those of Christianity and Islam. There was a time when the more orthodox section of the Arya Samaj used to proclaim from the housetops that they were non-Hindus; and that they were free to eat and drink and marry with non-Hindus; and that even Hindus should undergo a certain amount of Shuddhi before they could be admitted into the Arya Samaj.

The other section, which was believed to be more political-minded, was opposed to all these claims of the Mahatma party of which Swami Shraddhanand (then Lala Munshi Ram) was the head. Shuddhi with the latter was purely the ritual of conversion, i.e., admission into their Church. It had no political significance whatsoever. For a time, Lala Munshi Ram's party maintained this attitude, and some of them attempted to put into practice what they believed in theory. It was then that the now-famous Dharmpal was made a hero. Soon after, however, they found that by insisting on this idea and putting it into practice they were bound to lose the practical sympathy of the Hindu community. This they could not afford to do, as it was the general Hindu community that greased the various mills they were running. So better counsels prevailed, and they changed their attitude.

I know it as a fact, however (as I was an active member of the Arya Samaj then), that serious efforts were made even then to bring the Malkana and other Rajputs of the United Provinces and Rajputana into the fold of the Arya Samaj. Some were actually so brought at Aligarh and in the neighbouring districts. The Malkanas, however, did not want to be "Aryas"; what they desired was to be readmitted into their own caste, and brotherhood on equal terms. To this the orthodox Rajputs would not agree.

So the matter remained in suspense for a number of years, until the orthodox Rajputs consented to take them in. What was at the back of the latter's mind in this change of attitude, is also clear. It was the communal demands of the Muslim community, the policy of Mian Fazl-e-Husain and the Multan riots, which created the necessary atmosphere. The principle of Shuddhi has now been accepted by the Hindu Mahasabha, and I am free to confess that the idea at the back of this decision is partly political, partly communal, and partly humanitarian, the latter element being more in evidence in the Shuddhi of the untouchables.

It was, it must be confessed, only natural that the Muslims should be exasperated at this change in the attitude of the orthodox Hindus, because the change opens out an entirely new chapter in Indian history. The question raised by the movement is a fundamental one, and although one can understand and appreciate the Muslim point of view, one can see no way of stopping the movement as long as non-Hindu agencies are free to carry on their proselytising work. The movement has come to stay, and this fact should be philosophically accepted. That it has direct political bearings cannot be denied, and the only way to minimise its importance is to do away with communal representation. For the present, the decisions arrived at by the Delhi Unity Conference may be accepted as the final word in the matter.

At this stage we might discuss the Sangathan and the Tanzim movements too. The Sangathan Movement also (or to call it by its proper name, the Hindu Sabha Movement) represents an old idea. The object was present to the mind of the founder of the Arya Samaj. But the Samaj signally failed to realise it, as it went on developing its sectarian proclivities. I remember that when I was a student of the Lahore Government College in the early-80s, a Hindu Sabha was formed at the house of Raja Harbans Singh of Sheikhupura in Lahore. That Sabha died in its infancy. Then the movement was revived towards the end of the last century at the house of the late Lala Balmokand, Reis, Lahore. Even this organisation, however, remained almost lifeless until the late R. B. Lal Chand put life into it.

But somehow or other, the movement never took root. It has benefited individual members, but it has done no good to the Hindu community as a whole. It had two formidable rivals: on the political side the Indian National Congress, on the socio-religious side the Arya Samaj. Fixed between these two mill-stones, it was never able to lift its head sufficiently high to be a success. The present movement is a reaction of the Hindu-Muslim situation. There is nothing in its aims and objects or its Constitution that need make it anti-Muslim, but to be frank, the fact that it is anti-Muslim is the only thing that keeps it alive.

The Khilafat Committees which were originally established to support the Khilafat agitation have regularly and systematically carried on a religious propaganda to which is directly traceable a part, at least, of the present bitterness between Hindus and Muslims. At Cocanada, it was given out that the Khilafat Committee would be used to organise the Indian Muslims. Tanzim is its other name. It is obviously anti-Hindu.

Personally, I would welcome both the movements, i.e., the Sanghathan and the Tanzim, if they could unite the different sections of the Hindus into one organisation, in one case, and all the different sections of the Muslims, in the other; for then it would be a comparatively easy thing for the two main organisations to come to terms with each other. But the task is hopeless. In my judgement the only purpose which the two movements are likely to serve is to increase the already existing estrangement between the two communities.

The Muslim Movement is also intended to keep the Pan-Islamic Movement going. One cannot help noticing, and noticing with regret, that while the Muslims do not open their purses for the relief of Indian sufferers from famine, floods, earthquakes, etc., and that while very little Muslim money is spent to improve the educational and economic condition of Indian Muslims, thousands and lakhs [hundreds of thousands] are sent abroad under one name or other.

The phenomenon is confined to India. One finds no evidence of it in other Muslim nations like Egypt, Turkey, Morocco, Sudan, Syria, etc., etc.

As far as internal organisation is concerned, both movements are bound to fail. The canker of sectarianism is as fatal in one case as in the other.

In the case of Sanghathan, the Arya Samaj and the Sanatan Dharam Sabha will not allow it to flourish and succeed. They do not seem prepared to transfer any of their functions or influence to the Hindu Sabha. In the case of Tanzim, the different Muslim sects will not unite to let it be a success. Both the movements will, however, be much advertised though, to keep alive anti-Muslim feeling in one case, and the anti-Hindu feeling in the other.

Some Suggestions for Political Improvement

I have so far touched [on] the past history of Hindu-Muslim relations and given a picture of how matters stand at present. I will now offer a few observations on how the present situation can be improved, in the political field.

It is suggested on behalf of Muslim leaders that:

- Communal representation with separate electorates in all the legislatures, local bodies, Universities, and other official or semi-official bodies should be provided.

  Mr. M. A. Jinnah is the latest recruit to this party, and I really cannot understand how he calls himself a nationalist still. The euphemism that this is only tentative, and that a time will come when the Muslims will be ready to give up communal representation, should deceive no one. Once you accept communal representation with separate electorates, there is no chance of its being ever abolished, without a civil war. A civil war will, again, actually mean the supremacy of one of the communities over the other. This lends weight to the fear entertained by some Hindus that some, at least, of the Muslim leaders are counting on the help of foreign Muslim states to establish Muslim rule throughout Hindustan. Whether this fear is [or is] not well-founded, it is only natural that those who entertain it should oppose communal representation with all the strength they can command. Their opposition, however, cannot be effective, as the Government seems determined to adopt their [this?] course. Therein they see the best guarantee of the permanence of the present conditions.

  Communal representation with separate electorate is the most effective reply to the demand for Swaraj, and the surest way of India never getting it. I have never been able to appreciate the mentality of those who constantly talk of turning out the British, and at the same time insist on communal representation with separate electorates. I really don't understand what they mean. The second is the surest way of the first being never realised. The experience of the last three years is the most conclusive proof of it. The

Muslim demand strengthens the position of anti-Swarajists both among the Hindus and the Muslims, and supplies an effective reply to the contention that India is ripe for Swaraj. Communal representation by itself is a sufficiently bad principle, destructive of, and antagonistic to, the idea of a common nationhood, but separate electorates make this vicious principle immeasurably worse. If our Muslim countrymen are really earnest in their belief in nationalism and in their demand for Swaraj, the least they can do is not to insist on separate electorates.

- Representation in provincial legislatures and local bodies should be on the basis of population, in provinces and places where the Mussalmans are in a majority. In other provinces and places, they should have "effective" minority representation.
- Posts and offices under Government should also be distributed on the principle stated in clause (b).
- In the provinces where the Muslims are in a minority, as well as m the All-India Departments, the Muslims ought to have 25 per cent to 33 per cent of the total posts.

We will take these clauses one by one, in their serial order.

The principle of clause:

- Is both theoretically and practically a negation of the united nationhood. It provides for a complete division of India, as it is, into two sections: a Muslim India and a non-Muslim India. I say deliberately non-Muslim India, because all that the Muslims are anxious for, is a guarantee of their own rights. All the other communities they lump into one as non-Muslims. Let those who demand communal representation with separate electorates in all the representative institutions of the land, honestly confess that they do not believe in nationalism or in a united India. The two things are absolutely irreconcilable.
- The demand for proportionate representation in the Legislatures is perfectly reasonable, provided the principle is accepted through and through. The plea for "effective" minority representation is, however, untenable. Mr. Jinnah

has placed a special interpretation of his own on this term. Let us examine it in the light of facts. In Bengal and the Punjab, the Mussalmans are in a majority, and if this principle is accepted, they will rule over these Provinces. The Hindus in these Provinces, according to the interpretation of Mr. Jinnah are an effective minority already, so they are not entitled to any special representation. But what about the Sikhs? Are they or are not entitled to special representation? And from whose share are they to get it? From the share of the Hindus or that of the Muslims? Under no principle can they get it from the share of the Hindus. They must get it, if they must, from the Muslims' share, on the same principle on which the Muslims themselves claim it in the UP, or the other Provinces where they are in a minority. This will interfere with the absolute majority which Muslims demand over the Hindus and Sikhs combined.

Some Mussalmans realise this, and contend that they will be content with a bare majority of one or two. But it is obvious that they cannot have everything in their own way. Assuming, however, that they are allowed their own way, do they imagine that they will be able to make their rule effective in the Punjab? The Punjab occupies a unique position among the Provinces of India. It is the home of a community who were the rulers of the Province when the British took possession of it. That community is virile, strong, and united. Will this community readily consent to occupy the entirely subservient position which this arrangement involves? If nothing else helps them, they may oppose Swaraj, as they did not long ago.

Under the circumstances, I would suggest that a remedy should be sought by which the Muslims might get a decisive majority without trampling on the sensitiveness of the Hindus and the Sikhs. My suggestion is that the Punjab should be partitioned into two provinces, the Western Punjab with a large Muslim majority, to be a Muslim-governed Province; and the Eastern Punjab, with a large Hindu-Sikhs majority, to be a non-Muslim-governed Province. I do not discuss Bengal. To me it is unimaginable that the rich and highly progressive and alive Hindus of Bengal will ever work out the Pact agreed to by Mr. Das. I will make the same suggestion in their case, but if Bengal is prepared to accept Mr. Das's Pact, I have nothing to say. It is its own look-out.

Maulana Hasrat Muhani recently said that the Muslims will never agree to India's having Dominion status under the British. What they aim at are separate Muslim States in India, united with Hindu States under a National Federal Government. He is also in favour of smaller States containing compact Hindu and Muslim populations. If communal representation with separate electorates is to be the rule, then Maulana Hasrat's scheme as to smaller provinces seems to be the only workable proposition. Under my scheme the Muslims will have four Muslim States: (1) The Pathan Province or the North-West Frontier, (2) Western Punjab, (3) Sindh, and (4) Eastern Bengal. If there are compact Muslim communities in any other part of India, sufficiently large to form a Province, they should be similarly constituted. But it should be distinctly understood that this is not a united India. It means a clear partition of India into a Muslim India and a non-Muslim India.

- From a national point of view, I strongly object to any communal distinction being adopted for Government service or in the Universities. Yet it cannot be denied that Muslim dissatisfaction at the present condition of things is well-founded and genuine. Hindus must make up their mind to concede to the Muslims their fair share of the loaves and fishes obtainable from Government. They must put themselves into the position of the Muslims and see the things from their point of view. Mian Fazl-e-Husain embodies in his person a real grievance. Only he has been hopelessly wrong in his method of removing this grievance. He ought to have appreciated the Hindu point of view, and proceeded in a way to make the seemingly bitter pill easily swallowable by the Hindus. The thing ought to have been done gradually.

Mian Fazl-e-Husain's rule in the Punjab, and that of Chaudhri Shahabuddin in Lahore, have given the Hindus a sample of what they are likely to have under Muslim rule. To provide them with the sample was perhaps a moving spring of Sir E. Maclagan's and Sir John Maynard's policy during the last five years.

They have gained their object. But is that a fact of which Mian Fazl-e-Husain, as an Indian patriot, can be proud? If I had been in Mian Fazl-e-Husain's position, I would have tried to gain the same object in a different way, and only resorted to open attacks in the last resort. What the Muslims of the Punjab (I say Muslims as distinguished from Muslim landlords, Muslim lawyers, and Muslim graduates) stand in the greatest need of, is educational and economic openings. There are Muslim districts where illiteracy is more widespread than anywhere else in the Province.

There are millions of Muslims who are exclusively at the mercy of their Muslim and Hindu landlords. What have the Muslim leaders done to improve their educational and economic position? Providing posts under the Government for a few educated Muslims is no remedy for the present condition. Safeguarding the interests of the few, and neglecting the interests of the many, is hardly a laudable thing, but that is exactly what Mian Fazl-e-Husain has achieved, and at such tremendous cost!

The Muslims all over the world have yet to learn that there are other ways of making money and thriving economically than through and by Muslim rule. Those who are doing nothing to place modern progressive ideals before the Muslims, and simply emphasise ingenious dogmas, hair-splitting doctrines, and reliance on Government, can hardly be called good friends of the Muslims.

If the Muslims of India were to link their fate indissolubly with that of the Hindus, it would be the religious duty of the Hindus to help them towards progress in all spheres of life, but if the present communal ideals are to prevail, then they can scarcely complain of Hindu apathy towards their alleged backwardness. The present communal struggle, with the atmosphere of violence and coercion that has been created throughout Upper India, can only produce a reaction in the minds of the Hindus.

A Summary of My Conclusions and Advice

In the last article I observed that Mian Fazl-e-Husain embodied, in his person, a real grievance. But a grievance against whom? Certainly not against the Hindu community. If the Hindus occupy a larger number of posts under the Government than they would be entitled to on a purely numerical basis, they are not to be blamed for it. The Muslim community ought to recognise that the fault is principally their own. They did not take sufficient advantage of the educational facilities provided by the Government in the early days of the British rule, and it is that fact which is responsible for the present condition of things. For the last fifty years the Government has been giving them special facilities for making up for lost time, with the gratifying result that they are now in a position to hold their own against every other community.

They are perfectly justified in claiming that in future they should receive their due share of Government posts. But are they justified in holding that until their proper proportion has been secured to them, no one from the other community should be employed? The contention is absurd on the face of it. The claim that the number of Government posts allotted to each community should be in proportion to its strength in the population, is equally absurd. How are the figures to be made up? Is the proportion to be fixed according to the number of posts, or according to the amount of salaries? Are promotions, *sub protem* appointments, and retirements also to be regulated by the same standard? If so, why not say that all the Departments of the Government should be divided into "Muslim" and '"Non-Muslim" sections, entirely separate and independent of one another? Even these would then have to be subdivided into "Urban" and "Rural," and agricultural and non-agricultural. The whole thing is so ridiculous that one wonders how such a claim could be seriously put forward by men of intelligence and common-sense.

Again, are the Muslims quite sure that, taking all-India figures, they will gain much by these principles being enforced? On what principle will the Ministerships be divided? Is it not a fact that in some Provinces, and within the Provinces in some Departments, they have got a larger number of posts than the ratio of population would justify?

I would beg of my countrymen to consider the matter in the light of practical difficulties, and then suggest a scheme by which their reasonable demands may be satisfied. I am free to confess that in the present state of communal feeling no Department should be monopolised by anyone community or class. All reasonable safeguards against this contingency should be provided. Precautions must also be taken against communal intrigues or machinations. I think the appointment of a properly representative Public Services Commission will be a sufficient guarantee that no community shall, in future, be improperly deprived of its due share of Government posts. I can think of no other solution which would meet the needs of the situation. When, however, Swarajya is attained, the solution will probably be simple. The Provincial Governments will have full powers to appoint their servants, and the Provinces having Muslim majorities will, if the present state of feelings continue, automatically have a majority of Muslim Government servants. In the All-India Services, a Services Commission will continue to make appointments.

In the meantime, may I make a respectful appeal to the Hindus not to make much fuss about Government appointments? No community can economically prosper which relies too much on Government patronage. What percentage of the population earn their living that way? It is true that Government servants influence communal life otherwise than through their salaries. The amount of such influences can easily be exaggerated. As long as the present conditions last, I would leave the Government free to distribute the loaves and fishes at their disposal as they choose. The cream is, in any case, reserved for Europeans; then come Anglo-Indians; Indians come last of all. To me this fight over crumbs seems to be the most insensible [senseless] thing for any patriotic person to indulge in. Under Swarajya, the Government of every Province will determine the complexion and the character of its administrative agency. It is perfectly futile to enter into any pact about this matter now or to quarrel over it.

From Government Services we descend to Local bodies. I think the Constitution of Local bodies must be settled on lines different from those of the Legislatures. The population rule will not be sound in their case. The Local bodies do not legislate. They only manage local affairs. Local affairs are local, after all, and must be managed according to the special circumstances of each locality. But if the Muslims insist on the population basis, I will let them have it that way. While they will be the gainers in some Provinces, they will be the losers in others.

As for Universities and other educational institutions, they are the last places where any communal distinction should be allowed. That will be poisoning the whole intellectual life of the nation. I can understand and appreciate special facilities being asked for classes considered backward. Give them special scholarships, open educational centres in areas largely occupied by such classes; even assign larger or special grants from public revenues for their benefit, without dislocating or injuring existing institutions.

In this connection I will say at once that I did not like or approve of the opposition offered by some Hindu members of the Punjab Legislative Council to the opening of Intermediate Colleges at Campbellpur, Lyallpur, and Gujarat. If they objected to more money being spent on Arts Colleges, the best thing for them was to suggest the transfer of one or two Colleges from the East to the West. I am afraid an analysis of the conduct of some Hindu members of the Punjab Legislative Council, both in the last Council and in the present one, will not convince any fair-minded person that the whole blame for the present communal tension in the Punjab can be laid at the door of Mian Fazl-e-Husain.

The responsibility for much of what the Mian has done, or is doing, rests with the bureaucratic Government. Perhaps he has been its ready and willing tool, as his own views coincided with that of the Government. Hindu critics should have seen into the game, and should not have allowed themselves to be made the unconscious instruments of the bureaucracy in creating more bad blood between the communities. In any case, the future generation will not acquit them of all share in helping, however unconsciously, to bring about the crisis through which we are passing. In my judgement the Non-cooperation Movement is also partly responsible for it. Personally, I do not care at all about posts or about admissions into the Government Arts Colleges. The case is, however, different with the Professional Colleges. In their case the allocation of numbers to different communities, regardless of merit, would lower the standard of education and the subsequent efficiency of the successful units. These are, however, minor matters to which undue importance should not be attached.

Now to summarise the suggestions I have made:

- Free your minds from the pernicious doctrine of absolute rights.
- Purge your politics of "religion" (dogmatic religion).
- Rationalise religion as much as possible, and lay emphasis only on essentials.
- Remove social barriers which separate and estrange one community from another.
- Love India above any other country in the world, and be Indians first and last.
- Concentrate all efforts on improving conditions at home. That does not debar you from sympathising with your fellow-religionists abroad and helping them occasionally, provided that your duty to your own countrymen permits of it. In this respect follow Turkey and Egypt.
- Don't fret at Shuddhi. It has come to stay.
- You can try Sanghathan and Tanzim, if you can purge them of anti-Muslim and anti-Hindu feelings, which, in my opinion, is very difficult.
- Have proportional representation in Legislature if you may, but do not insist on separate electorates.
- Divide the Punjab into two Provinces to make majority rule effective.
- Don't insist on population being the rule of representation in local bodies. But if you must, do not insist on separate electorates.
- Have Public Service Commissions to regulate the filling of Government posts on certain general broad principles.
- No communal representation in Universities and educational institutions. But special facilities for backward

classes may be provided, with special grants from public revenues for their benefit.

A Plea for Mutual Cooperation

No Indian who loves his country can look upon the prevailing state of things except with the most excruciating pain and anguish. There are men in the public life of the country, who have given their all in the hope that before they die they may see the Goddess of Liberty ruling over their beloved native land. They have put up with all kinds of humiliations, sufferings, and losses, and sacrificed every comfort and convenience, and even neglected their children for the sake of this, the one single object of their life. Absorbed in this their one passion, they have treated with supreme contempt all kinds of calumnies, libels, and slanders, that have been heaped on their devoted heads by the foreign rulers of the land, and also by some among their own countrymen. They have seen their juniors rise over their heads to the highest offices under the State and to the most alluring positions in life. They have suffered insults and rebukes at the hands of men who were not even worthy of unloosening the strings of their shoes. They have been followed like criminals, imprisoned and banished like common felons, but have never lost hope.

And after all this, they are told most seriously and solemnly, both by Hindus and Mussalmans, that Hindu-Muslim unity is impossible, which means that Swaraj is impossible, or in other words, that they have been pursuing a shadow, a phantom, and living in [a] fool's paradise and wasting their lives!

How crushingly painful it is. Yet in the light of what is happening, how plausible and apparently unanswerable! Amongst those who hold that unity is impossible there are men of light and leading, men of learning and scholarship, men of influence and position, even men who have a record of great service and sacrifice in fields other than political. On the other hand there are men who assure us that this is a passing phase, that Hindus and Mussalmans can be made to, and will eventually, forget what has happened at Multan, Saharanpur, Delhi, Allahabad, Lucknow, Shahjahanpur, Lahore, Amritsar, Amethi, Sambhal, Gulbarga, and Kohat, that they will not only shake hands but embrace each other in love and fraternity, as soon as Englishmen will have left us, and that therefore, all that is wanted at present is a union which will result in the expulsion of [the] foreigner. They do not tell us, however, how, in face of the prevailing distrust, this union is to be brought about, how the foreigner is to be expelled, and lastly how the expulsion of the foreigner, even if it was practicable, would, by itself, solve the problem of Hindu-Muslim differences. Is it the foreigner that loots and desecrates temples and mosques? Is it he that kills people and burns property? Is it his hand that strikes children and women or dishonours the latter? No, they say, the hands are those of the Indians, but the brains are of foreigners.

Assuming that to be so, how are we going to put these brains out of operation? The reply is, by conceding Muslim demands in almost every respect. Mahatmaji himself said that the average Mussalman was a bully, and the average Hindu a coward, and also that cowardice was worse than death; and yet the remedy he suggested was that Hindus must concede to the Mussalmans and other minorities all that they demanded in the political field. Applying that rule to the Punjab, the result will be Muslims 55, Sikhs 33, and non-Muslims and non-Sikhs 12. Is that the remedy? No, say the Muslims, we do not want concessions, we want our rights; and the rights, as they view them, are what have been stated above.

Some of their spokesmen add: "If you don't do that now, you won't have Swarajya." Another says: "If you don't do that now, we shall declare Jehad against you, when you have got it." Nationalist Muslim leaders, men who advocate communal representation in all institutions in the land and a fixed proportion of Government services, say "Oh! Don't listen to Ziauddins and Fazl-e-Husain, they represent nobody. They are in alliance with the foreigner."

They forget, however, that the demands put forward by themselves are exactly the demands of Ziauddins and Fazl-e-Husains, the difference being no greater than that between tweedledum and tweedledee. The only difference is that one is called M. A. Jinnah, Esquire, and the other Dr. Ziauddin. These friends of ours forget that there are as many Ziauddins and Fazl-e-Husains among the Hindus as among the Mussalmans, and if the Hindu Nationalists had listened to them, there would have been no movement for political freedom. And without that movement there would have been no Shafis, Sarmas, and Saprus in the Government of India; nor would there have been Fazl-e-Husains and Mahmudabads in the Provincial Governments.

At least this much credit must be given to the Hindu Nationalists: that their efforts have been principally instrumental in bringing the country nearer to Swarajya than it would possibly have been otherwise. The Muslim educated community, with a few honourable exceptions, had in the past and until only a short while ago, consistently opposed these efforts. The Hindus do not want any special favours. All they ask for is justice and fair play. If the present situation is in any way unfavourable to the Muslim community, they will be only too willing to agree to any changes which the Muslims desire, subject only to one condition. They will not willingly and voluntarily be parties to any compromise or arrangement which will make real and lasting unity impossible.

For God's sake, don't threaten us with Jehad. We have seen many Jehads! For the last twelve hundred years we have heard that cry every day of our national existence. Yet, Jehads have not suceeded in killing us, and God willing, no threat of Jehad will influence us by one hair's breadth in our determination to continue to live. We are prepared to subordinate our communal life to national life. For united national existence, we would do anything, but we shall not submit to threats or to coercion. It is true that Muslim distrust of Hindus can successfully block the avenues of Swarajya, but brother Muslims! don't forget that active Hindu hostility may also be productive of some harm to the Islamic world. Away, then, with these threats and distrust. Let us live and struggle for freedom as brothers whose interests are one and indivisible. Let us live and die for each other, so that India may live and prosper as a Nation. India is neither Hindu nor Muslim. It is not even both. It is one. It is India.

To the Hindus, I will say, "If there are any among you who still dream of a Hindu Raj in this country; who think they can crush the Mussalmans and be the supreme power in this land, tell them that they are fools, or to be more accurate, that they are insane, and that their insanity will ruin their Hinduism along with their country. For God's sake don't listen to them and don't be guilty of patricide. You have no one outside India to help you. You are like a lonely waif in the world, and your position is extremely delicate. Be sensible, and show your readiness to listen to the dictates of justice, fair play, and patriotism. Be even ready to make sacrifice, if such sacrifice does not stultify you or nullify your desire for nationhood. Give up your pride and listen to reason and common-sense. That is the only way to salvation."

To leaders like Mahatma Gandhi I would say in all humility: "Sirs, do not put the cart before the horse. Do not assume the existence of conditions which do not exist. Listen to the voice of experience and caution. It is better to proceed slowly than to run away with assumptions and presumptions which would not only do no good but might land your country into pits. Do not try to change human nature simply by resolutions and exhortations. Give it time." I am convinced that if in 1920 and 1921, Mahatma Gandhi had listened to the voice of those who had greater experience of the public life of the country, the reaction of 1923 and 1924 would not have been so terrible. The assumption that seven crores of Muslims had accepted non-cooperation, was absolutely unwarranted. It was too much to expect educated Muslims to give up opportunities of preferment and promotion which they were just beginning to get, the Hindus being already much in advance. This was a demand which was bound to, and did eventually, strain their loyalty to the leaders. I don't blame them for "not listening to the latter." Let us restart our work with greater regard to the actualities of life and the possibilities of human nature, and we may yet live to see our efforts proving fruitful. Amen!

I have not said all that I wanted to say. I have deliberately kept back some important and unsavoury facts that recently came to my knowledge, in the hope that there will be no need to give publicity to them.

Open Letters to Sir Syed Ahmed Khan

First Letter

Would you excuse me if I encroach upon your valuable time for a short while? Before I address you on the subject matter of discussion I think it advisable to state for your information that I have been a constant reader and admirer of your writings. From childhood, I was taught to respect the opinions and the teachings of the white-bearded Syed of Aligarh. Your Social Reformer [the Urdu journal *Tahzibul Akhlaq*] was constantly read to me by my fond father, who looked upon you as no less than a prophet of the nineteenth century. Your writings in the [English-language journal] Aligarh Institute Gazette and your speeches in Council and other public meetings, were constantly studied by me and preserved as a sacred trust by my revered parent.

It was thus that I came to know that you once approved of the contents of John Stuart Mill's book on "Liberty," and it was thus that I came to know (if my memory does not deceive me) that the present Chief Justice of Hyderabad [Mehdi Hasan Khan], a staunch opponent of the National Movement, once translated Jeremy Bentham's book on "Utility" for the readers of your Social Reformer. Is it strange then that I have been astonished to read what you now speak and write about the "National Congress"?

Any person, in my circumstances, would shout out. Times have changed; and with them, convictions! Flattery and official cajoleries have blinded the eyes of the most far-seeing; cowardice has depressed the souls of the foremost of seekers after truth, and high-sounding titles and the favours of worldly governors have extinguished the fire of truth burning in many a noble heart. Is it not a sad spectacle to [see] the men whose days are numbered, whose feet are almost in the grave, trying to root out all the trees planted with their own hands!

Under these circumstances, Syed Sahib, it is, surely, not strange if I ask what has been true cause of this lamentable change in you. Old age and exhaustion of faculties may, perhaps, have some share in causing you to forget what you once wrote and spoke. Has your memory lost its retentiveness, or is it the blindness of dotage which has permitted you to stray into your present unhappy position? If the former, I from amongst your old admirers will take upon myself the duty of reminding you of what, in moments of wisdom, was recorded and published by your pen and tongue, and this duty, I promise, I will fulfil with the utmost pleasure and with feelings of the highest satisfaction.

I will begin with your book on the "Causes of the Indian Revolt," which was written in 1858, though only translated and published in English in the year 1873. It may be worth while to note here that the translators of this were no others than Sir Auckland Colvin, the present Lieutenant-Governor of the North-West Provinces, and Lieutenant-Colonel Graham, the writer of your biography [The Life and Works of Sir Syed Ahmed Khan, 1885]. In this book, after having tried to prove that the Mutiny of 1857 was no "religious war," nor the result of a preconcerted conspiracy, you say that "most men, I believe, agree in thinking that it is highly conducive to the welfare and prosperity of Government — indeed, that it is essential to its stability — that the people should have a voice in its Councils. It is from the voice of the people that Government can learn whether its projects are likely to be well received. The voice of the people can alone check errors in the bud, and warn us of dangers before they burst upon and destroy us."

To make the matter more clear you go on saying that "this voice, however, can never be heard, and this security never acquired, unless the people are allowed a share in the consultations of Government. The security of a government, it will be remembered, is founded on its knowledge of the character of the governed as well as on its careful observance of their rights and privileges." These are noble words, nobly spoken; words of sterling honesty and independence of spirit. Can they bear any other meaning than that which attaches to that resolution of the National Congress which prays for the introduction of a representative element into the Constitution of our Legislative Councils? Pray, tell me how can the people have a voice in the Councils of a Government if not by representation? How can the people of a country have their voice constantly heard if not through representatives?

But, to leave no doubt on the subject, I will go on giving quotations in proof of my assertion that you have yourself in former times strongly advocated the introduction of a representative element into the Legislative Councils of India. After laying much stress upon the necessity of a Government respecting the opinions of the people it governs, you say: "The evils which resulted to India from the non-admission of natives into the Legislative Councils of India were various.... It (i.e. the Government) could never hear, as it ought to have heard, the voice of the people on the laws and regulations which it passed." Again you say: "But the greatest mischief lay in this, that the people misunderstood the views and the intentions of the Government. They misapprehended every act." After this you proceed to say that "if Hindustanis had been in the Legislative Councils, they would have explained everything to their countrymen, and thus these evils which have happened to us would have been averted."

In your opinion, as expressed there, this non-representation of the voice of the governed in the Legislative Council of the realm was "the one great cause" and the "origin of all smaller causes of dissatisfaction," Nay, further, not to leave any doubts in the matter, and to prove that in your book you even go to the length of saying that your countrymen should be selected to form ar assembly like the English Parliament (which demand, at the time you advanced it, was certainly more premature than it now is though the National Congress, with all the advantages that the country has had in the way of education and enlightenment since that miserable year of 1858, only advocates the partial introduction of a representative element in the Legislative Councils), I shall give some more extracts from the same work.

There you say: "I do not wish to enter here into the question as to how the ignorant and uneducated natives of Hindustan could be allowed a share in the deliberations of the Legislative Council, or as to how they should be selected to form an assembly like the English Parliament. These are knotty points. All I wish to prove is that such a step is not only advisable but absolutely necessary, and that the disturbances are due to the neglect of such a measure."

Could clearer words be used than what have been quoted above? Is there any doubt as to their meaning? Because if so, I shall be obliged to quote the exact Hindustani words used by you to express the ideas propounded in the above lines. But no, I do not suppose you can feel any doubt on that point, because the English rendering was undertaken by no others than Sir Auckland Colvin and Lieutenant-Colonel Graham, the former of whom, at least, is now being proclaimed (whether rightly or wrongly, God knows) as an opponent of the National Congress.

Sir Syed, does it not sound strange that the writer of the words above quoted should put himself forward as the leader of the anti-Congress Movement? Is it not one more proof of India's misfortune, that the writer of the above words should impute bad motives to the supporters of the National Congress, mainly because they advocate the introduction of some sort of representation in the Legislative Councils of India? Is not your charge of sedition against the promoters of the Congress, in the face of these, a mere mockery, a contradiction in terms?

Thirty years ago, you advocated the institution of a Parliament, and yet you chide us saying that we want an Indian Parliament, notwithstanding that we protest that for the present, and for a long time to come, we do not claim any such thing? Mark the difference. India is no longer what it was thirty years ago. In the course of this period it has made a marked advance towards a higher civilization. The natives of India are no longer, with very few exceptions, ignorant or uneducated. The rays of education are penetrating and shedding their wholesome light inside most Indian homes; hundreds of thousands of Indians are as well educated as any average English gentleman, and we see scores of our countrymen every year crossing the "black waters" to witness with their own eyes the proceedings of the great British Parliament, and personally familiarise themselves with the political institutions of the English nation.

Can you in face of these facts still call us "seditious"? According to your writings, we are the most loyal subjects of the Government, and if, notwithstanding what you have written, you still deserve to be called "the ablest of our loyal Mahomedan gentlemen," why do we not deserve to be styled as "the ablest of the most loyal subjects of the English Government"?

To give a still more clear idea of what you thought about the fitness of India for this sort of Government, I give one more extract to the point, and then I will have done with your old writings for the present. After giving many arguments in proof of your position that the law which allowed the sales of land for "arrears of Government revenue" was also a cause of the outbreak of disturbances in 1858, you say: "A landed estate in Hindustan is very like a kingdom. It has always been the practice to elect one man as the head over all. By him matters requiring discussion are 'brought forward' (mind, not decided — LLR), and every shareholder, in proportion to his holding, has the power of speaking out his mind on the point."

You are wrong when you say "in proportion to his holding." However, let it remain as it is. You proceed and say: "The cultivators and the choudhries of the villages attend on such an occasion and say whatever they have to say. You have here, in great perfection, a miniature kingdom and parliament." How is it that now you have changed your mind, and have come to opine that these kingdoms, as you called them, should have no voice in the making of laws which materially affect the person, the property, and the reputation of the people?

Some persons insinuate that these writings which I have quoted came from an honest, uncorrupted mind, at a time when the writer had no prospect of being raised to the Legislative Council by mere favour. No, Sir Syed, no! I, on my own part, do not want to make such an insinuation against the fearless writer of those noble words which have been quoted above. Then the problem to be solved remains the same, viz., why this change, why this inconsistency"?

I pause for a reply, with a promise of more in my next; and in the meanwhile beg to be allowed to subscribe myself,

The Son of an old Follower of Yours

27th October 1888

Second Letter

It is more than two weeks now since my first letter was published, and I think I have waited long enough for the reply which, it seems, you have no mind to send. However, in fulfilment of my promise, I am bound to go on giving quotation after quotation, bringing home to you your own former political teachings, and I hope I shall be able clearly to prove that you once believed in all the principles upon which the different Resolutions of the National Congress are based. This will leave you no alternative but either an open and unreserved confession of your apostasy, or an unreserved retreat from politics.

Do not think, Sir Syed, that I shall rest satisfied with the publication of these letters in India. No, they will be duly published and distributed in free England, side by side with the pamphlets of your own pet [United Indian Patriotic] Association of yesterday [August 1888]. In the book already so often referred to, i.e. "The Causes of the Indian Revolt," you say: "Government were but slightly acquainted with the unhappy state of the people. How could it well be otherwise? There was no real communication between the Government and the governed, no living together or near one another, as has always been the custom of Mahomedans in countries which they subjected to their rule. Government and its officials have never adopted the course without which no real knowledge of the people can be gained." Further on you say that "this cannot be expected from the English, as they almost all look forward to retirement in their land, and seldom settle for good amongst the natives of India."

Now I take the liberty of asking, has there been any improvement of late in this direction? Have the majority, or even one per cent, of the retired English officers, permanently settled in India? On the contrary, we find that they are birds-of-passage just as much now as, or perhaps more than, they were when the above sentences were written. Then, have the Englishmen and the natives taken to living together, or near one another? Do you ever see Englishmen living in the Mahallas [neighbourhoods] of your towns, however large the towns or however respectable the Mahallas may be? None of the Englishmen have ever been seen doing that. In fact, their mode of living is so peculiar that they cannot.

Or, do you think that the point has been gained by a few Anglicised natives like yourself having taken to living in bungalows? If that is what you argue, I assure you are sadly mistaken. Your living in Europeanised houses cannot be said to be a gain to native society. It is rather, if I may be allowed to say so, a very severe and deplorable loss. In the sentence quoted above, you admit that living together or near one another enhances our sympathies and gives us more occasions of seeing, mixing with, and obtaining a more intimate knowledge of, each other. It is thus clear that Europeans can only really know us if they see us in our native homes, in our small thatched huts full of misery and sickness. How poor and miserable India is, they can feel only if they live amongst or near the houses of our agriculturists, and there see with their own eyes respectable native families sleeping in rooms into which an English beggar would scorn to step.

Why is this? Is it because we Indians do not know how to live? Now, if you say that, go to those Indian residences which are occupied by our few rich or even well-to-do countrymen, and there you will find that our mode of living is quite on a par with that of Europeans. Does anyone then ask how it is that I say that respectable natives live, everywhere, in buildings which can only properly be called hovels? The answer is, because they are miserably poor and cannot afford to build comfortable houses. Taxation is so high that they never feel themselves secure of their respectability. In fact, that is always in danger. The poor fellows are daily and nightly engaged in making the two ends meet.

What I mean to say is that the fact of you or a few other natives having to live in bungalows and imitating the English customs of eating and drinking and dressing cannot do any good either to India or to England. In fact, this will never help the English to realise the unhappy state of the people. Then the question is, how can the Government know the wants and wishes of its subjects? They cannot know them through official reports, because these reports are almost all prepared by persons who seldom see the real state of the people whom the reports concern. You yourself said: "But even these officials themselves were ignorant of the real thoughts and opinions of the people, because they had no means of getting at them" (vide your Biography by Colonel Graham, p. 49.)

Then, can the Government get this knowledge through the petitions of their subjects? I say, as you said, no. You said that these petitions "were," and I say they are, "seldom if ever attended to and sometimes never heard" (vide the same page of your Biography). I add to this that even if they are ever attended to, enquiry into the allegations made in them is often entrusted to the same officials whose conduct forms the subject of complaint. Their reports are taken to be gospel truth and the petitions are thrown out.

Then, can the Government know the real opinion of the people through the Native press? No, because the Government officials have always been hostile to it, and have even asserted that these papers represented nobody but themselves.

Public meetings even are not effectual, because these are invariably declared to be the work of professional agitators, stump orators and wire-pullers.

The question then is that, admitting as you do that it is essential for the purpose of good administration that the people should have a voice in the consultations of the Government, how should that voice reach the Council Chambers, and how should the people be consulted before laws are passed? You once said that "laws affecting the subjects should be made after consultation with the representatives of the people" (vide Social Reformer of the 15th Shawwal 1290, Hijri, equivalent to the 6th December, 1873, p. 163), and there cannot be any other answer to this question. Further on you said: "I am very sorry that this is not being done in India, and in not doing so Government is in error to a certain degree, but in a larger measure it is owing to the incompetency of the subjects, but I am confident that after a certain period sufficient education will remove both" (vide the same Journal, same page).

It is fifteen years now, Sir, since the above lines were written, and it is surely time to ask, or at least to consider, whether that period, or *chand roz* [some days], to speak in your own words, has not expired yet. I am ready to concede, though it may be for argument's sake only, that the period has not expired, but are we now making steady progress towards the desired end? Your objections, unfortunately, are not based upon considerations of time, but are put forward as matters of principle.

Then admitting, as you do, that this voice can only reach the Council Chamber through the representatives of the people, the only question to be solved is — who should be those representatives, or in other words, how should they acquire that position? Can men like Raja Shiva Prashad and yourself, be properly considered as representatives of the people, and can the method of selection by which you were sent to the Council Chamber, be accepted as of any value? I think no reasonable man would contend that it would have been possible, if Raja Shiva Prashad had been an elected representative of the people of India, for him to have libelled the whole Indian nation, as he did in his notorious speech on the Ilbert Bill [1882]. Could Raja Peary Mohan Mukherjee and other native members have consented to the raising of the Salt tax [1886], if they had thought that their seats depended on the voices of the people, whose throats were, so to speak, to be cut by that obnoxious and inhumane measure?

Then the correct solution is this and no other, that the people must be represented by delegates elected by themselves; and subject of course to the restrictions to be imposed by the Government. Co-sharers in the business of governing or legislating, these representatives must be such as to be totally independent of official favour or disfavour. If the selection of members for the Legislative Council is to be entrusted to officials, I say it is a downright farce, and there can be no representation.

The majority of the quotations given above come from a book which was written about thirty years ago, and you may find an excuse by saying that the state of people has since then undergone a mighty change, and that in consequence of this, the remedies then suggested are no longer suitable. My dear Sir, this reply cannot stand a moment's examination. I am going to show that in 1881, which is only seven years ago, you held the same views and felt rather proud of them. When it was proposed to raise the old Punjab University College to the status of a University, you were one of the foremost opponents of the proposal. You, [and] your admirers and followers, should not have forgotten that you wrote certain articles under the heading "Our Vernacular," and got them published and circulated in a pamphlet form. These articles were published in almost all the leading vernacular papers of Northern India, and the educated community of the Punjab, who were strongly opposed to the establishment of a University on the [traditionalist] lines suggested by Dr. Leitner, obtained effective support from these writings of "the ablest of the loyal Mahomedan gentlemen."

In one of them (paper 2nd perhaps), which was published in your Social Reformer for 1297-98 Hijri (equivalent to 1881), at p.135, you say: "National progress and National Government are both sisters born of the same mother. When a nation loses its independence, its progress only depends upon its learning the language and sciences of the conquerors and thus taking a part in the Government of the country. By way of flattery whatever may be said, and as a matter of policy whatever may be stated, the fact is that in reality the relations of Hindustanis to their rulers are no better than those of slaves to their master." The italics are mine. I have tried to give a faithful translation of your Urdu sentences. If I have erred, I hope to be excused, and that my mistake may be pointed out.

However, to satisfy the scruples of sceptical readers, I prefer to give the last portion of the sentence in Roman characters and leave them to judge for themselves whether the rendering is correct or not. The original words are: *Khushamad ki baten jo chahe kah le, aur 'political' tariq men jo kuchh bayan karna ho, kiya jawe, magar Hindostaniyon ka hal apni fatahmand qaum ke sath gulami ke halat se kuchh ziyada nahin hai.* In the same article, further on, you said that the "University College was being raised to the status of a University with the object of throwing obstacles in the way of our National advancement, and that the result of the clamour after Oriental studies could be nothing but that of keeping ourselves in the state of serfdom."

Sir Syed, would you still call us "seditious"? Remember that we are the product of that education which you so strongly recommended and which you have never been known to condemn. Our English education, the study of eminent European minds and European sciences — alas! that you cannot feel this — has expanded our souls, and we can no longer be selfish "Sat Bachnia" prodigies of your Oriental language. Sir, your fall seems to remind me of the fall of Adam. Just as Satan is said to be the cause of the fall of that progenitor of our race, this seeking after worldly honours seems to be real explanation of your decline. It is nothing to you, because your term in this world must at no very distant period expire; but to us, who are yet, we hope, to live long and to fight out the bloodless battle of liberty, it is destined to remain a permanent disgrace. The line of argument against us would be that the races which produce such inconsistent philosophers are not fit to receive the boon of Local Self-Government.

Sir Syed, if you have changed your political opinions, the sooner you announce it the better it will be, both for yourself and for us. It is simply childish to persist in your claim to consistency in the face of the above quotations. Better announce this change, and explain why and how this took place. Again pausing for a reply, with a promise of more in my next, I beg to subscribe myself,

The Son of an old Follower of Yours

15th November 1888

Third Letter

Well may we apply the opening sentence of Dickens' Tale of Two Cities to the present times in India. Well may we say that it is "the best of times" as well as "the worst of times." Best as the country is on the point of having a nation, worst as a particular section of the community wants to check the progress of the country; and unfortunately is headed, or at least is said to be headed, by a man who has been a frequent advocate of representative Government in India. It is "the age of wisdom" as the country has risen from its deep lethargy and made up its mind to assist the Government by wise counsels.

It is "the age of foolishness" as a particular party has the audacity to believe that their opposition will cause the national movement to die in its infancy. It is "the epoch of belief" because the different sectional interests have begun to believe in each other's sincerity; it is "the epoch of incredulity" because you, Sir, are said to be nowadays against the introduction of a representative element into the Legislative Councils of India. It is the "spring of hope" when we see eminent English statesmen advocating the rights of the dumb millions of India. It is the "winter of despair" when we see her own sons deserting the cause of awakened India.

Sir Syed, I must remind you that it is the same India for the welfare of whose sons you established "The Siddor's Union Club" at Aligarh. Do you remember, Sir, that in that Club the alumni of the Mahomedan College were trained in the art of discussing public matters in public councils? I ask you, Sir, why you established that Club? Why did you formulate those rules of discussion which predict the establishment of representative institutions in the country? Oh, if we had only known that it was to end in this! I feel that I have gone astray, and must look to those extracts from your writings and sayings so dear to me, which foretold the establishment of representative Councils in India.

Will you please turn to page 49 of your Biography by Lieutenant-Colonel Graham, where you are described as saying: "The people were isolated, they had no champion to stand up for their rights and to see justice done them, and they were constrained to weep in silence." Can you in the face of these words still say that the people never needed such champions, and that the Government has been doing and will go on doing, without demand, what it has thought and what it will think necessary for the welfare of the people? That it never needed the voice of such champions for the redress of grievances and the attainment of rights?

Having pointed out what the Government ought to have done to make itself popular (quotations as to which have been given in letters Nos. I and II), you said in the end of the same book, "The Causes of Indian Revolt," that "it was necessary for the Government to win the friendship and the good feeling of its subjects." Further on you said: "As yet, truth compels me to state, Government has not cultivated the friendship of its people as was its duty to do: the father loves his child before the child loves him. If a man of low degree tries to win the esteem of one in high position he is liable to be styled a flatterer and not a friend. It was, therefore, for Government to try and win the friendship of its subjects, not for the subjects to try and win that of the Government. If Government say that what I say is untrue — that they have tried to cultivate friendship and have only been repaid with enmity — I can only say that if it had gone the right way to work, its subjects would most undoubtedly have been its friends and supporters instead of, as in many instances, rising up in arms against it. Now, friendship is a feeling which springs from the heart and which cannot be kindled by 'admonitions'. Government has hitherto kept itself as isolated from the people of India as if it had been the fire and they the dry grass — as if it thought that, were the two brought in contact the latter would be burnt up."

I have given this large quotation to recall to your mind some of the reasons upon which you formed the opinions which I have already quoted in my letters Nos. I and II. These reasons may also go to prove that the prayers of the National Congress as to the concession of volunteering to be allowed to the native subjects of Her Majesty, are nothing but reasonable and consistent with the noble principles involved in the above lines. Now I have done with your book on "The Causes of Indian Revolt" so far as it concerned that resolution of the National Congress which prays for the introduction of a representative element in the Legislative Councils of India. Most of these extracts, except one or two here and there, were abstract, and perhaps you may, with your usual calmness, have the boldness to say that there is nothing in these quotations which goes to prove that you ever meant to say that these representatives to the Council of India should be elected by the subjects.

Very good, I will search out quotations which will leave nothing doubtful. You may not have forgotten that months after the opening of your Scientific Society you delivered "a vigorous speech" at the laying of the foundation stone of the New Ghazipore, now the Victoria College. In the course of that address you said: "Bear in mind, gentlemen, that Her Gracious Majesty Queen Victoria has had proclaimed in this country that her servants and subjects, European and native, are to be considered as being on an equal footing; and this assurance, gentlemen, is not a mere matter of form, but a reality." Now, Sir Syed Ahmed, will you still laugh at us because we believe this — this very proclamation — to be our Magna Carta?

Further on in the course of the same address you said: "The appointment of Natives to the Supreme Council was a memorable incident in the History of India. The day is not far distant, I trust, and when it does come you will remember my words, when that Council will be composed of representatives from every division or district, and that thus the Laws which it will pass will be laws enacted by the feelings of the entire country."

"You will see that this cannot come to pass unless we strive to educate ourselves thoroughly. I once had a conversation with one in high authority on this very subject, and he said that Government would be only too glad if a scheme such as I have sketched above were practicable, but he felt doubtful; if it were stated that there were qualified men in every District, Government would gladly avail itself of their knowledge and give them seats in Council. I knew this only too well, and felt ashamed that such was the case. What I have above stated is only to inculcate on your minds the great fact that Her Most Gracious Majesty wishes all her subjects to be treated alike; and let their religion, tribe, or colour be what it may, the only way to avail ourselves of the many roads to fame and usefulness is to cultivate our intellects and to conform ourselves to the age."

Sir Syed, have the happiness to know that the day which you in 1864 said was not far distant, is coming nearer, and that you need no longer feel so much ashamed of your countrymen for not conforming to the age. Your prophecy is not fulfilled yet, but we are certain that sometime or other it is sure to be fulfilled, and then you will have the satisfaction of feeling that you did not prophesy in vaiń. Sir Syed, do you wish to withdraw this prophesy of yours, and if so why? Please explain - I and others like me are waiting in suspense. Only say that with the return of sobriety and the calmness of old age you have come to know your own errors, and we will no more trouble you with these prophecies. Sir Syed, would you please point out what else could be the meaning of the above sentence except that — that India would some (in 1864, not far distant) day be governed by Councils composed of members elected by the people themselves? If not this, how can the laws be said to be "enacted by the feelings of the entire country"?

Two months before you spoke the words quoted above, you, on the 9th January 1864, started a Translation Society now known as the Scientific Society of Aligarh; and in the course of a speech then delivered, pointing out the ignorance of your countrymen, you said: "From their ignorance of the events of the past, and also of the events of the present; from their not being acquainted with the manner and means by which infant nations have grown into powerful and flourishing ones, and by which the present most advanced ones have beaten their competitors in the race for position among the magnates of the world — they are unable to take lessons and profit by their experience." Sir, we took your advice, and your countrymen have learnt the means and the manner by which they can advance the growth of their "infant nation" to the position of a "powerful" and a "flourishing" one.

How is it that this growth which you so much desired in 1864 is an eyesore to you now? How is it that now at this period you cannot feel any pleasure in seeing a combination of all the different races and sects towards the accomplishment of the great end for which you have been until recently struggling so hard? How is it that you are going to prove that you did not deserve the distinctions so deservedly, as we thought, bestowed upon you? By your present attitude, by your present utterances, you mean to prove that all that you once said, all that you once did, for which you were rightly honoured both by the Government and the people, and for which you were said to be deserving of being "awarded a conspicuous place on the list of benefactors" of India, was, after all, but utter nonsense — because that is the phrase you now apply to the repetition of those same principles — which you once so strenuously advocated — by the supporters of the National Congress.

On the 10th of May, 1886, you addressed a large and influential meeting of the European and native residents of Aligarh on the necessity of Indian affairs being more prominently brought before Parliament, and of forming an association for this purpose (at least so says your biographer on pp. 88 and 89). In the course of this speech you compared the British rule with that of the "former Emperors and Rajas" of India. You said "it" (i.e. the rule of the latter) "was based upon nothing but tyranny and oppression; the law of might was that of right; the voice of the people was not listened to; the strong and the turbulent oppressed the feeble and the poor, and usurped all their privileges with impunity for their own selfish ends. It is only therefore by such usurpers and turbulent spirits that a despotism such as flourished in Hindustan for many long centuries, is at all to be desired."

Know, sir, that the National Congress wants nothing but that [the] voice of the people be listened to, and that "the strong and turbulent" may not oppress "the feeble and the poor." The National Congress wants to achieve these ends by peaceful means, and in fact by prayers; while it can only be the usurpers and the turbulent who desire to threaten, as you now do, the use of arms. It can only be the self-assumed "strong" who can threaten "the poor" with the use of the arms by "the followers of the prophet." Further on you regretted the indifference with which the affairs of India were treated in the Parliament, and laid the blame of it to a great extent upon the shoulders of your own countrymen. You said: "India, with that slowness to avail herself of that which would benefit her so characteristic of Eastern nations, has hitherto looked on Parliament with a dreamy apathetic eye, content to have her affairs, in the shape of her Budget, brought before it in an annual and generally inaudible speech by Her Majesty's Secretary of State for India."

You entreated your countrymen to discontinue this apathy, and you asked them to exert themselves towards securing the proper representation of their interest in the governing body of the British Nation. You appealed to the "entire native community" to "cooperate" with the London Association established for the purpose. To your countrymen you continued to say: "You will have only yourselves to reproach when in after years you see the European section of the community enjoying their well-earned concessions, whilst your wants remain still unmet." Sir Syed, the country then responded to your call, though imperfectly, and it is now that the country has felt the value of your words and begun to throw away the deep indifference which you so forcibly lamented.

Pray will you tell me whether, prior to the movement of National Congress, there was no agitation for the redress of the grievances of the Indians in India? If so what was all this which you were doing? Why did you establish and support all these: associations? Why did you call upon the entire country to "cooperate" with these associations, if the Government had of its own accord been doing all that was needed for the welfare of India? In your criticism upon the Lucknow speech of the Hon'ble Pandit Ayudhia Nath of Allahabad you meant to ask (if I did not err in understanding and reproducing it from memory) the Congress-wallahs if any of their agitations had been existing when the Government granted all the boons which we enjoy. I have quoted largely from your own writings to show that such an agitation did exist, and that you yourself were one of the most prominent agitators.

You even went to the length of saying that no fear need be entertained of your (i.e., of those who meant to take part in such associations) being called discontented by the Government. To quote your own words, you said: "I am afraid that a feeling of fear — fear that the Government or the district authorities would esteem you factious and discontented, were you to inaugurate a measure like this — deters you from coming forward for your country's good.... Believe me that this moral cowardice is wrong — the apprehension unfounded; and that there: is not an Englishman of a liberal turn of mind in India who would regard with feelings other than those of pleasure and hope, such a healthy sign of increased civilization on the part of its inhabitants. The natives have at present little or no voice in the management of the affairs of their country, and should any measure of Government prove obnoxious to them, they brood over it, appearing outwardly satisfied and happy while discontent is rankling in their mind."

Further on you said that the natives were in the habit of inveighing against such measures in their homes, but to the Europeans they represented that they were satisfied with the justice and wisdom of these very measures. You loudly proclaimed "that such a state of affairs is inimical to the welfare of the country. Far better would it be for India were her people openly and honestly to express their opinions as to the justice or otherwise of the acts of Government." Would you pray tell me, Sir, why we are sedition-mongers; is it because we speak "honestly" as to the justice or otherwise of the acts of the Government; is it because we have overcome the moral cowardice with which you charged us? Are we seditious because we do not want to keep "discontent ranking" within our hearts? Are we disloyal because we, according to your own teachings, have come forward to speak up for our country's good?

If we deserve all these epithets on account of all these I must say, Sir, that you are the father of all this. You taught us to do exactly what we have begun doing now. You not only taught but encouraged us by your own example. Why do you now deprecate "this healthy sign of civilization," as you once called it, on the part of Indians? If we, the followers of your old principles, have exceeded the proper dimension — which, I humbly maintain, we have not — it is surely not advisable to root out these instincts from within us, but rather to point out the place and the occasion where we have exceeded. How have you come to oppose the principles themselves, the principles so lovingly promulgated by you?

Say that the principles are not to be discarded, but the men abusing these principles are to be despised. We will then know how to love the principles and not the men. We loved you because you held these principles, because we thought you loved your country above everything, because we considered you to be one of the fathers of the present India; and if we have erred, we must say we think that you should have pointed out our error in time. Truly has a poet said: *Khwab tha jo kuchh kih dekha tha; afsanah tha jo kuchh kih suna tha*; i.e., "What I saw was but a dream; what I heard, an idle tale." Ah! human delusions are then destined to delude the human eye for ever!

Again with a pause, with a promise of more in my next.

I am yours,

The Son of an old Follower of Yours

22nd November 1888

Fourth Letter

The fourth meeting of the Indian National Congress is soon to be held at Allahabad, and so I think I must hasten to give some more of the most important quotations in this letter of mine. The less important ones I leave for some future occasion.

When this letter reaches you, you will be, possibly, smiling over [Lord Dufferin] the ex-Viceroy's [anti-Congress] speech delivered at the St. Andrew's Dinner, Calcutta. If you will only take the trouble of reading that speech with your eyes open, you will find that your uproar against the introduction of some representative element in the Legislative Councils of India is not liked even by those whom you have undertaken to flatter, and whose national traditions you try to belie. Sir Syed, for God's sake, reconsider your position, and do not disappoint us just when the morning of hope has begun to dawn over us and our motherland.

Now to proceed with your old writings and sayings; please turn to pages 207 and 208 of your Social Reformer for 1298 Hijri, equivalent to the year 1881 AD. There, while giving an account of your voyage to London, you said that on the way you happened to see Mr. D. Fitzpatrick, the former Deputy Commissioner of Delhi, with whom you talked about "goodness or badness of the Punjab administration." Therein you profess to have said that the Government of the Punjab was a despotic one, though a thousand times better than that of the Sikhs.

Further on you say "the people of the Punjab may be happy and perhaps may like it because they have been just taken out of fire and made to sit in the sun. But we cannot like it. The goodness or badness of the Punjab Government, i.e. of the Government of the non-Regulation Provinces, should be asked of the inhabitants of Delhi, Panipat, Rohtak, Hissar, and Sirsa districts, which once used to belong to Regulation Provinces and have now been subjected to a non-Regulation (or beqanuni) Punjab Administration. As far as I know, people think that of many other punishments which had been awarded to the inhabitants of Delhi and its adjacent districts in the Mutiny, this was also one: that they were made over to the Government of the Punjab and thus made the subjects of non-Regulation Provinces."

These lines were written at a time when the North-Western Provinces did not enjoy the blessing of having a Provincial Legislature of its own, and so the only superiority in the administration of the NWP over that of the Punjab then, was the existence of a High Court instead of the Chief Court in the Punjab, and the Constitution of a Board of Revenue instead of a Financial Commissionership here. The word "despotic" is your own, and is used in your Urdu style, and thus you cannot say that the word has been unwittingly thrust upon you by the translator. Even at the risk of unidiomatic English I have tried to give a literal translation of your Urdu sentences. If you think that this translation is incorrect, I trust you will not, for the sake of your own reputation, fail to publish a true translation of the sentences quoted.

Now, will you please explain on what principles you designated the Government of the Punjab as despotic, and how you distinguished it in that respect from the Government of India or that of NWP? I can venture to say that the Government of the Punjab was never more despotic than the Governments of other sister Provinces. No doubt the merit of each Government to a considerable degree depends upon the personal character of its head. The Governments of Montgomery, Aitchison, and even that of Sir James Lyall cannot be said to be more despotic than that of any of the Governors of other Provinces. Can you, Sir, in the face of this broad accusation of yours, still designate us as reckless accusers of Government and its policy?

Further on in the same article you go on saying: "In fact the present time is not one in which people may like a despotic Government, nor are those virtues (which in ancient times used to be mixed with a thousand vices) of a despotic Government, and by which the influence of the former were an antidote for the latter, to be found in these days. Nowadays it is not possible for those virtues to exist in any despotic Government, and the people who think that in India a despotic Government, such as it used to be in bygone times, would be more appropriate and useful than the constitutional form of Government, are greatly mistaken. They are just like one who judges a garden by its state in the autumn, without caring to think what it will be in the spring." The word "despotic" throughout this quotation is your own, Sir.

At another place, on page 132 of the same journal for the same year, under the heading of "The Eastern Arts and Sciences," you exhort us not to devote ourselves to them but to the study of Western ones. You ask us even "to forget our mother-tongue" (an impossibility in itself), because you said our national advancement only "depended upon the spread of Western Sciences." You said, "Let us by all means remain loyal to the Government, let us always regard it to be our patron and well-wisher, and let us at the same time try to extricate ourselves from that servile and savage state in which we are." Nobly and truly did you say that thus, and thus only, should be the subject of a generous kind-hearted Government who rules over a nation for the good of the latter, or, say, for the good of the human race.

In the course of the same article on the same page of your *Tahzibul Akhlaq* you say, "No nation can ever advance in parallel lines, all travelling from one point to another. Nations always advance in the shape of a triangle, whose one corner projects in advance of the others. To think that we may be divided in different sects is to pray that we may not be enlightened by the light of

Western ideas." In contrast to this, please reconsider your Meerut speech [of 1888], in which in fact you wanted to express that the whole nation must remain in the background because you think that the Mahomedan community has not sufficiently advanced to fully reap the benefits to be enjoyed by the granting of the boons prayed for by the National Congress. (I do not admit that the Mahomedan community is not sufficiently advanced).

On page 136 of the same Journal you say, "I sincerely believe and wish to assure the Government that the same discontented educated critics" (meaning those educated gentlemen who severely criticise the Government measures and who are blamed for it) "yield to none in their appreciation of the British rule; hence it is not just to effect the ruin of our education on account of any apprehension of such criticism." These are the words which you addressed to those politicians who advocate the closing of Government Colleges and schools, and who are of opinion that education in Western ideas and sciences has made the Indians disloyal.

You would, I suppose, like to re-read those words also, by which you encourage your own educated countrymen to fight out the battle of their national advancement bravely and without fear. You say, "Without doubt, there are many difficulties in the way of our doing so" (i.e., promulgating those blessings of education, instruction and enlightenment which we acquire in those civilized countries to which we go on completing our education).

"On one side we are to contend against the prejudices and ignorance of our own countrymen, and on the other side we are to bear the opposition of those narrow-minded men of the conquering nice to whom our social and political advancement is an eyesore, and who dislike us because we have adopted English life, English politics, and the manners of an English gentleman; and change of dress even infuriates them to such a degree that they look at us with angry eyes as a pious man looks at a great criminal. But we should keep the good of our nation at heart, and should bear all the difficulties and troubles which beset our way with the greatest possible forbearance and perseverance. I do not wish to conceal that Time, the Great Reformer, will let all these things be, and no opposition or discontent will be able to keep them back. But still there is no doubt that this narrow-mindedness is kindling the feelings of discontent, and is surely calculated to cause all sympathy and love between the governors and the governed to be banished."

Sir Syed, have the happiness to learn that your countrymen took you to be a true prophet, that they are going to stick to every word which you wrote — are not to be daunted or baffled by any opposition, no, not even by yours. How is it that you preached to us to persevere, and yourself could not do this? We have persevered, but the old man has fallen: what a pitiable spectacle of human weakness!

Next I will give an extract upon the great question of native volunteers with which one of the Resolutions of the National Congress deals. On page 332 of your Biography, says your Biographer, that in March, 1883, when Mr. A. O. Hume (the beloved General Secretary of the National Congress) advocated the cause of native volunteers in India, and stated that in the Mutiny he had a brigade of infantry, cavalry, and artillery in the Etawah yeomanry levy — all Volunteers — he (i.e. Lieutenant-Colonel Graham) addressed a letter to the Editor of the Pioneer in which he tried to rebut many of the arguments advanced by Mr. Hume, which letter he says brought you (Sir Syed Ahmed) down upon him in a letter which you wrote to him.

He gives an extract from that letter on page 334, which runs thus: "I have perused your reply to Mr. Hume's letter advocating the volunteering of the Natives of India. In not allowing the natives to become Volunteers, the Government mean to say that they do not trust the Natives of India. Its consequences should be judged from the saying: 'If you want us to trust you, you should also trust us.' There yet exists a wide gulf between the Europeans and the Natives of India, and unless it be filled up nothing can secure and improve the prosperity of the country." The italics are mine.

This you wrote in the middle of 1883, and now in 1887 and 1888 you say Indians do not want anything. On the same page Lieutenant-Colonel Graham writes as follows: "What I would advocate would be the selection by the local authorities in all large stations in India of a certain number of picked Native Volunteers — men of good family and well known for their loyalty — to be placed under the command of the officer commanding the

European Volunteers. I would let them select their own company officers, and once started I would also permit them to select their own recruits as vacancies occurred."

I say "give us this much and we will be satisfied for a long time to come."

A few important extracts more and I will have done with your old writings and sayings for the present. Contrast the meanings attached to the words "Nation" and "National" by you in your Meerut speech with those promulgated by yourself at Gurdaspur on the 27th of January, 1884. At Gurdaspur you said that "we (i.e., the Hindus and Mahomedans) should try to become one heart and soul and act in unison; if united we can support each other. If not, the effect of one against the other would tend to the destruction and downfall of both. In old historical books and traditions you will have read and heard, and we see it even now, that all the people inhabiting one country are designated by the term one nation. The different tribes of Afghanistan are termed as one nation, and so are the miscellaneous hordes peopling Iran distinguished by the term.

Europeans, though abounding in variety of thoughts and religions, are still known as members of one nation, though people of other countries also do come and settle with them, but being mixed together they are called members of one and the same nation. So that from the oldest times the word Nation is applied to the inhabitants of one country, though they differ in some peculiarities which are characteristics of their own. Hindu and Mahomedan brethren, do you people any country other than Hindustan? Do you not inhabit the same land? Are you not burned and buried on the same soil? Do you not tread the same ground and live upon the same soil? Remember that the words Hindu and Mahomedan are only meant for religious distinction — otherwise all persons, whether Hindu or Mahomedan, even the Christians who reside in this country, are all in this particular respect belonging to one and the same nation. Then all these different sects can only be described as one nation; they must each and all unite for the good of the country which is common to all."

Again in your Lahore speech, which was delivered in reply to the address of the Indian Association of Lahore, you, on the

3rd of February, 1884, said as follows: "Even granting that the majority of those composing this Association are Hindus, still I say that this light has been diffused by the same whom I call by the epithet of Bengalees. I assure you that Bengalees are the only people in our country whom we can properly be proud of; and it is only due to them that knowledge, liberty and patriotism have progressed in our country.

I can truly say that really they are the head and crown of all the different communities of Hindustan. I myself was fully cognizant of all those difficulties which obstructed my way, but notwithstanding these I heartily wished to serve my country and my nation faithfully. In the word Nation I include both Hindus and Mahomedans, because that is the only meaning which I can attach to it (i.e. Nation or *qaum*)." Here in the end, the word nation is originally used by yourself.

To Resume: "With me it is not so much worth considering what is their religious faith, because we do not see anything of it. What we do see is that we inhabit the same land, are subject to the rule of the same Governors; the fountains of benefits for ali are the same, and the pangs of famine also we suffer equally. These are the different grounds upon which I call both those races which inhabit India by one word, i.e. Hindu, meaning to say that they are the inhabitants of Hindustan. While in the Legislative Council, I was always anxious for the prosperity of this nation." This letter of mine has already exceeded its proper dimensions, and therefore I think I must not give more extracts, and must leave the rest to be commented upon by abler hands than mine.

Anybody reading these extracts will be once for all convinced of the former loftiness and present lowness of your position. Foreigners reading these extracts will not believe that your now famous Meerut and Lucknow speeches were in reality delivered by the same Sir Syed Ahmed Khan who was once proud (whether rightly or wrongly, God knows) of his broadmindedness. This much seems certain: either you were not the author of those ideas reproduced in the above quotations, or your recent utterances were inspired by some mind other than your own. Poor Sir Syed, you must feel sorry for all this inconsistency, though you may not have the boldness to say so.

Sir, I assure you that you should not despair; a small sacrifice at the altar of your country, a renewed profession of the faith that was once in you, will suffice to regain for you the confidence of your countrymen. If you are not prepared to do so, I must think myself justified in impeaching you in the name of consistency, in the name of honesty and fair play, in the name of the great Muhammad whose descendant and follower you profess to be, in the name of Mahdi Ali, your old devoted friend who once felt proud of showing to the world that the original Mahomedan rule was based upon democratic principles; and lastly in the name of the pupils of your own Mahomedan Anglo-Oriental College, Aligarh, whom you trained in the principles which you now affect to detest.

It is a year since you actually engaged yourself in creating and keeping up an opposition to the National Congress, but up to this time your countrymen have not been clearly enlightened as to what it is that you object to in the proceedings of the National Congress. You say we are not fit for a republic, and so do we say. You say we are not yet fit for a Parliament, and so do we say.

If you say that the introduction of some representative element even into the Government would be injurious to our community, we ask why and how, and pray when did you receive that revelation — because up to 1884 you yourself acknowledged the necessity of these Legislative Councils being reconstituted upon some representative basis. Then, again, when were you inspired with the idea that the Hindu and the Mahomedan interests are sure to clash at least in this respect? Because up to 1884 you believed in the doctrine of Hindus and Mahomedans having one and the same political interests, and being members of one and the same nation.

To your friends Maulvis Mahdi Ali and Mahdi Hussain, whose tergiversation is not less amazing than your own, I have only a few words to say. To the former, that he had better now suppress his lecture published in the Social Reformer for 1290 Hijri on pp.136, and those preceding and following it. To the latter, that he should now publicly recant the views set forth in his article under the heading of "Liberty" published in your Social Reformer for 1298 Hijri, 1881, from pp.23l to 341. Until they do this I will ask them to abstain, if they desire any human being to credit them with common honesty, from abusing us and denouncing our principles; and to my other countrymen as well as to our rulers, I have only to say further:

"I know a maiden fair to see,
  Take care,
She can both false and friendly be,
  Beware! Beware!

Trust her not,
  She is fooling thee.
She has two eyes so soft and brown,
  Take care.
She gives a side-glance and looks down,
  Beware! Beware!

Trust her not
  She is fooling thee!

And she has hair of a golden hue,
  Take care!

And what she says is not true,
  Beware! Beware!

Trust her not,
  She is fooling thee,
She has a bosom as white as snow,
  Take care!

She knows how much it is best to show.
  Beware! Beware!

Trust her not,
  She is fooling thee."

With a promise to begin afresh in the year 1889,

I beg to subscribe myself, Sir,

Yours,

The Son of an Old Follower of Yours

20th December 1888

7

Golden Words of Lala Lajpat Rai

- I am not one of those who believe that the students, particularly University students, ought not to meddle in politics. I think it is a most stupid theory.
- At first sight it seems absurd to give one name to all Indian civilization. But a close examination for facts and data amply proves the unity of Indian civilization, at least for the present geological period.
- The shrine in our heart which shall live for ever in golden letters shall be the Jalianwala Bagh and not the Montford Reforms.
- Melodrama and excess of sentimentality have no place in politics.
- A campaign of political emancipation of a nation under foreign rule imposed and maintained at the point of bayonets cannot be based on an attempt to change human nature quickly. Such attempts are bound to fail.
- Then I began to suspect that I was being spied on by my own servant who lived with me in the same compound. Life became intolerable and I lost my sleep and appetite, so I decided to leave India.

1886: He was associated with the founding of the DAV College at Lahore and out of his income from a lucrative practice at the District Court in Hissar and the Chief Court at Lahore he contributed a lion's share to it.

1893: The Arya Samaj split into two in Punjab, one section lead by Lala Hans Raj and Lala Lajpat Rai retained the control over DAV College Lahore, while the radical section was under the leadership of Pandit Lekh Ram and Lala Munshi Ram.

1895: PNB has the distinction of being the first Indian Bank to have been started with Indian Capital. The Bank was founded by the great freedom fighter Lala Lajpat Rai. PNB has been a part of Indian history and from its humble beginning with initial capital of Rs. 20000/-, the bank has grown to become one of the largest banks in the country.

February 1897: Lala Lajpat Rai, a leading moderate in the Arya Samaj, announced that the samaj would shelter any orphan sent to them. He began to collect funds for this orphanage.

1899-1900: When a dreadful famine raged in Punjab, the Central Provinces, Rajputana and the United Provinces, Lajpat Rai planned and implemented the relief work on an extensive scale.

1905: On his return from England, Lala Lajpat Rai told that neither the British government nor the British Press was prepared to do anything for the suffering Indians. He exhorted the people that if they really cared for their country, "they would have to strike a blow for freedom themselves and they should be prepared to give unmistakable proof of their earnestness".

July 1906: Leaders like Bal Gangadhar Tilak, Lala Lajpat Rai and Bipin Chandra Pal were convinced that resolutions alone unless backed by force will not bring India an inch nearer to her goal of freedom. They began to doubt the efficacy of peaceful methods and stressed the need of forceful constitutional agitations. Lala Lajpat Rai and Sardar Ajit Singh launched Peasants' Movement in the Punjab.

May 1907: He took active part in the movement against the British Rule. The Lal-Bal-Pal (Lala Lajpat Rai, Bala Gangadhar Tilak and Bipin Chandra Pal) group was very famous in our freedom struggle. The British Govt. deported Lajpat Rai to

Mandalay, Burma (Myanmar), without trial. But he could return in November as the authorities could not prove any evidence against him.

1911: He re-entered the Lahore Municipal Council. When he stood for election to the Municipal Council his popularity was immense. Even the deaf, the dumb and disabled' people turned up to vote for him. A dumb voter brought a photograph of Lalaji to indicate that he would vote for Lalaji.

1922: During freedom struggle, National College Lahore, established by Lala Lajpat Rai, on the pattern of Kashi Vidyapeeth, Varanasi and Gujarat Vidyapeeth Ahmedabad, established by Mahatma Gandhi as part of freedom movement, being parallel centres of higher education, played a major role in shaping Bhagat Singh and hundreds of other youth towards freedom struggle. Lala Lajpat Rai was Chancellor of this college.

1925: Communist Party of India was formed. Lala Lajpat Rai though never joined the CPI but was the founding president of the All India Trade Union Congress (AITUC), the Labour wing of the Communist Movement.

November 1927: The most prominent Congressman in the Punjab was Lala Lajpat Rai. He had been part of the trinity of Extremists known as Lal-Bal-Pal. Through the years, however, Lajpat Rai had become a wily politician who no longer wished to remain in politics but to retire instead.

October 30, 1928: An all-parties procession, led by Lala Lajpat Rai, marched towards the Lahore railway station to protest against the arrival of the Simon Commission. Stopping the procession, police made a lathi charge at the activists. The confrontation left Lala Lajpat Rai with severe injuries and also led to his death after some time.

November 17, 1928: A meeting was held the same evening where he spoke with such vigour that his words, "Every blow aimed at me is a nail in the coffin of British imperialism", became historic. Though he recovered from the fever and pain within three days, yet his health had received a permanent setback and on this day, he succumbed to the fatal injuries.

Bibliography

Anil Kumar Jana: *Quit India Movement in Bengal: A Study of Contai Subdivision*, Indian Pub, 2004.

Arvind Kumar Singh: *Encyclopaedia on Lala Lajpat Rai*, Anmol, 2009.

Bakshi, S. R.: *Indian Freedom Fighters: Struggle for Independence*, Hardcover, 2002.

Bhattacharya, B. K.: *India's Freedom Movement: Legacy of Bipin Chandra Pal*, Deep and Deep, 2007.

Chand, Feroz: *Lajpat Rai: Life and Work*, Publications Division, Government of India, New Delhi, 1978.

Chandra, Bipan: *India's Struggle For Independence*, Penguin Books India (P) Ltd., New Delhi, 1989.

Dhanki, J. S.: *Lala Lajpat Rai and Indian Nationalism*, ABS Publishers, Jalandhar, 1990.

Diraviam, Leila: *Diraviam -Our Treasure*, Asian Printers, Chennai, 1999.

Erwin Neumayer and Christine Schelberger: *Bharat Mata: India's Freedom Movement in Popular Art*, Oxford University Press, 2008.

Gandhi, Rajmohan: *Rajaji, A Life*, Penguin Books India (P) Ltd., New Delhi, 1997.

Ganjoo, S.: *Muslim Freedom Fighters of India*, Anmol, 2002.

Goyal, P. K.: *Battle of India's Freedom Movement*, Vista International, 2005.

Hardikar, N. S.: *Lala Lajpat Rai in America,* Servants of the People Society, Delhi, 1966.

Hari Hara Das: *The History of Freedom Movement in India (1857-1947),* National, 1998.

Isaacs, Harold: *Scratches on Our Minds: American Image of China and India,* New York, 1980.

Iyengar, A. S.: *Role of Press and Indian Freedom Struggle: All through the Gandhian Era,* APH, 2001.

Joginder Singh Dhanki: *Perspectives on Indian National Movement: Selected Correspondence of Lala Lajpat Rai,* National Book Organisation, 1998.

Joshi, V. C. *Lajpat Rai: Need for Publicity Abroad, Writings and Speeches,* University Publishers, Delhi, 1966.

Kailash Khanna: *History of Indian Freedom Struggle,* Commonwealth Pub, 2004.

Kaushik, A. S.: *Great Freedom Fighters of India,* Indian Pub, 2007.

Khairul Anam, Md.: *Indian Freedom Movement and Murshidabad District 1905-1947,* Bagchi, K. P., 2008.

Krishan Mohan: *Encyclopaedic History of Indian Freedom Movement (4 Vols-Set),* Book Enclave, 1999.

Krishan Mohan: *Revolutionary Politics and Indian Freedom Movement,* Book Enclave, 1999.

Krishna, B.: *Indian Freedom Struggle: The Pathfinders From Surendranath Banerjea to Gandhi,* Manohar, 2002.

Lal Lajpat Rai: *Europeanization and the Ancient Culture of India,* Annals of the American Academy of Political and Social Science, 1929.

Lion Agrawal, M. G.: *Freedom Fighters of India (4 Vols-Set),* Isha Books, 2008.

Majumdar, R. C.: *History of the Freedom Movement in India (3 Vols-Set),* Firma KLM, 1997.

Manju Verma: *The Role of Women in the Freedom Movement in Punjab (1919-1947),* Abhijeet, 2003.

Maulana Syed Mohammad Mian: *The Prisoners of Malta (Asira'u-E-Malta): The Heart-Rending Tale of Muslim Freedom Fighters in British Period*, Manak, 2005.

Mazhar Kibriya: *Gandhi and Indian Freedom Struggle*, APH, 1999.

Muthaiah, S.: *Women Freedom Fighters*, The Hindu, 2004.

Nagar, Purushottam: *Lala Lajpat Rai: The Man and His Ideas*, Manohar, Delhi, 1977.

Nanda, B. R.: *The Collected Works of Lala Lajpat Rai*, Manohar, 2005.

Nanda, S. P.: *Freedom Movement and Constitutional Development in India*, Dominant, 2004.

Norman Barrier, G.: *The Arya Samaj and Congress Politics in the Punjab*, The Journal of Asian Studies, 1967.

Omesh Saigal: *Shaheed Bhagat Singh: Unique Martyr in Freedom Movement*, Gyan Pub, 2002.

Parmanand Parashar: *Kashmir and the Freedom Movement*, Sarup, 2004.

Pradhan, K. B.: *Freedom Movement in India*, Arise Pub, 2007.

Prafulla Kumar Pattanaik: *The First Indian War of Independence: Freedom Movement in Orissa, 1804-1825*, APH, 2005.

Puri, Harish K.: *Ghadar Movement: Ideology, Organisation and Strategy*, Guru Nanak Dev University, Amritsar, 1993.

Rafiya Nisar: *Shaikh-Ul-Hind Maulana Mahmud Hasan and Indian Freedom Movement*, Manak Pub, 2008.

Rai: *India Home Rule League of America*, Columbia University, USA, 1990.

Raj Kumar: *Essays on Indian Freedom Movement*, History and Culture Series, Discovery, 2003.

Ram Sharma, S.: *Education of Women and Freedom Movement*, Discovery, 1996.

Ram, S. and Kumar, R.: *Quit India Movement: 1942-1945*, Commonwealth Pub, 2008.

Ramanathan, K. V.: *The Satyamurti Letters, Vol. II: The Indian Freedom Struggle Through the Eyes of a Parliamentarian*, Dorling

Kindersley for Pearson Longman an Imprint of Pearson Education, 2008.

Rathore, Naeem Gul: *Indian Nationalist Agitation in the United States: A Study of Lala Lajpat*, 1965.

Ratna Ghosh: *Netaji Subhas Chandra Bose and Indian Freedom Struggle (2 Vols-Set)*, Deep and Deep, 2006.

Ravindra Kumar: *Champaran to Quit India Movement*, Mittal, 2002.

Shachi Chakravarty: *Quit India Movement: A Study*, New Century Publication, 2002.

Shailesh Chandra: *90 Years of India's Struggle for Independence: 1857-1947*, Alfa Pub, 2008.

Shantinath Gupta: *Great Freedom Fighters of India*, Anmol, 2006.

Sharma, S. R.: *Life and Works of Lala Lajpat Rai*, Book Enclave, 2005.

Sirisa Kumar Shadangi: *The Prisons of South Orissa and the Freedom Fighters in Incarceration, 1900 - 1947*, Punthi Pustak, 2005.

Sumiti Malhotra: *Thoughts of Great Personalities in 20 Century*, Raj Publishing, 2003.

Sundaram, V.: *Great Crusader for Women's Emancipation*, News Today, 2005.

Sundararaja, Saroja: *March to Freedom in Madras Presidency, 1916-1947*, Lalitha Publication, Chennai, 1989.

Surinder Singh: *The Political Memoirs of an Indian Revolutionary: Naina Singh Dhoot (1904-1989)*, Manohar, 2005.

Taneja, Anup: *Gandhi, Women and the National Movement, 1920-47*, Har-Anand Publications, Delhi, 2005.

Thapar-Bjorkert, Suruchi: *Women in the Indian Nationalist Movement*, Sage Publication India (P) Ltd., New Delhi, 2006.

Vishnoo Bhagwan: *Indian Freedom Movement and Constitutional Acts*, Atma Ram, 1999.

Warrier, Shoba: *Quit India Movement: 60 Years*, Dr. Sarojini Varadappan, 2002.

Index

❑❑❑